Homebound Teaching

Homebound Teaching
A Handbook for Educators

by
Nancy R. Macciomei
and
Douglas H. Ruben

McFarland & Company, Inc., Publishers
Jefferson, North Carolina, and London

British Library Cataloguing-in-Publication data available

Library of Congress Cataloguing-in-Publication Data

Macciomei, Nancy R.
  Homebound teaching.

  Bibliography: p. 191.
  Includes index.
  1. Domestic education — United States.   2. Domestic
education — Law and legislation — United States.
I. Ruben, Douglas H.   II. Title.
LC37.M145   1989   371.9'046   89-42732

ISBN 0-89950-381-0 (lib. bdg. : 50# alk. paper) ∞

Printed in the United States of America

McFarland & Company, Inc., Publishers
  Box 611, Jefferson, North Carolina 28640

To our parents,
Chuck and Belle Ruben

Contents

Introduction

Welcome to the mysterious world of "homebound teaching." Mysterious is perhaps an understatement considering the myriad of tasks, and sometimes ambiguous responsibilities, assembled in one job. At a philosophical level, homebound teaching represents the essential but often overlooked rights of handicapped students in public education. It is for school-age children injured in accidents or suffering from congenital disabilities that make them physically unable to endure regular classroom instruction. What happens to them? Do injured students vanish into oblivion for a short while and then reappear on the school scene? What about permanently handicapped students?

Prior to the adoption of Public Law 94-142, signed by President Gerald Ford on November 29, 1975, many physically and emotionally impaired students were ignored, relegated to an inferior status, or simply hidden away. Untold thousands of hard-to-teach children with handicaps dropped out of school. Public Law 94-142, called the "Education for All Handicapped Children Act," was designed to alleviate these conditions. By this law, implemented September 1, 1978, schools were legally mandated to offer equal educational opportunities to all handicapped students.

Rapidly the school systems worked to develop innovative programs tailored for "special education." Children labeled as "exceptional" or "disabled" now met in special classrooms, instructed by specially trained teachers, on lesson plans specially designed to better serve the needs of handicapped students. Proponents of special education naturally welcomed the attention at last being paid to handicapped students, who after their long wait were entitled to some extra privileges. Critics said special education became a dumping ground for slow learners with no real handicaps, relieving regular, nonspecial education teachers of the burdensome task of teaching difficult pupils.

However regarded, the enforced growth of special education within the last 15 years has produced widespread programs for the large number of children in need. The assigned placement of students in resource rooms, self-contained rooms and in mainstreaming reflects a workable system, a system quickly maturing against constant budget threats, policy changes, and teacher turnover.

And amid this growth is a certain type of educator whose job begins outside the classroom setting. This teacher responds to another P.L. 94-142 requirement, that disabled students be taught in the most normal environment possible — closest to home and with normal peers where possible. Where there is temporary or permanent injury or disability, the closest normal environment is home itself.

The homebound teacher travels to one or more counties instructing school-aged children who are medically unable to attend school. Homebound teachers work out of all sorts of facilities — homes, hospitals, rehabilitation agencies — and adapt to situations atypical for normal learning. Although a homebound teacher's duties still primarily involve educational planning, the teacher does not function in the same way as a regular teacher, teacher consultant, or independent specialist. Somewhere between these occupations, borrowing a little from each, lies the unique expertise of the homebound teacher.

Little if any descriptive material on homebound teachers is available for special educators other than the sketchy outline provided in each state's legislation. Responding to this need, we have assembled a comprehensive handbook full of practical strategies for teaching the homebound. All these strategies are based on personal experience. *Homebound Teaching* is the first collection of basic concepts, behavioral interventions, and instructional procedures pertaining to various chronic and acute disabilities encountered on the homebound trail. Special educators faced with homebound responsibility may rely on this text as a reference manual for interpretation of law (e.g. P.L. 94-142), for modifications of curricula, for methods to manage inappropriate student behavior, and for medical background on different orthopedic handicaps.

Homebound Teaching follows seven chapters to introduce major practices of homebound instruction. Chapter 1 introduces the philosophy of homebound service under P.L. 94-142 and individual state laws. Chapter 2 draws from practical implications of the services in defining proper criteria of homebound instructors. Discussed are educational evaluations, Individualized Educational Programs (IEP), and testing modifications. Chapter 3 emphasizes curriculum modification and implementation across a vast array of subject areas taught, as well as across grade levels in most school systems. Formal and "informal" teaching techniques are covered.

Chapter 4 presents a compendium of behavioral management interventions, organized for rapid reference. A listing of behavioral disorders refers the reader to appropriate numbered interventions. Each intervention is described in terms of procedure, indications, contraindications and limitations.

Chapter 5 outlines needed background to cope with individual and family crises, examining the homebound child and society. Chapters 6 and

7 address common orthopedic handicaps found in homebound visits. Specifically covered are short-term and terminal illnesses, issues of death and dying, and community services that are available in both rural and urban areas.

Educator responsibility also entails awareness of state legislation on credentials for homebound instructors. This is the purpose of Appendix A. This appendix summarizes defined criteria and interesting features of nearly all 50 states' regulations concerning enactment of P.L. 94-142. Appendix B provides addresses for support agencies nationwide. Finally, educators will find the glossary a welcome resource amidst the deluge of medical and psychological terms they are expected to know.

It is so important that teachers of the homebound offer practical and meaningful lessons to disabled students, while also undertaking the broad role of liaison between parent, school, and other professionals. The authors certainly believe any teacher can demonstrate the tactics and strategies of good teaching. But employing those strategies under circumstances that are sometimes bizarre, sometimes highly restrictive, and nearly always adapted to special needs calls for extraordinary instructional competence. This enhanced competence is the natural reward of being a homebound teacher.

In preparing this book we embarked on a mission at times requiring the sacrifices and cooperation among our family and colleagues. Recognition is especially owed to our spouses, Barry and Marilyn, for their abiding patience and schedule readjustments. Their thoughtful and supportive roles gave continued impetus to our energy during all phases of manuscript preparation.

N.R.M.

D.H.R.

1. Theory and Practice

The homebound teacher travels to one or more counties instructing school-aged children that are medically unable to attend school — that is, limitations in their physical health necessitate their absence from school for brief or extended periods of time. Homebound teaching is the result of federal and state laws which mandate that handicapped children have a right to free, appropriate public school education. Thus the Homebound Program is available in all public school systems in the United States.

Homebound services enable the children confined to home settings to make cognitive and affective progress toward overcoming their limitations. Educational, psychological, and sociological interventions are applied directly. Through these services, children receive an adjusted and individualized curriculum, toward helping them in recovery or adaptation.

Homebound Teaching: A Handbook for Educators is a guide to the one-on-one instruction of teaching the homebound child. Methods, materials, and practical case analysis will be discussed. Our intention is to provide awareness and understanding of this virtually unknown, unconventional, and extremely challenging system of instruction.

Classroom vs. One-on-One Instruction

Classroom instruction provides cognitive as well as affective growth in the most traditional ways. When traditional classroom instruction is not appropriate for a student's needs, alternate teaching structures are considered. Homebound fits into this "alternate" category.

Many key elements such as instruction, motivation, and emotional and behavioral adjustment can be offered through homebound services in the modest "classroom" settings created in each household. The homebound program allows the health-impaired student to continue with his or her schoolwork and to maintain contact with the educational system. Homebound teachers should have the flexibility and specialized skills to extend or modify the curriculum and design a holistic educational approach to instruction. Education takes place wherever and whenever a teacher and student are communicating.

1

Perspectives in Philosophy

The educational philosophy of homebound is that every person should have the opportunity to be educated to his fullest potential, including health-impaired students who cannot attend regular or special programs outside the home. Whether a student is out of school for two months with a broken bone or debilitated indefinitely by acute leukemia, that child is entitled to continue with his education following a somewhat "normal" routine. The teacher-student relationship and hourly sessions may represent the only "normal" function that the child has each day.

From a psychological standpoint, the program is invaluable. Families are often in crisis: They are frightened by an uncertain future, shocked by the seriousness of the disability or illness, and overwhelmed by rising medical bills. The homebound teacher and service can provide a worthwhile activity for child and family to focus on while coping with the related variables of crisis in the family.

Introduction to the Population

There are three general categories of health problems that cause students to require homebound services: *short-term disabilities, chronic illnesses, and long-term illnesses or disabilities.*

Short-Term

The short-term disabilities might include multiple fractures or broken bones, rheumatic fever, corrective surgery, and medical problems related to school-aged pregnancy. The overall goal of short-term students is to comply specifically with their classroom teachers' structure and materials. Because the short-term student returns to school in four to ten weeks, assignments and testing are treated as an extension of the regular classroom. It is mandatory that the homebound teacher make initial and continuous contact with the regular classroom teachers and principals to clearly establish the guidelines and evaluation methods used.

Although the short-term student's academic program may resemble his classroom instruction, the physical setting is quite different. Homebound sessions take place in the kitchen of many households; possibly on a couch in the small surroundings of a tenement house; in a chair pulled up to the sickbed of an eight-year-old with cystic fibrosis; or in the formal dining room of a suburban household. Compliance with the classroom structure coupled with flexibility, informality, a sense of humor, and a holistic outlook can be the true mode of success. Case One exemplifies this complex situation.

CASE ONE: TASHA

I was on my way to the first appointment with the first student of the year. The worn-out county map was on my front seat as I drove past dense forest on a bumpy country road. The small, weather-worn shacks balanced on stilts made of brick. These homes were scattered throughout miles of countryside. Some had grey, wooden porches while others had cracked brick steps leading to torn screen doors. A few women with their babies were enjoying conversation or just silently sitting on their porches. Mechanically searching for the house, my thoughts drifted to my hometown of Detroit. I could easily remember the poorer sections of the downtown area, but none that resembled what I was now seeing.

My two-year-old Cutlass Supreme stood out like a sore thumb as I pulled into a cleared patch that most resembled a driveway. Although my student did not have a phone, I had contacted a neighbor to let the family know when I would arrive. I turned off the motor of my car and just stared at my student's home which seemed little more than a weather-worn wooden shed. Two of the windows were boarded up and the door was half hanging, half resting on the top step. This little shack rested on a few unsteady-looking bricks. Being a large person, I hesitated to go in at all. What if I fell through? Or worse, tilted the whole house to one side? I drew up my confidence, my ten years of teaching experience, and my raw nerve. I opened my car door. This was the first day of school.

Cautiously, I walked up the three brick steps and gently tapped on the door, trying not to unhinge it. I could hear someone yelling, "Teacher's here!" The television was on, and the sound of a dramatic conversation, probably a daytime soap opera, competed with babies wailing. The door opened and an elderly, overweight woman smiled a toothless grin.

"You Tasha's teacher?" she asked.

I smiled and carefully entered their home. I began talking about the homebound services they could expect for the next few months until Tasha went back to school. As I spoke, my eyes took in the broken furniture, an antiquated television set, and the hotplate near the fireplace.

There were two other rooms, their entrances blocked by hanging beads. Two babies were lying on the couch, sucking happily on their thumbs. There were two younger women, one of whom was Tasha's mother. As I finished my introduction, a few oblong dark spots I could see out of the corner of my eye began crawling toward the ceiling. I was evidently the only one to notice.

I was then led through the beads to meet Tasha. The stuffy, small room had three beds next to each other. Tasha was in a full body cast, plastered from chest to her toes. Each leg was plastered separately with a long bar stretched between each leg at the knees. She was a small 12-year-old who looked like a large, white turtle. She gave me a sweet smile, and I sat on the bed next to her.

The grandmother wanted to stay in and listen to our sessions. I asked her to wait a few sessions, until Tasha and I became acquainted. She promised she would be quiet but said she wanted to stay because she had never learned to read. I looked at her tired eyes, which seemed to be silently asking for a chance. I quietly said, "O.K." I took out my record book, each subject's sixth-grade textbook, and general information sheets.

As we began to work, Tasha answered my questions. She was a soft-spoken, friendly girl who had been struck by a hit-and-run driver a few weeks earlier, and she was concerned about keeping up in school. As we spoke, Tasha's grandmother sat closer and asked us to "quit jabbering and start the lessons!" I couldn't help smiling. My anxieties diminished and I began to feel comfortable in this unusual situation.

I saw Tasha and her grandmother every other day for three months. Each of them always turned in a set of homework, and I corrected both. Tasha and her grandmother were both working hard to digest the material. During each session, Tasha's mother, her sister, and the two babies would watch television and stay as quiet as possible while the eldest daughter and senior mother were keeping up in reading, math, spelling, science, social studies, and health. I had rarely had such motivated students.

As time went on, I couldn't wait to get to Tasha's house. Although my student load was becoming full, I arrived early and stayed late. I was absolutely captivated by their desire to learn. The bugs on the wall and floor no longer distracted me. The poverty of these people no longer devastated me. I now knew the love and support this assembly of in-dividuals gave to each other.

After three months, Tasha had her cast removed. The family and I knew the sessions and my service were coming to an end. Thoughts of returning to school became the conversation during our time together. On Tasha's last day, I arrived with home-baked cookies. I also brought one progress report for Tasha, and one for her grandmother. I left fifteen minutes later, feeling I had learned as much as I had taught during this special teaching experience.

Chronic

Chronic illnesses are characterized by an imbalance of health and ill-ness. The children appear normal, but will have acute onsets of coughing, wheezing, seizures, weakness, or pain. Chronic illness is considered an "in-visible" ailment. Klienberg (1982) explains, "The unique commonality among these disease entities is their virtual invisibility to the outside world. Children with these diseases often seem healthy to others. This paradox often creates special problems for these children thus affected. They want to, and do appear, normal. However, they may be betrayed by their disease at any moment" (p. 85).

Many times a severe, invisible health problem causes an added physical problem. Consequently, a referral is made through special education ser-vices for a new school placement. This usually means the student is assigned a homebound teacher, a situation illustrated in Case Two.

CASE TWO: STEVEN

It had started to rain as I walked up to the door of an apartment in the city's oldest housing project. As I knocked, I hoped my first session would be remembered. It was only 8:30 A.M. I knocked again and heard a small voice say, "Come on in." Poking my head in the door, I strained to see through a darkened apartment. All the lights were off. One small kitchen window let in a single ray of light over the wooden table.

"Steven?" I asked as I approached a young boy sitting at the table.

"Is that you, Miss Nancy?" he asked in a deep Southern accent.

I felt relieved that he remembered our appointment. I pulled up a chair and strained to see my new student. Due to his recent blindness, Steven had not considered turning on the lights.

As I sat in Steven's darkness, I told him about the homebound services that he would receive for the next few months. I recalled his file while I talked. Steven's brain tumor was diagnosed in the spring, and within months his vision had deteriorated from a visual impairment to total blindness. When school started, he was placed in the Homebound Program to learn to cope with his new disability and failing health.

Steven was a tall, chubby ten-year-old. He lived with his father, who worked first shift in a mill. I told Steven that we would work on his fifth-grade subjects, but his most important homework would entail learning to read with his fingers. We would spend most of our sessions learning pre-braille skills.

I flipped on the light switch, picked my purse and briefcase up off the floor, pulled my chair closer to Steven's and took his hands in mine. I explained how different and challenging this new way of learning and living would be. As I showed him his new braille tape recorder, tapes, pre-braille books, and games, I studied his face.

Steven listened intently, looking directly at me. He had red, swollen stitches beginning at the front of his ear and encircling his entire hairline like a giant horseshoe. He had a boyish, round face and a happy grin. At the close of our session, Steven took my arm, squeezed it and said, "Miss Nancy, you got a nice, fat arm just like me! I'm glad you're my teacher!"

Although my session with Steven was at an end, I hated to leave him all alone in the apartment. I turned on the television and told him to expect me in two days. He answered, "See you soon, Miss Nancy."

During the next few months, Steven worked diligently on pre-braille reading skills and a minimal fifth-grade curriculum. He acquired the light yet definite touch needed to differentiate the variations of raised dots, became adept with the tape recorder and tapes, and played a mean game of braille dominoes.

After Thanksgiving, it was decided that Steven would try returning to fifth grade in a program for the visually impaired. I accompanied him the first two weeks. We counted steps from his classroom to the cafeteria, the cafeteria to the bathroom, and the bathroom to each classroom. Many times we would start talking about his favorite TV show, "What's Happening," and then talk about what was for lunch. We would get so distracted that we would have to start counting all over again. Steven learned to fold his money appropriately, put his food on the plate like a clock: potatoes at 3:00, meat at 6:00. He made it through the transition of nine years of sight to the beginning of his tenth year as a blind individual. He seemed to accept the situation, looking forward to each day as an adventure.

I learned through Steven that declining health and blindness are only as devastating as we make them. The spirit and motivation of children, especially this ten-year-old boy, could not be shattered. I hugged Steven goodbye on the last Friday of the two weeks and told him how proud I was that he could make it on his own. He just smiled his ear-to-ear grin and said, "See you soon, Miss Nancy."

Long-term

Students who remain in the homebound program for a prolonged period of time generally do so for one of two reasons. First is the onset of degenerative disease in latter stages, such as muscular dystrophy, Friedreich's Ataxia, or cystic fibrosis. These children remain in the program for orthopedically handicapped until they are too weak or too ill to actively participate in a self-contained situation.

The second reason is terminal illness, such as childhood leukemia, tumors, or a variety of cancers. These students can remain in school until their condition cannot withstand the demands of a regular classroom. Physical condition can weaken rapidly as a side-effect of various radiation therapies. Many families start these therapies initially, only to terminate radiation because of the vomiting, loss of hair, and accelerated physical decay.

Since families usually focus on the child's disease, part of the homebound teacher's job is to help the family realize that children continue to develop despite their illness. There is a need for educational continuity in a child's immediate future. Although the instructional goals may vary from those of the classroom, homebound education still provides the pupil with needed direction. Many of the sessions also may be devoted to basic coping skills or support for the family in their grief process. As Kleinberg (1982) relates, "If the goal for education is to help children develop a sense of efficacy, mastery of their environment, and self-worth, then continued educational experiences are essential" (p. 31). Kleinberg clearly articulates the "many hats" worn by the homebound teacher. The following case study relates this situation to an additional barrier to learning — a language barrier.

CASE THREE: DONNY

I stood at Donny's door a few minutes without knocking. On each side of the square, cement porch grew a vegetable garden the size of a large posterboard. Neat rows of purple onions, cucumbers, and green beans bloomed unaware of the city dust and noises. The cars whizzed by not ten steps from the healthy stalks of green and purple, oblivious to their surroundings. As the door opened, I was introduced to sights, sounds, and smells that were undoubtedly of Grecian origin. A small, smiling, grey-haired woman dressed in black opened the door. As she gestured for me to enter, I heard instrumental music on the record player.

Donny's brother and father, both slender, dark-haired men, were talking on the couch. A woman barely five feet tall looked up at me and said, "Please come in. I'm Donny's mother." She ponted to her husband and son. They shook my hand and began including me in their conversation, as if I understood their native Greek tongue. I politely nodded and smiled at what seemed the appropriate times. Finally, she pointed to Donny, sitting in a wheelchair by a table in the living room.

I sat down and introduced myself to him. I studied Donny's eyes. He was only eighteen years old, but his face revealed deep-set lines from sleepless nights. His dark brown eyes were shaded by weakened eyelids and dark shadows. I was aware of how far and how swiftly his muscular dystrophy had progressed. Yet he was clearly willing to struggle to continue with his schooling and his life.

I took out the books I had brought for Donny. His English was minimal, marking the priority for the first few months of school. As I showed him the workbooks, tapes, and readers, I could hear his mother puttering around in the kitchen. Soon she appeared with thick dark coffee in a miniature mug, and baklava, a delicate Greek pastry. She smiled, saying something that might have translated to, "Eat! Eat!" Quickly she scurried back into the kitchen.

The next few sessions proved how ambitious and conscientious Donny was. Confinement to a wheelchair did not prevent his completion of all assignments. Even though his arms, hands, and fingers were slow, his homework was painstakingly neat, almost as if it had been typed. He had a talent for languages and was picking up English quite readily. We covered diction, basic grammar, and sentence structure. I emphasized survival English phrases such as telephone conversations; we practiced asking for information from the operator. We began to role-play situations.

Donny and I began to work on algebra after the Christmas break. He had a genuine thirst for knowledge and tackled algebraic expressions as if they were simple addition problems. By May, we were through the third book in the English series, the entire first-year algebra book, and at least two dozen varieties of Greek pastries.

The year came to an end too quickly. Donny was conversing in English sufficiently to help his family with daily interactions. He had even taught me a few Greek phrases. I was impressed with his progress, his desire to learn, and his will to live.

Declining health in the long-term or terminally ill pupil calls for unusual flexibility in educational planning. Besides academic needs, emotionally caring for the child's adjustment may deserve utmost attention to conveying the value of learning against medical odds. Donny's case diplays the much-needed flexibility of the homebound teacher during visits with a teenager with muscular dystrophy. In this case, a secondary complication presented itself as the student needed to learn another language.

Homebound Legislation and Funding

P.L. 94-142 states: "It is the purpose of this act to assure that all hand-icapped children have available to them, within the time periods specified, a free, appropriate public education emphasizing special education and related services designed to meet their unique needs." This law applies to all handicapped or orthopedic impairments. Specifically, other health impairments (OHI) include pupils with "limited strength, vitality, or alertness due to chronic or acute health problems, such as a heart condition, epilepsy, tuberculosis, rheumatic fever, nephritis, asthma, sickle cell anemia, hemophilia, lead poisoning, or diabetes, which adversely affect a child's educational performance" (P.L. 94-142, 1977, p. 42478). This law puts the chronically ill child within the range of the special education law. The homebound program therefore operates under federal and state special education guidelines.

The mandatory special education law can be further summarized in the following way:

1. Every handicapped child has a right to a public school education of high quality and one that is designed to develop the child's maximum potential.

2. Decisions on program placement for the handicapped, in public schools, must be a result of a committee decision.

3. The parents of a handicapped child are members of this committee and have an equal right to participate in all decisions affecting the education of their child. Due process is the right of each parent and should be explained in full.

4. Regardless of the severity of a handicap, that child is entitled to a quality education.

Where homebound education funds are appropriated is currently a debate in most school systems. It is an issue that confronts regular educational funds on a local or state level, and it affects federal funding for students certified as having a handicap. Because regulations are so vague, each state follows its own funding practices, with possibly little or no overlap between states. In North Carolina, for example, state special education funds and local funds are used to finance the homebound program. When Title VI-B funds are used, however, only children evaluated as "handicapped" in accordance with federal definitions are eligible for service.

In recent years there has been progress in the allotments for the chronically ill. Because education is tax-supported, some revenues "trickle down" to this area of education, but not without criticism. Tax revenues for education historically have been unpopular among lawmakers and their constituents. When, in addition, programs and their purposes are ambiguous, as in the case of homebound programs, funding is often diverted to more defined services in education. Thus attention is deflected away from the needs of the handicapped and from federal laws intended to provide for those needs, and consequently state compliance with these laws suffers.

There are two funding rules that do apply in every state where a district elects to hire a regular teacher to serve homebound students. First, special education reimbursement for such personnel is not available. Second, state reimbursement for specialized equipment is not available. Barriers within the state or local system thus prevent or minimize an adequate budget for the homebound child's adequate needs.

Legal and Ethical Concerns

Like all educators, homebound teachers are required by law to provide a high quality of services to all students. Because of large caseloads, homebound programs often suffer a lack of communication between support services and the homebound instructor. For example, as most communities are naive about homebound education, trained instructors are often regarded as intruders in the household, or fanatics pushing "education in the home." Mistaken beliefs abound as superintendents, principals, and other administrators remain unaware of homebound philosophy; their varying degree of ignorance of the purpose and practice essentially can ruin community acceptance of services and cause further restraints on instruction funding policies.

Community support thus becomes an integral part of homebound practice. Teachers deliver an educational service but also wear the hat of publicist in advancing the benefits of personalized instruction. To this end, solicitation of support is woven into the overall fabric of homebound interaction, from contacts with the student's teachers to the dyadic interaction with the family. Increasing awareness of the positive aspects of the teacher certainly is not the complete solution, but it does inform the tax-paying public of a special service to which they can contribute.

Conclusion

This chapter has introduced the fundamental educational philosophy and basic population associated with the homebound program. There is a great need, mandated by legislation, to service and fund programs for homebound school-aged children.

Homebound education is a professional link between the public school system and the community. The teacher acts as a liaison for medical, educational, and social services. In this way homebound bridges the gap created by a child's absence from school. Individual attention and family counseling help guide the acutely or chronically disabled pupil and his family through their time of crisis.

2. Homebound Criteria

Who teaches homebound children? Several types of professionals do. Many retired secondary school teachers are hired to tutor a few homebound students for the school systems. Teachers on maternity leave are also contracted hourly to tutor. Experienced regular classroom teachers or special education teachers might also transfer into a homebound program. Special education teachers may or may not have had classroom experience. The variety of teachers is manifold.

Homebound teachers who became employed full-time before the passage of P.L. 94-142 remained in employment. A minimum of additional coursework, such as workshops or a college class was required for these teachers. They avoided returning to school for upgraded certification and avoided undergoing further education now expected of trained homebound teachers.

It is difficult, if not impossible, for a few continuing education courses to provide sufficient training in areas of importance to the homebound teacher, such as orthopedic handicaps, other health impairments, and curriculum modifications. Over 80 percent of current homebound teachers lack this kind of training as well as other qualifications for the field.

This chapter focuses on teacher training and responsibilities in educating the homebound student. Where training matches responsibilities, the teacher is sure to feel more comfortable and competent in this demanding situation.

Educating the Homebound Teacher

Basic Training

General college education is encouraged for all teachers, but it cannot possibly supply all the background and mechanics of one-on-one instruction. Theoretically, all homebound teachers need training in all subject areas, curricula and regular school policies. A second training area is school counseling, theory of abnormal and normal psychology and behavioral techniques. A third area is in social work; awareness covers community networks, available agencies and funding and basic public relations. Obtaining all three areas of study, in most colleges, is unlikely.

Instead, certification programs attempt a logical overview of prevalent methods and issues in the special education field. The process to become a homebound teacher then is more obvious. First, individuals seek certification in orthopedic handicaps at an accredited college or university. The skills acquired are appropriate for application in both classroom and hospital settings. Classroom experience affords educators insight into the mechanics of public instruction, school policies and varying cognitive and affective learning conditions of exceptional children.

The course of study in homebound certification typically entails required and elective courses on teaching methodology, emotional disturbance, mental retardation, learning disabilities and normal children. Classroom practice and internships generally are the first "real-life" use of book knowledge, and students make their first acquaintance with the difficult amalgam of learning, health and community problems. Ultimately this confrontation with student needs guides educators toward a unified or specialist direction, whereby they identify a special population or disability in which to gain stronger competence.

Oddly enough, school policy often conflicts with graduate training. Current trends in national public educational systems discourage unified specialization. Programs emphasize cross-categorization or "combining" children with various handicaps to be taught on similar levels of instruction. Consequently colleges and universities now offer generic special education programs preparing teachers for a mélange of learning, emotional, and health problems. Educators of tomorrow will likely be generalists, not specialists, and they will have only skimmed the surface of topics needed to make them even minimally skillful and efficient.

Movement away from specialization clearly is a step backward. Also threatening progress in special education are reduced faculty and low enrollment in college programs in the field. One consequence of this decrease is that fewer states are regulating standards for teachers who administer homebound programs. In a recent study, Klienberg (1980) reported that of 39 states researched, only 8 (Florida, Georgia, Iowa, Maryland, Michigan, Nebraska, Utah and West Virginia) required either special certification or had established some temporary form of competence standards. Since 1980, additional states have ratified standards for either homebound teachers or homebound and special education (see Appendix A).

Role of the Homebound Teacher

Ideally the homebound teacher should be employed to instruct only homebound children. Pupil caseload usually varies from six to twelve and will depend on such factors as health of student, student's grade range, and distance teacher travels to homes. Qualified teachers acknowledge there is an inconsistent schedule, with some students canceling because of relapse, return to school, or family reasons. As pointed out earlier, entry into these delicate situations following traditional classroom curricula is essentially futile. Instead, homebound programs share the following main objectives:

1. To provide for the development of basic skills, including those which will help each child to speak and write correctly, to read and listen intelligently, and to think critically.

2. To provide opportunities that meet each child's basic human needs for security, sympathy and success; this fosters a healthy personality development.

3. To provide an atmosphere that promotes independence and self-direction in the student.

4. To prevent education deprivation when there is long-term hospitalization or home confinement.

5. To promote learning experiences so that grade-level skills can be maintained and strengthened.

6. To isolate subject-area deficits and apply individualized remediation.

7. To grant school credit for work completed satisfactorily while students are at home.

8. To take advantage of one-on-one learning for enhanced acquisition of skills and for stronger motivation, particularly with students failing in the classroom.

9. To provide an effective, sequential educational program for permanently homebound students.

Teacher Competencies

Homebound teachers face the dilemma of wearing many different professional hats. Flexibility to shift from topic to topic, maintaining a coherent flow of instruction, keeps the ailing student awake and interested. Teachers can plan for this versatility ahead of time with certain "outside competencies." Among these needed tools:

1. Knowledge of organizations and agencies providing special experiences, materials or equipment that enrich the student's lesson plans.

2. Familiarity with computerized materials and their application to homebound instruction.

3. Skills in interpreting to parents and schools the advantages and disadvantages of the homebound program.

4. Knowledge of basic curricula, K-12.

5. An unfailing sense of humor.

By comparison, the state of Florida supplies a resource manual on homebound programs and suggests, in addition, some general competencies:

1. Broad knowlege of curriculum.
2. Knowledge of individual instruction.
3. Ability to interpret task analysis.
4. Ability to evaluate resource programming.
5. Knowlege of exceptional children.
6. Use of behavior management methods.
7. Ability to provide supportive environment.
8. Ability to be perceptive and flexible.

Careful attention to the curriculum becomes a task in communication. Homebound teachers, as liaisons, describe and interpret health and learning facts to the regular school teacher. Explaining health limitations in easy, understandable language makes the student's teacher more sympathetic to homework delays and poor performance. Properly informed teachers are also less prone to stereotypes of unproductive students who "also were lazy in class."

Teacher Responsibilities

Homebound teachers, like most teachers, have routines with different tasks that keep their operation running smoothly. Here we review nine basic tasks: coordination, family introduction, scheduling, evaluation, testing, record keeping, Individualized Educational Plan, supporting the family, and coping with student loneliness.

Coordination. It is the responsibility of homebound teachers to work closely with principals, teachers, guidance counselors and other school personnel to provide services for students confined to home. For hospitalized students, educational services take second priority, the immediate need being empathy. Teachers become a central link to medical and school personnel, apprised of the child's condition, restraints and capabilities.

Family Introduction. A teacher presenting him- or herself in a student's home can be perceived either as a welcome visitor or as an invader of privacy. Parents generally are particular about which professionals are close to their homebound children. Following hospital discharge, parents naturally are suspicious of demands upon their children and may resist this educational service unless properly informed beforehand. The following list of questions and answers is an example of a "pre-introduction" mailed to parents and discussed in advance of the first teacher visit.

1. *What is homebound teaching?*

Homebound teaching is that part of the instructional program which is designed to care for school-age children who are unable to attend a regular classroom and are eligible to receive such instruction.

2. *What are the limitations of homebound programs?*

Every subject cannot possibly be covered by one teacher in the limited time available. The homebound teacher will try to keep the student up to date in the major subject areas.

3. *What facilities do I need for my child to be taught at home?*
The home should provide a comfortable, convenient place where the teacher and student can work effectively. The teacher and pupil must have a place to work that is free of interruptions from family members and unnecessary noise.

4. *How can the parents help?*
Parents can help by giving the child encouragement and praise, thereby boosting his or her morale concerning instruction. They can also help by establishing a permissive child-parent-teacher relationship through parent-teacher cooperation in carrying out all projects designed in the child's best interests. Finally, parents can help by keeping study periods relaxed and free from interruption.

5. *Should parents be present at any time during instruction?*
Parents should not stay in the same room that class is held in, but a parent (or responsible adult) should be in the home at any time the homebound teacher is there.

6. *How long is the instruction and how often does the teacher visit the student?*
Homebound continues for as long as the child's condition warrants it during the regular school year. A physician's statement is issued as proof of the condition. Usually, students are seen for a weekly total of two to five hours on an alternating-day basis (Monday and Wednesday, or Tuesday and Thursday, etc.).

7. *Will I need to make continuous contact with my child's school?*
No. The homebound teacher will confer frequently with the child's grade teacher(s). Children will receive assignments and take tests and earn test credit just as if they were in regular classrooms.

8. *Do I have any responsibility in paying the homebound teacher's salary?*
No. The school system pays the teacher from the school budget.

9. *Should I help my child with school work in between teacher visits?*
This depends on the individual child. Remind your child that school time is work and study time. Parents can assure students have a special time each day for study and that they follow the homework schedule.

Scheduling. Although the number of hours of instruction typically are preset by the school, teachers will be responsible for scheduling students on an hourly or weekly basis. Hours of appointment are not arbitrary. Factors computed into the schedule should include (1) caseload at any given time; (2) ages and ability levels of pupils; (3) physical and other limiting conditions of pupils; and (4) travel time: geographical location of homes.

Evaluation. The student's performance should be observed and evaluated over a designated period of time, according to rules in each school system. For temporarily confined students, evaluation may be a team effort between regular teachers and special education and homebound teachers. Data at this evaluation must document the student's progress, regression, and behavioral problems; collected information forms the basis for decisions about instruction.

Besides monitoring progress, evaluation also pertains to method of grading. Each student deserves an individualized grading system, based initially on the criteria established by the regular classroom teacher. The rule of thumb is to accept all work completed by homebound students, whether grading it "exceptional" or "passing." This is because grades given by the homebound teacher are averaged in with grades documented by the regular classroom teacher, in that grading period or semester.

Testing. Periodically homebound students should receive educational testing in accord with testing protocol in practice for regular classroom cohorts. Testing also assists in development of new learning goals for long-term or chronically ill students unlikely to return to classroom instruction.

Test administration for homebound poses many real problems, as does the interpretation of results. Giving the test in standard format may be impractical due to facility restraints (e.g. hospital room) or physical restraints. One way around these obstacles is altering administration procedures. The idea of modifying test protocol may at first seem strange, even a threat to test validity, causing concern that answers may be misrepresentative of true scoring potential. However, test modifications done carefully will at best accommodate the student and at worst yield insufficient data for evaluation. All test modifications must be documented in the Individualized Educational Plan (IEP) as an instructional strategy used for the student. Acceptable modifications vary for state public school systems but are reasonable and necessary according to federal legislation (P.L. 94-142). Places to apply modifications are on Minimum Skills Diagnostic Tests (MSDTs), End of Course testing (EOC), and State Competency Testing Programs (Competency).

Approved standards for test modification should be consulted in your own school system and state. Rules on modifications are most generally available for "annual testing programs"; e.g., in North Carolina the following aids may be used in annual testing of children with special needs:

1. *Braille writer/abacus*: Braille versions of all test forms are made available to blind and low-vision students who are trained in this writing system. This modification may include the use of the Crammer abacus to perform calculations or the braille writer to write essays when appropriate. Students with visual impairment who have less than Level II braille skills have the brailled version of the test read to them while their responses are recorded by the proctor. A copy of the braille test is provided in regular print to each proctor.

2. *Magnification or large print*: Students may use any magnification device that they *normally* use during instruction. Large print editions of, for example, the California Achievement Test may be provided at all grade levels for low-vision students who qualify for this modification. If students will be in special education after homebound services end, use of these modifications must be in accord with recommendations of a school-based committee and receive "administration placement committee approval."

Students utilizing a large print edition may need further modifications, such as ample space that will allow movement of the large-size book. Magnifying instruments for reading may not enlarge the page sufficiently for clarity. In such cases, answers can be made in the text booklet and later transferred to the answer sheet by the proctor. Answer sheet and booklet must be verified by the proctor to ensure that no errors in transcribing occurred.

3. *Reading test aloud*: The proctor may read the test aloud for students with specific learning disabilities that affect their ability to perceive printed words or numbers. These handicapping conditions must be documented and evidence shown that prior instruction was attempted exclusively through auditory means.

4. *Signing the test directions*: Test administration sessions for hearing-impaired students may include an interpreter using signed English for test directions or to answer questions. The proctor, present at all times, reads the test directions aloud as presented in the manual, so that they can be signed. Interpreters should also sign test questions that are read aloud as part of the test directions.

5. *Answers recorded by proctor*: Students unable to respond to test items by marking an answer sheet or test booklet may have a proctor record the answers. This modification applies to students with orthopedic impairments, severe learning disabilities, or severe mental or emotional handicaps. For example, when a math test is administered, students must dictate all math operations to the proctor, use a worksheet, a typewriter or word processor as a worksheet. Upon completion of test, the proctor and student should sign a document indicating that all calculations were written by proctor, as dictated by the student. This document must be filed with the student's permanent record.

6. *Marked responses in test booklet:* This modification applies only to students who experience problems in recording responses on an answer sheet. Use of this approach must be in accord with recommendations of the school-based committee and other committee approval.

7. *Dictation to a scribe:* This modification is available only to sutdents who are orthopedically impaired to the extent that they cannot use a typewriter or word processor to complete the examination. The session between student and scribe must be recorded on cassette tape and given to the test coordinator along with the transcription. However, dictation to a scribe is not the same as the *answer recorded by proctor* modification.

8. *Dictation to a recorder:* Another option available to orthopedically impaired students is dictation to a recorder which is later transcribed by the proctor. This modification can be used only by students unable to use a typewriter or word processor.

9. *Use of typewriter or word processor:* This modification is available for blind or low-vision students who do not read braille, and students who are orthopedically impaired or have severe learning disabilities.

10. *Hospital and home testing:* All hospitalized or homebound students should have equal opportunities for testing while confined. Parents or guardians may elect to defer testing until students return to school or are physically recovered.

Record Keeping. Homebound teachers assume the responsibility to complete and submit all required reports and forms to the designated individuals and students' permanent file. Records will vary by educational policy, but generally include (1) teacher's travel (mileage), (2) pupil attendance, (3) pupil's grades, (4) pupil's books, (5) materials covered, and (6) student/school contact.

Individualized Educational Plan. For most homebound students, confinement to home is temporary with plans to return to the classroom. In the interim, parallels between routine classroom process and homebound process are made to preserve continuity. This begins by writing a formal Individualized Educational Plan (IEP), a document of goals and techniques for execution of the curriculum. Development of the IEP is the most essential aspect of application consistent to P.L. 94-142. Each plan is written by an interdisciplinary team and covers student instruction for a given period, such as thirty days. Contents include (1) student's present needs, (2) annual short term goals and objectives, (3) services projected or utilized, (4) duration of program services, and (5) evaluation procedures.

Figure 2.1 illustrates an IEP for John Doe, a seventh grader receiving homebound for general health problems. Three categories on this form appear on nearly every IEP form throughout the nation: Short-term Objectives

STUDENT NAME ____John Doe_____ I.D. ____32986_____

Individual Responsible _____Homebound teacher_____ SCHOOL __Smith Middle School

Statement of Current Performance:	Long Term Goal:
PERFORMING ON GRADE LEVEL — (7th) Modification due to health problems are suggested below	TO PROVIDE ACADEMIC INSTRUCTION TO MAINTAIN GRADE LEVEL

Short Term Objectives and Evaluation Criteria	Strategies	Date Attained
1. To provide Homebound services when student is too ill to go to school.	TEXTS: English IN our World The Adventures of Tom Sawyer	All assign-ments due according
2. The homebound teacher will provide continuity by seeing student in hospital (if hospital teacher is not available)	Spelling (7th grade) Principles of Science The New Exploring the NON-Western World	to agreement between homebound and class-
3. Teacher will make weekly visits to school to provide current assignments and guidance.	General Mathematics	room teacher
	SUPPLEMENTAL ACTIVITY: Journal	MASTERY LEVEL
3. The homebound teacher will provide quarter and/or semester grades based on completed assignments.	MODIFICATIONS:	80% on all assign-ments
	Spelling tests administered	
5. The homebound teacher will plan all curriculum using school system guidelines.	orally All Math assignments modified to completing (no less than) ½ of total problems on each page.	

White: Cumulative folder
Yellow: Parent
Pink: Service Provider

Figure 2.1. A sample IEP.

and Evaluation Criteria, Strategies, and Date Attained. In this case, dates for work completion coalesce with the classroom teacher's schedule, rather than being tied to a separate, specified timetable.

Supporting the Family. Attitudes of the family represent a major force in the child's rehabilitation process. Optimistic, uplifting praise for minor steps of achievement can boost morale for a physically weak child. Conversely, resentment of "invasion" by the teacher and parental neglect can accelerate the downward spiral to physical decay and sloppy homework. Entering the household also means entering into the height of family affection or family dysfunction. Teachers alert to characteristic emotional conditions during family crises stand better prepared to offer family support. Common mistakes parents make to which teachers should be particularly attentive include:

1. *Overprotection:* This develops when the child is prevented from doing for him- or herself. This is particularly common when children are in body casts for three months or longer. In some instances, parents have answered questions for the child, until the child no longer is eager to be independent. Teachers may wish to point out that despite children's disabilities, independence begins immediately by having them do whatever they can do.

2. *Guilt*: Frequently parents feel they are to blame for the child's condition. This is especially true for accident victims, yet equally common in cases of corrective surgery, sports injuries or terminal disease. Assurance can help parents to realize accidents are commonplace and that their guilt will only relieve the student of feeling responsible and being independent.

3. *Overindulgence*: Parents consumed by guilt may also react by compensating or overcompensating for lost time with their children. Parents may spend unusually long hours with the student, purchase too many gifts, or may plan elaborate trips and excursions hoping to redeem their children's trust. Unfortunately the real consequence of such action is serious delay of physical recovery and prevention of emotional stability. Teachers can best help parents understand that maintaining a normal, routine lifestyle conveys a passage of time and expectation of recovery.

4. *Sentimental pity*: Empathic understanding and pity are very different. Empathic understanding verifies for the student that his or her anguish is real, experiential, and engenders normal emotions shared by other people. The teacher who demonstrates such understanding is perceived as caring, trustworthy and warm. By contrast there is an instinctive tendency to show pity, to reveal our own inadequacy to deal with polymorbidity. Homebound children resent pity because it reminds them of their vulnerability, helplessness and disruption of normal life patterns. Teachers can remind parents of this point.

Coping with Student Loneliness. Depression and loneliness are normal reactions to prolonged disjointment of one's social life pattern. When children remain confined either in the hospital or at home they lose faith in restoring daily routines, they forget friendships and associated pleasures, and they resent being disabled. Faced with helplessness, teachers must wear their social worker hat. The challenge is to awaken a fresh perspective on life by encouraging introspection of the student's feelings.

General interventions for showing compassion include the following:

1. Accept the child's feelings and reassure the child it is natural to have such feelings.

2. Spend the first few minutes of every session asking questions about things students are interested in.

3. Be aware that your concern with their learning and progress is a way of expressing positive feelings.

4. Encourage all children to keep a journal.

5. Reward the process and effort as well as the final result.

6. Make each student conscious of his or her progress.

7. Help students feel that accomplishment is its own reward.

Certain "feeling games" are designed to evoke self-awareness of emotions and resolution to anger. Outlined below are four games for easy, practical implementation either before lessons begin or immediately afterwards.

1. *Free Association Word Test:* The teacher constructs a list of words related to school situations, interpersonal relations and general school information. For example: teacher, hookey, pencil.... Then, the teacher gives out the stimulus word to the child and he or she responds with the first word that comes to mind. Responses can be oral or written and the "game" can be played as a language arts exercise.

2. *Sentence Completion Game:* The child is asked to complete these sentences:

    a. When my teacher ...
    b. My friends ...
    c. Report cards are ...
    d. I'm unhappy in school when ...
    e. Now that I can't go to school ...
    f. I feel that school ...
    g. Other children in school ...

3. *Story Completion Game:* The teacher introduces a story plot and then asks the student to complete it, adding as many characters and details as possible from imagination. Another version is re-creating a story plot from a newspaper headline.

4. *Six Wishes Game:* Teacher asks the child different questions for a writing or oral assignment. Such questions include:

    1. If you could have a kind of world to live in, what kind of world would it be?

    2. If you could have any kind of family, what kind of family would it be?

3. If you could have anybody in the world for a friend, who would it be?

4. If you could be anything or anybody, what or who would you be?

5. If there was one thing you could do all day long without stopping, what would it be?

6. If you could pick your dreams at night, what would one be?

When Homebound Time Is Over — Who Really Cares?

Hours are spent on planning, providing direct lessons under the most unusual and challenging conditions ... and all for what? Homebound teachers expend a tremendous amount of energy but may be the last to reap rewards from their services. Feedback in any bureaucracy — and school systems are no exception — is delayed, ambiguous and frequently absent. This is why teachers need another, more immediate closed-feedback loop to gain recognition for the student's homebound experience.

A useful solicitation for feedback is to ask students finishing homebound to reply in writing to the following questions: How did they perceive homebound? Did they like the teacher and program? How did they feel about the demands put on them? Below are replies from four students the senior author, Nancy Macciomei, had over the years.

Cancer hits the family

It was in the month of July that I found out I had cancer in the leg and the lungs. It shocked everyone in the family. The word "Cancer", by itself, makes anyone scared. I know what it could do to you or what can happened. So, I took it one day at a time. A week passed by I started taking the treatments. The medicine I was taking had side effects. I would go to the hospital every Monday and stay until friday. I usually get out on the weekend, that was good too. The Doctor told us I would be sick and my hair may come out. A week passed. I was losing weight even my bones were showing. Some of my hair had come out. After four treatments I stopped. I said, "that I was going to leave it up to Jesus Christ." My mother agreed. Two weeks later I started gaining my weight back. I had a new growth of hair. I tried to go back to school but, I was too weak and I started hurting all over. My homebound teacher started to come back again she's a very nice lady. I tried and tried to go back to school but the same thing occurred. I am doing fine thanks to the Good Lord up above. I would also like to thank my family and my friends. And my teacher Nancy M. for understanding my situation.

•

Homebound teachers

I think homebound teachers get the worst part of the deal. This is because the homebound teacher has to run back and forth between homes and schools. All the student has to do is sit back and relax while (s)he is waiting on the teacher to arrive.

Every day before class the homebound teacher has to go to the student's school before class to start. She must chase down eight to nine teachers before class starts. This is no easy job, because these teachers are in all different places around the school.

After she talks to the teachers, she heads out to my house to begin class. On the way over she reviews over the assignments.

When she gets to my house we begin class by going over the past assignments from yesterday. This includes all the homework given in regular class from the previous day.

Class lasts about one or two hours depending on where my homebound teacher must go to next. During this period we must cover all subjects sufficiently in order to stay up with the regular classes.

Towards the end of class, Mrs. Macciomei informs me of my assignments due tomorrow. Also, I am told what time she is coming by in the morning.

After class is over, it is usually off to another school or to another homebound class. She is constantly on the "run" all day.

These are a few elaborations on why a homebound teacher has it so rough. In order to withstand this torture, one must be well qualified and very patient. Also, they must have a numbered of injured students.

•

Having a homebound teacher has many advantages. The teacher comes to my home and I don't have to worry about getting up early to make sure that my hair and make-up are perfect. It is a casual teaching session and it doesn't matter how I look. Since I had knee surgery, I have not been able to hold my leg down so I couldn't stand to wait on a bus to go to school. With Nancy coming to my home, I am able to elevate my leg to where we can study and I am in as little pain as possible. Nancy is a great tutor and I feel comfortable being around her. Not only has she been a great tutor, I think of Nancy as my friend.

We have an hour to an hour and a half session every other day. We go over all my subjects in each session. I have quality time in these sessions. If I have a problem or just don't understand how to do something, Nancy is always patient and works with me until I understand how to do it. The teachers at school do not have the time and will tell you to figure the problem out by yourself. Sometimes that just can't be done.

Nancy makes learning fun. The subjects I don't really care for, Nancy teaches in a way that makes it fun to learn more about it. Homebound teachers seem to care more about the education of their students than the teachers in the school system do.

I have more work to do on a daily basis because my classes are every other day instead of every day. But that is alright with me. In order to keep up with my classes I have to work harder between sessions. Nancy always praises my good work and if I would mess up on something, she will explain what I did wrong so that I don't make the same mistakes. She has never yelled at me or raised her voice at me because I had made a mistake. She keeps me updated on things that are happening at school and with the things that she feels that I would like to know about the functions at school. She takes my education seriously and makes sure that I do my very best at everything. I wish that all the teachers at school could be as caring, pleasant and understanding as Nancy is. Nancy has made my stay out of school a more enjoyable one because she has been such a good friend and teacher. I will miss her very much when I return back to school. She is always smiling and cheerful when she comes to my home to tutor me. If I knew of a friend who was going to be homebound, I would tell them to try to get Nancy as their tutor. She is the greatest.

The only disadvantage I have found with being homebound is that I don't get to see my friends at school.

•

I like the HomeBound Program because it helps me keep up with my studies at school. It also gives me something to look forward to during the week.

One of the things I don't like about the HomeBound Program is that I can only spend a short time, and just a few days a week with my teacher. I would like for us to have more time to discuss my lessons with each other.

I will feel better about returning to school because of the Home-Bound Program and my teacher.

3. Modifying the Curriculum

Homebound instruction provides a continuous educational program for children who otherwise would be separated from the school group for short or long periods of time. Adjustments in the curriculum are needed to maintain an education for these children. Homebound instructors *should* follow the general curriculum of the current grade level and basic prerequisites for the next grade level. But there is ultimately a problem with this. Following the grade-appropriate curriculum to the letter is an inflexible approach. It overlooks the emotional and social benefits which come from keeping the child constructively occupied.

When a student has idle time, he spends it being restless, irritable, unreasonable, and hard to work with overall. Boredom often undermines the teacher's efforts and delays progress in recovery. One alternative we suggest is to *modify the existing curriculum*. It seems daring, but don't be afraid to twist, turn, alter and essentially invent your own rendition of assignments relative to the student's capacity to learn.

This chapter reviews methods of modifying standard curriculum within a range that preserves the integrity of academic study. Key alterations of the simplest sort, from writing a journal to introducing calm discussion, relieve teachers of the endless struggle to make assignments fit. Orthopedically handicapped children, for instance, will not automatically fit into regular reading drills, nor is their socialization mature enough for the plot of many stories.

Below are some general and specific guidelines to design lesson plans according to student ability. First we present general curriculum modifications, then curriculum modifications for math, and finally, curriculum modifications for reading.

General Curriculum Modifications

Profile of Homebound Student

What do you know about this student, anyway? Some students are quite capable of reading the assigned textbook. However, their pace of reading is slow. What else do you know about this student? Usually not much.

25

Before the first visit to the home, teachers need background information on the child's physical condition. Was he in a car accident and now confined to a body cast for three months? Does he have cancer and feel fine, yet progressive degeneration is imminent? Or perhaps this student suffers cystic fibrosis and needs to lie down on the couch or bed during instruction. Whatever the disability, homebound teachers must understand the student's condition and be prepared to accommodate it.

What level of skills does the student demonstrate . . . or lack? Homebound children vary along a continuum from skillful to illiterate. Grade level is a poor gauge of aptitude. Students in any grade ranging from kindergarten to high school, and including some who have never been to school, represent a challenge because they may have major deficits undetected by a classroom teacher that are suddenly visible during individualized instruction.

How normal or abnormal is this student's ability to learn? Homebound instruction operates on the worthwhile assumption that all impaired students experience some degree of life disruption. The severity of this disruption depends entirely on whether the incapacitation has been temporary or since childhood (congenital). A good rule of thumb to follow for any delayed education is to *start where the student is.* For example, students whose performance was superior before an accident rendered them aphasic now require extensive relearning at a slower, more tolerable pace; with smaller units of instruction approached in a gentle, remedial format, mistakes will be fewer, and the correction of them easier.

Principles for Modifying Curriculum

Once the student's background is known, the next task involves simple adjustments in curriculum. Over time, curriculum adjustments become a natural step in daily lesson planning for the homebound teacher, much as the classroom teacher figures out a daily order of subjects. Preparation, in other words, follows a routine set of rules or principles from which decisions are reached about appropriate materials.

We can identify six principles, in particular, having special relevance to curriculum modifications in homebound. Appropriate adjustments in any subject are based on (1) individualizing the problem, (2) level of instruction, (3) degree of instruction, (4) readiness for instruction, (5) tolerance of instruction, and (6) multisensory instruction.

Individualizing the Instruction. Homebound students are a unique population. The teacher must understand the student's characteristics, home background, academic strengths and weaknesses, medical and personal needs. This entails a holistic or total picture of the situation. Awareness covers physical, psychological, social, cultural, ethnic and religious factors plus other observable influences upon the student.

Level of Instruction. It is important that any assessment of a "learning deficit" is relative to experiences of that student. Traditionally the diagnosis of skill deficit resulted from formal school testing or after considerable evaluation of academic failures. Methods of testing alone certainly can alert an educator to underdeveloped skills but will overlook other factors, such as confinement and reactivity to medical condition, that deteriorate student motivation at home or school.

Degree of Instruction. Lesson materials should be meaningful to students and their medical situation. Try not to overwhelm the students with a multitude of assignments. Instead, understand the medical problems and associated side-effects. One solution is budgeting appropriate time for selected subjects. For instance, many students fatigue quickly because of ailments, but after a period of rest can regain a burst of energy and produce excellent work. Tired students only become frustrated and irate and will tune out your carefully planned instruction.

Readiness for Instruction. Homebound instructors should be aware of the different levels of reading that exist, as well as the reading level of a particular student. Reading, writing and other academic skills vary, and it is best to begin at the level comfortable for the student, rather than at the level where he "should" be.

Tolerance of Instruction. At first students may seem overwhelmed by assignments. This is perfectly understandable considering the sequence of events. They have suffered a medical crisis; they are out of a regular school routine; family and friends treat them differently; and now a new teacher assigns them homework to be completed entirely on their own. Overloading students without assigning proper priorities to their needs is a real mistake. If the emphasis is on quantity rather than quality, not only will students refuse to work, but their motivation may decay.

Multisensory Instruction. The multisensory approach is an attempt to integrate various teaching approaches, materials and methodology. Alertness to the many strategies used in education and behavioral sciences assures the greatest flexibility with instruction and accommodation to complex learning situations.

In general these principles outline simple reminders when advancing to the step of actual instruction. Application is evident in the following case.

CASE FOUR: JIMMY

Jimmy had been diagnosed as having cystic fibrosis when he was only eight months old. For six years he had battled increased breathing difficulties and colds that turned instantly into pneumonia. He was no stranger to the children's ward at the hospital in town. But despite his severe illness, Jimmy remained high-spirited, loving, and especially interested in school.

I saw Jimmy for approximately two years. Each session he would greet me at the door, holding "Huggy Bear." He was ready to give me a big hug. We would sit on the floor with our legs stretched under the rectangular coffee table. His schoolbooks would be on one side and his latest projects (trains, airplane models, etc.) would be set proudly in the middle for me to praise.

The sessions could never begin until Jimmy set up our school. Jimmy had never been to school, so he tried to imagine what it was like. For one session he set up pillows behind, to the side, and in front of our feet to pretend we were in the back seat of a car. For another session he placed his toy trains and tracks around our work so we could have school in an imaginary caboose. During our two years we had sessions in the cockpit of an airplane, on a city bus, in the jungles of Africa, and on a farm. I could usually tell what Jimmy had watched on television the last few days, depending on what situation he created.

After designating our school environment, we worked for one hour, every other day. We covered pre-primer reading skills, beginning math concepts, and basic aspects of social studies.

After a year, Jimmy's health began to deteriorate at a rapid pace. Our sessions became shorter, and less school work was accomplished. We would work for thirty minutes, during which he constantly coughed up mucus that was collecting in his lungs. He started to keep a few large grocery bags to his side so he did not have to make a mad dash to the bathroom every few minutes. Each coughing spell seemed to empty an ounce of energy along with the choking mucus that he dispelled.

After ten or fifteen minutes of continuous coughing, Jimmy would stop working; pale and exhausted, he would lie down on the davenport. During the last few weeks in November of the second year, Jimmy would be lying on the sofa when I entered, exhausted from a sleepless night. The two of us would simply talk briefly and watch a little television.

I would sit on the couch, holding Jimmy's hand or just sitting by his side, enjoying ten to fifteen minutes of his favorite cartoon, "Scooby Doo." The rest of the hour I spent with his mother, discussing Jimmy and his rapidly declining health. She was a remarkably open and honest woman, willing to share her fears about the inevitable future. We spoke about death and dying. I listened to her talk about how she loved Jimmy but hated to see him so ill. She wanted him to stop hurting, possibly to die soon, instead of struggling against the lingering pain. She was overcome with mixed emotions and a deep sense of guilt. She, too, had nights without sleep, holding Jimmy's hands until he could rest each night.

Christmas came with a bang. Jimmy suddenly found energy that we thought he had lost forever. He seemed to perk up during the festivities. He wanted to get up and play with his new toys and stuffed animals. The Christmas spirit gave Jimmy and everyone new hope. He asked to do schoolwork and talked endlessly about his Christmas tree and gifts. Although school was on break, I came to see Jimmy and brought him home-baked, chocolate-chip cookies that he wolfed down instantly. Jimmy and his mother took outings to the store and the pizza parlor. With Huggy Bear beside him, he made a major comeback into the world of the living.

After the first few days of the new year, Jimmy was back on the couch, unable to catch his breath. His burst of energy had vanished. His pink, full cheeks had changed drastically to pale grey and sunken. Jimmy was too weak to eat or use the bathroom on his own.

Although school resumed, my visits consisted of a hug for Jimmy, a few positive words, and a thiry-minute conversation with his mother. In a low whisper she asked for information on funeral arrangements, costs and whom to contact when the time came. Two days after one of my visits, Jimmy died. He was lying on the couch, took a loud, final gasp for breath, and passed away silently.

Jimmy was buried with Huggy Bear at his side. I could not concentrate on the praises the minister had for Jimmy. I just sat on the pew, silently recalling the last two years. For the next few weeks, I stopped by Jimmy's house to see how his mother was getting along. She deeply mourned the loss of her son, and yet was relieved to know he was out of his misery. I helped her pack up all of his toys, which she donated to the children's ward at the hospital in town.

I left the house giving Jimmy's mother a gentle hug, knowing that although our time together had come to an end, I would remember Jimmy and his mother forever.

Tips for Individualized Lesson Plans

An unfortunate but common error is presenting the school teacher's lesson plans verbatim. Mechanically assigning math problems or reciting text to read and write creates a sterile and chilly atmosphere. Students already realize the special nature of a visiting-teacher arrangement and expect assignments to move at a slower pace than in their classroom. Animated, more creative lesson plans may not disguise the obviously slower pace of assignments, but they can allow for a degree of flexibility in teaching style.

Listed below are adaptations common in standard homebound curricula. Explanations are given for each adaptation for further clarity (see Chapter 4 for more specific interventions).

1. *Reduce quantity of instruction.* Begin with what the student already knows and teach it in small steps. For example, give 10 spelling words instead of 25 per week.

2. *Allow various steps to get the final requirements.* Move at a slow pace, but also break down goals into small, achievable steps. This process is known as "task analysis" and is described procedurally in Chapter 4. Reduction of steps also is easier for learning.

3. *Identify an interest or strength of the student and encourage expression of it.* Identify what the student enjoys doing, whether it be a hobby, project, or favorite book. Incorporate that interest into a focused assignment such as writing a research paper on it.

4. *Grade each student by ability and effort produced.* Use your in-

tuitive sense about this. Certainly the work of a normal classroom student will differ greatly from that of a homebound student with muscular dystrophy. Spelling errors that are unacceptable for regular students can be viewed as successful instances of perceptual-motor coordination, of writing by firmly grasping a utensil; efforts this delicate for the dystrophic student are milestones deserving much praise.

5. *Be creative about tests.* Traditional testing by booklets, forms, or memorization may be impractical for certain disabilities. Accident-induced aphasics surely are incapable of memory-based or power (time-pressured) testing. Creative variations, adapted to the student's handicap, can evaluate needed academic skills and be more representative of lessons learned.

6. *Mark only correct answers; leave wrong answers to be corrected.* There is twofold logic in this simple strategy. First, drawing attention to incorrect answers overlooks small units of progress and can discourage further work in that subject area. Secondly, an unmarked correction signifies the opportunity for students to remedy mistakes "before the teacher checks it again."

7. *Do not grade all the assignments.* Review the assigned work at each visit, but grade only a representative sample of the work. Feedback in the form of comments or written notes can be given for the remainder of work, sending a message to the student that *anything* he does is acceptable.

8. *Always couple the completed assignments with a generous amount of praise.* Recall a fundamental rule that homebound students usually require long hours to complete a minimal amount of work. Praise even for incorrect papers acknowledges the struggle of time and concentration endured by that student.

9. *Always allow students to use aids.* Whereas in the classroom certain aids such as rulers, numberlines and calculators may be prohibited, aids can facilitate completion of work that otherwise may be ignored when the student is home. Again, primary focus at all times is upon enhancement of opportunities for students to attempt and, one hopes, complete the lesson; accuracy of work is a second priority.

10. *Always present one new concept or skill at a time.* Multiple concepts in a single lesson will easily confuse the student even on areas already mastered while the student was in school. This is because homebound suspends the rapid, pressured, and sequential pace of classroom learning, offering fewer chances for trial and error and interaction with teacher.

11. *Review after two or three new concepts.* Never assume serial learning occurs along the same predictable progression as it would in the classroom. Once there is mastery of a concept, repetition of that concept either in combination with new concepts or alone should be a regular part of daily lessons.

12. *Contract study units.* Unique to homebound is individualized instruction. Students can select which subject to do first — for example, spelling precedes math, followed by social studies. Students can choose this order as well as the order of units within a subject area. Contracts set up an informal agreement that lessons will follow the student's preferred order in exchange for completion of assignments.

13. *Interpret the lesson through art form.* Verbal instruction alone is a weak medium for the student's comprehension. Use visual aids, collages, murals, papier-mâché and story boards for illustration of new and particularly complex concepts.

14. *Include role-play.* In social studies or history, an enactment between teacher and student frequently conveys the theme or storyline more persuasively; role-play and role-reversal stimulate immediate application of material that is particularly difficult or warrants a longer attention span than is normally possible for the student.

15. *Write postcards or letters to a fictional or real character in assignment readings.* Stories acquire significantly more meaning when students can participate in them. Letters, journal entries or any written variation of expression about the antagonist and protagonist adds dimension to these characters, lending more insight into the storyline.

16. *Encourage students to do independent reading.* Reading outside the prescribed order of fiction or nonfiction books is an excellent method for generalization. Discussion of newspaper and magazine articles or novels that the student has read further sharpens attention to critical details, description, and of course pronunciation of different words. On a more important level, it extends learning beyond the confines of teacher-student dyad.

Curriculum Modifications for Math

Teaching math in regular classrooms poses several complications, from remembering number order to theoretical comprehension. Outside the classroom complications are more pronounced because students lack the needed day-to-day repetition of facts and concepts. Approaches to homebound mathematics thus deviate sharply from classroom approaches. Several practical adaptations of classroom math lessons are possible for homebound teachers faced with a curriculum that is unrealistic for the student's current level of functioning.

Tips for Individualized Math Lessons
Following are 10 useful guidelines for dealing with student aptitude differences and complex lesson plans.

1. *Find the level of skill mastery and proceed according to the student's pace.* Obvious as this point seems, the unseasoned teacher may be tempted to proceed through a given math unit verbatim. Resist this temptation: First identify at which level or unit in the math book the student is competent, even if it is several chapters behind the assignment; then go forward from there.

2. *Use concrete materials to model concepts.* Physical aids such as geometric cubes, rulers, and other templates sharpen awareness of concepts. Case illustrations using real or imaginary situations also add clarity.

3. *Assign all material in a simple, sequenced presentation.* Math units tend to move rapidly from elementary to complex as the practice problems become more difficult. Concentrate on creating, when needed, examples that lie between simple and hard math problems or that simplify the step-by-step operations.

4. *Repetition should be routine.* Computations at any level require a good memory, not only of the basics of multiplication, division, addition and subtraction, but also of intricate conversions and numerical properties. Frequent rehearsal of math formulas, methods, and basics will help to achieve mastery over new concepts.

5. *Develop accuracy, then speed.* Probably because of the pressure for passing scores on standardized testing, today's teachers are emphasizing shortcuts for faster solutions to math problems. Speed performance at the homebound level poses obvious hazards, in that a student may know enough simply to solve a math equation but misunderstand essential logistics. Attention is best redirected toward a slower, more calibrated approach to learning.

6. *Teach the essentials only.* Classroom math units often cover points of relevant history or theoretical underpinnings of some concept. Knowing the origins of the Pythagorean theorem, for example, can broaden the student's appreciation of the application. In homebound teaching, however, it is wise to spare these embellishments and reserve the student's limited endurance for relevant concepts.

7. *Establish individual standards.* Rather than using group norms, evaluate the student's potential per math unit and agree upon criteria or standards that define mastery for that student. Once criteria are established, contract with the student on how much time or practice will be spent toward this goal.

8. *Be patient and provide motivation.* Memory of math concepts alone is a hard task. When memory tasks combine with rigorous practice sessions, disabled students are more prone to fatigue, self-doubt, and apathy. Overcome this performance decay with genuine praise on small approximations of progress.

9. *Write numbers by rhyme.* This creative device softens the hard-

ship of drawing or remembering new numbers. Phrases that combine rhyme with a description of how the number looks or is formed entice immediate interest from students. Try the following:

A straight line like one is fun.
Around and back on a railroad track: two, two, two.
Around a tree and around a tree is three.
Down and over and down some more, that's the way to make a four.
Fat old five goes down and around,
Put a flag on top and see what you've found.
Down to a loop, a six rolls a hoop.
Across the sky and down from heaven, that's the way to make a seven.
Make an S but do not wait.
Climb back up to make an eight.
A loop and a line is nine.
It's easy to make a one and a 0.
It is all of your fingers, you know.

10. *Emphasize problem-solving.* Mathematics is by nature a problem-solving exercise. Yet students can benefit from reminders that their calculated work on equations has direct value for coping with the hard adjustments of homebound education. Teachers may wish to extend problem-solving into domains of daily decision-making, assigning of priorities, and clarification of values.

Addition

Sequence of Steps in Addition. Teaching the operation of addition follows a very systematic forward process as the numbers increase in value. This process includes:

1. Basic facts with sums less than 11: e.g. $7 + 2$.
2. Tens plus one digit without regrouping: e.g. $20 + 6$.
3. Two digits plus one more: e.g. $25 + 1$.
4. Two digits plus one digit without regrouping: e.g. $42 + 6$.
5. Tens plus tens without regrouping: e.g. $40 + 30$.
6. Tens plus two digits without regrouping: e.g. $40 + 27$.
7. Two digits plus two digits without regrouping: e.g. $43 + 26$.
8. Basic facts with sums greater than ten: e.g. $13 + 4$.
9. Two digits plus one digit with regrouping to ten: e.g. $43 + 7$.
10. Tens plus tens with regrouping in tens place: e.g. $30 + 30$.
11. Tens plus two digits with regrouping in tens place: e.g. $60 + 74$.
12. Two digits plus two digits with regrouping in ones place: e.g. $15 + 36$.
13. Two digits plus two digits with regrouping in tens place: e.g. $75 + 62$.

14. Two digits plus two digits with regrouping in ones and tens place: e.g. $99 + 76$.

15. Addition with more than two addends: e.g. $45 + 6 + 32$.

Common Errors in Addition. Six of the most common error patterns in addition include:

1. The student does not understand the identity element for addition or confuses it with the multiplicative identity: e.g.

$$
\begin{array}{r} 47 \\ +40 \\ \hline 80 \end{array}
\qquad
\begin{array}{r} 41 \\ +12 \\ \hline 52 \end{array}
\qquad
\begin{array}{r} 38 \\ +11 \\ \hline 19 \end{array}
$$

2. Each column is treated as a separate problem instead of regrouping and the use of place value: e.g.

$$
\begin{array}{r} 26 \\ +18 \\ \hline 314 \end{array}
\qquad
\begin{array}{r} 19 \\ +29 \\ \hline 318 \end{array}
$$

3. The student adds ones to tens, or tens to tens and hundreds: e.g.

$$
\begin{array}{r} 37 \\ +3 \\ \hline 70 \end{array}
\qquad
\begin{array}{r} 342 \\ +12 \\ \hline 454 \end{array}
$$

4. The student does not grasp ones to tens: e.g.

$$
\begin{array}{r} 29 \\ +8 \\ \hline 27 \end{array}
\qquad
\begin{array}{r} 43 \\ +7 \\ \hline 40 \end{array}
$$

5. The student writes the regrouped figure instead of the remainder: e.g.

$$
\begin{array}{r} 34 \\ +19 \\ \hline 71 \end{array}
\qquad
\begin{array}{r} 28 \\ +17 \\ \hline 81 \end{array}
$$

6. Student does not complete the addition problem: e.g.

$$
\begin{array}{r} 35 \\ +9 \\ \hline 34 \end{array}
\qquad
\begin{array}{r} 23 \\ 5 \\ +2 \\ \hline 28 \end{array}
\qquad
\begin{array}{r} 25 \\ +42 \\ \hline 47 \end{array}
$$

Subtraction

Sequence of Steps in Subtraction. Here are the procedural steps, from simple and moving toward complex, for learning the operations of subtraction:

1. Basic facts with sums less than 11: e.g. $9 - 7$.
2. Tens minus tens without regrouping: e.g. $40 - 20$.
3. Two digits minus one digit without regrouping: e.g. $27 - 2$.
4. Two digits minus tens: e.g. $24 - 10$.
5. Two digits minus two digits without regrouping: e.g. $33 - 12$.
6. Three digits minus two digits without regrouping: e.g. $345 - 42$.
7. Basic facts with regrouping: e.g. $15 - 7$.
8. Tens minus one digit: e.g. $20 - 3$.
9. Two digits minus one digit with regrouping: e.g. $23 - 4$.
10. Two digits minus two digits with regrouping: e.g. $41 - 26$.
11. Hundreds minus tens: e.g. $300 - 40$.
12. Hundreds minus two digits: e.g. $400 - 23$.
13. Three digits minus two digits with regrouping from tens to ones: e.g. $290 - 31$.
14. Three digits minus two digits with regrouping from hundreds to tens: e.g. $326 - 94$.
15. Three digits minus two digits with regrouping from ones to tens and from hundreds to tens: e.g. $421 - 34$.
16. Three digits with zero in tens place minus two digits with regrouping: e.g. $402 - 36$.

Common Errors in Subtraction. Following are common mistakes easily detected in subtraction:

1. Student does not have mastery of basic subtraction combinations: e.g.

$$\begin{array}{r} 784 \\ -357 \\ \hline 426 \end{array}$$

2. Student does not understand the subtraction of zero or confuses it with the identity element for addition: e.g.

$$\begin{array}{r} 60 \\ -28 \\ \hline 40 \end{array} \qquad \begin{array}{r} 60 \\ -28 \\ \hline 48 \end{array}$$

3. Student does not complete subtraction problem. This usually occurs when there are fewer digits in the number being subtracted: e.g.

$$\begin{array}{r} 673 \\ -44 \\ \hline 29 \end{array}$$

4. Student subtracts small digit from larger digit instead of regrouping: e.g.

$$
\begin{array}{r}
373 \\
-189 \\
\hline
216
\end{array}
$$

5. Student does not understand regrouping in general: e.g.

$$
\begin{array}{r}
819 \\
-8 \\
\hline
819
\end{array}
$$

6. Student subtracts tens from hundreds, or ones from tens, or ones from tens and hundreds. This usually occurs when there are fewer digits in the number being subtracted: e.g.

$$
\begin{array}{r}
463 \\
-27 \\
\hline
236
\end{array}
\qquad
\begin{array}{r}
78 \\
-6 \\
\hline
12
\end{array}
\qquad
\begin{array}{r}
975 \\
-5 \\
\hline
421
\end{array}
$$

7. Student regroups from tens to ones but does not change tens digit accordingly: e.g.

$$
\begin{array}{r}
46 \\
-9 \\
\hline
47
\end{array}
$$

8. Student regroups from hundreds to tens but does not change hundreds digit accordingly: e.g.

$$
\begin{array}{r}
638 \\
-156 \\
\hline
382
\end{array}
$$

9. Student regroups when not necessary: e.g.

$$
\begin{array}{r}
33 \\
-22 \\
\hline
1
\end{array}
\qquad
\begin{array}{r}
21 \\
-10 \\
\hline
1
\end{array}
$$

10. Student regroups from hundreds to tens to ones but does not change the hundreds and tens digits accordingly: e.g.

$$
\begin{array}{r}
934 \\
-568 \\
\hline
376
\end{array}
$$

11. Student regroups from hundreds directly to ones without regrouping the tens. This usually occurs when there is a zero in the tens place: e.g.

$$\begin{array}{r} 905 \\ -408 \\ \hline 408 \end{array}$$

12. Student regroups from hundreds directly to ones and again from hundreds to tens, making the hundreds digit two less. This usually occurs with zeros in the tens and ones positions of the larger number: e.g.

$$\begin{array}{r} 600 \\ -263 \\ \hline 247 \end{array}$$

13. Student decreases digit value by one but does not regroup to its right-hand neighbor: e.g.

$$\begin{array}{r} 642 \\ -127 \\ \hline 415 \end{array}$$

14. Student regroups from hundreds to ones, making the tens digit a nine: e.g.

$$\begin{array}{r} 397 \\ -138 \\ \hline 269 \end{array}$$

15. Student subtracts from bottom up: e.g.

$$\begin{array}{r} 4563 \\ -1982 \\ \hline 7429 \end{array}$$

16. Student subtracts as if multiplying: e.g.

$$\begin{array}{r} 39 \\ -2 \\ \hline 17 \end{array} \qquad \begin{array}{r} 69 \\ -42 \\ \hline 47 \end{array}$$

Multiplication and Division

Common Errors in Multiplication. Operations in multiplication and division largely pertain to the multiplication table in addition to the basics of addition and subtraction. Frequently recurrent mistakes are:

1. There are errors in basic facts or multiplication aspects of zero or of one: e.g.

$$\begin{array}{r} 1 \\ \times 6 \\ \hline 9 \end{array} \qquad \begin{array}{r} 4 \\ \times 0 \\ \hline 4 \end{array}$$

2. Student brings down tens without performing multiplication: e.g.

$$
\begin{array}{r} 10 \\ \times 5 \\ \hline 10 \end{array}
\qquad\qquad
\begin{array}{r} 30 \\ \times 3 \\ \hline 30 \end{array}
$$

3. Student incorrectly regroups: e.g.

$$
\begin{array}{r} 32 \\ \times 4 \\ \hline 218 \end{array}
\qquad\qquad
\begin{array}{r} 31 \\ \times 5 \\ \hline 515 \end{array}
$$

4. Student neglects regrouping or regroups without completing multiplication: e.g.

$$
\begin{array}{r} 67 \\ \times 3 \\ \hline 181 \end{array}
\qquad\qquad
\begin{array}{r} 67 \\ \times 4 \\ \hline 81 \end{array}
$$

5. Student multiplies numbers of multiplicand after taking multiplier: e.g.

$$
\begin{array}{r} 67 \\ \times 3 \\ \hline 441 \end{array}
\qquad\qquad
\begin{array}{r} 74 \\ \times 4 \\ \hline 308 \end{array}
$$

6. Student records only the first product: e.g.

$$
\begin{array}{r} 21 \\ \times 13 \\ \hline 63 \end{array}
\qquad\qquad
\begin{array}{r} 18 \\ \times 22 \\ \hline 30 \end{array}
$$

7. Student does wrong operation: e.g.

$$
\begin{array}{r} 67 \\ \times 3 \\ \hline 70 \end{array}
\qquad\qquad
\begin{array}{r} 67 \\ \times 3 \\ \hline 64 \end{array}
$$

8. Student fails to complete initial stage of multiplication: e.g.

$$
\begin{array}{r} 15 \\ \times 15 \\ \hline 175 \end{array}
\qquad\qquad
\begin{array}{r} 46 \\ \times 12 \\ \hline 92 \end{array}
$$

9. Student does two separate problems: e.g.

$$
\begin{array}{r} 17 \\ \times 12 \\ \hline 114 \end{array}
$$

10. Student neglects tens place value: e.g.

$$\begin{array}{r} 17 \\ \times 12 \\ \hline 34 \\ 17 \\ \hline 51 \end{array}$$

Common Mistakes in Division. Four major mistakes plague division problems. These include:

1. Student ignores the place value in the dividend and quotient: e.g.

$$3\overline{)639}^{\,213} \qquad\qquad 4\overline{)510}^{\,142}$$

2. Student records answers from right to left: e.g.

$$\begin{array}{r} 52 \\ 3\overline{)75} \\ 60 \\ \hline 15 \\ 15 \\ \hline 0 \end{array} \qquad\qquad \begin{array}{r} 63 \\ 6\overline{)516} \\ 480 \\ \hline 36 \\ 36 \\ \hline 0 \end{array}$$

3. Student fails to record a zero to show that there is no tens value: e.g.

$$\begin{array}{r} 32\ R.3 \\ 9\overline{)2721} \\ 27 \\ \hline 21 \\ 18 \\ \hline 3 \end{array} \qquad\qquad \begin{array}{r} 78\ R.2 \\ 6\overline{)4250} \\ 42 \\ \hline 50 \\ 48 \\ \hline 2 \end{array}$$

4. Student regroups, but cannot divide any number. He therefore brings down or regroups again without recording to show that there are no tens: e.g.

$$\begin{array}{r} 830 \\ 6\overline{)4818} \\ 4800 \\ \hline 18 \\ 18 \\ \hline 0 \end{array}$$

Math Activities and Games for Rote Learning

DOT TO DOT NUMBERS
Some students have difficulties writing the whole or part of a number. Create a worksheet with numbers in two colors. A solid line in one, a dotted line in another.

GHOST BUSTERS
From white construction paper, make ghost shapes. Put number combinations on each ghost. (for all basic functions)

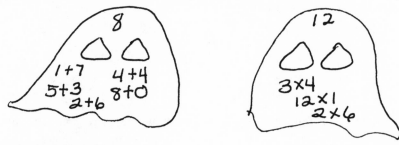

FLASHCARD STORIES
As flashcards are held up by the teacher, the student can make up a story about the combinations.

8	My brother has 8 gobots.
+4	I have 4 muppet babies.
?	How many toys do we have together?

PUMPKIN MATH
Draw a row of pumpkins. On each, write a math fact using the eyes for digits and the nose for the operation symbol.

MAGIC SQUARES

Draw the grid shown below, omitting the numbers. Students will place numbers 1 through 9 in the spaces as shown. The sums, when added together (down, across, or diagonally) will be 15.

4	9	2
3	5	7
8	1	6

NUMBER TREE

Draw the trunk of a tree with the figure ten in it. Ask the student to think of number combinations equaling ten. Have the student make a limb for each combination, as shown below.

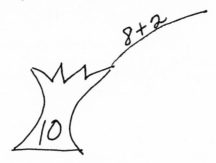

ROLLER DERBY

Draw a roller rink on the paper. Write a combination next to every loop the roller skater made. Each student "skates" the loops, answering the combinations as he goes. If he answers all of the questions correctly, he may be treated to a special reward (whatever is appropriate for that child).

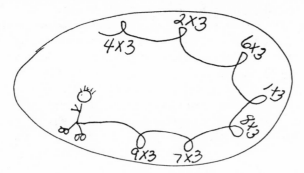

Curriculum Modifications for Reading

Reading levels vary so greatly among homebound students that a uniform starting point for lesson plans is impossible. As with math performance, students supposedly competent at one level of reading may actually be far below that level, or appear lower due to medical injury, confinement at home, or other factors. Whatever the case, assumed levels of reading must be checked against true observations during the homebound visit.

This section offers useful tips in the initial assessment and presentation of reading skills, tailored to meet the student's individual needs. First we should consider a series of questions about this new student; reflection of his needs will prove to be essential in later steps:

1. Can the student hear me?
2. Does the student have a vision problem?
3. Does the student understand what he is told or what he sees?
4. Can the student remember what he hears?
5. Can the student remember what he sees?
6. Can the student retrieve the information he has learned when he needs it?
7. Can the student recognize similarities and differences among pictures and printed symbols?
8. Can the student conceptualize and hold abstract ideas?
9. How long is the student's attention span?
10. Does the student have an interest in reading?
11. Does the student recall details of a story accurately?
12. Does the student distinguish reading for pleasure from reading for information?

Assessed reading skills indicate whether the student meets normal grade standards or falls seriously below his grade level and will require some extent of remediation. Notice that reading level fluctuates when there are visual impediments such as legal blindness or when instruction-following skills are weak. Influences beyond word recognition and formation per se thus are important to homebound teachers.

Clearly, then, reading ability must be evaluated. One approach, that of formal testing, examines elements of comprehension, vocabulary, pronunciation and so forth through a battery of distinct questions and applications. Referral for testing is the ideal solution, but practically speaking, there are many administrative obstacles to arranging testing and frequently the results go beyond answers of benefit to homebound teachers. Instead, informal testing is possible providing that the purpose is for *preparation of curriculum adjustments only*. (Informal testing that replaces formal testing for the sake of expediency and offers direction on speech therapy is unethical and unprofessional.)

Spelling Words

Pre-Primer	Primer	First Grade	Second (1)
a	all	about	across
ball	at	as	balloon
blue	boat	be	best
come	but	by	burn
father	to	color	care
get	duck	far	coat
have	find	four	dress
house	girl	green	fire
in	he	hello	gone
it	kitten	horse	knew
little	like	live	miss
make	now	met	off
mother	out	name	pig
not	put	of	right
play	saw	paint	shall
will	stop	road	six
ride	thank	so	table
want	there	street	together
see	three	tree	turn
to	train	walk	wood

Second (2)	Third (1)	Third (2)	Fourth
above	able	act	abandon
bark	block	beach	armor
brother	child	bounce	blush
corner	daddy	chance	charity
drink	edge	cottage	cooperation
fairy	fix	distance	Detroit
flour	half	except	elsewhere
gay	Indian	fog	firmly
hide	lit	hoof	gracious
kept	mind	journey	hunger
left	north	lever	isle
mouth	pole	nod	loyal
pay	pour	peak	moreover
push	rich	quite	oven
roof	secret	scared	pond
sheep	signal	shoot	reckless
sound	spoke	spill	sauce
such	swing	stupid	soak
those	trail	ticket	survey
wheel	wall	wire	truck

Fifth	Sixth	Jr. (7-8)	Sr. (9-12)
abode	abbey	abate	abandoned
artistic	artillery	armament	armada
bobby	blunder	blunt	blurt
chart	Charleston	charitable	Charlemagne
coral	coon	devoted	cookery
embarrass	Diana	Elsie	detestable
fireplace	embroider	fireman	elude
granite	fir	graciously	Finland
hurried	grammar	Hungarian	graduation
Jacob	hurrah	jeer	hundredth
Morgan	isolate	loveliness	lovable
loyalty	loving	morrow	morose
overflow	Moses	outstretched	outsider
Polly	outstanding	poorly	pollute
recovery	ponder	recline	recital
scar	recite	saucepan	Saul
so-called	sausage	snuff	snuggle
surroundings	snowy	Susan	surveying
trumpet	suspicious	trudge	truant

To this extent, informal diagnosis to determine the student's general reading level can be achieved with the following common tactics:

1. Select three or four paragraphs and have the student read silently and orally. As the student reads aloud, count as mistakes: mispronunciations, omissions, substitutions, hesitancies (over 5 seconds), distortions, and word assists by the teacher.

2. For *syllabication,* give the student eight words orally and ask the student to write the number of syllables (or "beats") to a word. Then, give him eight unfamiliar words to read and have him write the number of syllables.

3. For *phonic spelling,* dictate ten strange multi-syllable words as a phonic spelling test. Ask the student to spell the words as they sound. Score on phonic accuracy rather than on the actual spelling of the word.

4. For *spelling,* compile your own list of words to test general familiarity with words. The list on pages 43–44 is compiled from several graded word lists.

Basic Reading Skills: Writing the Journal

Once abilities and deficiencies are determined, homebound teachers face their next dilemma: should they proceed with the classroom teacher's lessons, or modify the lessons according to the deficiencies? Under most circumstances the decision is to adjust curriculum planning so that students will participate during each visit to the household. One effective way to generate enthusiasm while increasing reading ability is writing a journal.

The student's attitudes toward school and toward his or her medical situation can be expressed in a daily log—a journal. This is different from a diary. Attitudes and feelings serve as initial data to be interwoven into short creative writing assignments. Using certain "prompts," homebound students can display their daily thoughts by submitting written samples for teachers to review. Entries are reviewed with comments and serve for discussion between teacher and student. Journal entries directly strengthen ability in the following areas:

1. Following instruction.
2. Finding the main idea.
3. Finding details.
4. Finding relevant materials from a reading sample.
5. Distinguishing fact from opinion.
6. Organizing ideas.
7. Remembering personal attributes of characters.
8. Locating specific information in a story.
9. Determining the literary form of a story.
10. Drawing correct inferences.
11. Outlining sections of story.
12. Recognizing comparisons and opposites.
13. Using reference books and secondary resources.
14. Selecting the theme in a story.

Modified journal entries for children involve less writing detail and can focus instead on single sentences, pictures, or collage of pictures from another source (e.g. magazines). Figure 3.1, for example, provides pictorial prompts for children. This "Faces Attitude Inventory" presents a series of different facial expressions the child can relate to himself by circling the closest "feeling" that matches his personal feelings.

"Prompts" for older children take five forms. They consist of descriptive prompts, clarification prompts, anything-and-everything prompts, listing prompts, and seasonal prompts.

Descriptive Prompts. Following are sample instructions in this category:

1. Describe your favorite time of the day.
2. Describe the tools needed to play your favorite sport.
3. Describe a pair of your shoes.
4. Describe one person in your family.
5. If you could be anyone living today, who would you be?
6. Describe your favorite TV commercial.
7. Describe an object in the room.
8. Describe a car you would like to buy.
9. Name and describe your favorite dessert.
10. Describe your favorite TV personality.
11. How would it feel to be President of the United States?

Which face shows how I feel about school?

Which face shows how I feel about eating vegetables?

Which face shows how I feel about me?

Which face shows how I feel about my family?

Which face shows how I feel about summer vacation?

Figure 3.1. Faces Attitude Inventory.

12. Describe your favorite color; make a list of everything you have that is this color.

13. Describe your "special place."

14. Describe the most unusual gift you have ever received.

15. Describe your favorite candy.

16. Describe a monster. What are his destruction techniques?

17. You have just been transported in a time machine to the days of early man. Describe what you see and what you do.

18. You have been asked to make up a new kind of sandwich for a fast food restaurant. Describe the ingredients you use.

19. Describe your favorite animal.

20. A friend is coming to visit from another state for the weekend. Plan what you would like to do with him in this city.

Clarification Prompts. Following are sample clarification prompts for journal entries:

1. Choose your favorite fruit. Explain why it is your favorite.

2. Name your favorite day of the week. Tell why it is your favorite.

3. Name your favorite school subject and explain why it is your favorite.

4. If you could play a musical instrument, what would you choose and why?

5. Name an animal you would like to have as a pet and explain why you chose that pet.

6. Name your favorite sports team and tell why it is your favorite.

7. You can buy anything you want. What would you buy, and why?

8. My favorite horror movie is _____ because _____.

9. You have been given the power to change any aspect of your personality. What would you change, and why?

10. You are asked to rename each one of your family members. What names will you give them?

Anything-and-Everything Prompts. Here is a brief listing of prompts in this category:

1. You awake one morning to find that you are now 20 years old. What changes have occurred while you were sleeping?

2. If I were invisible, I'd _____.

3. One dark night you go outside because you hear a noise. Suddenly you hear the sound of huge, slushy footsteps coming closer and closer. What do you do?

4. The happiest day of my life was _____.

5. Your favorite sports personality rings your doorbell. He or she has chosen to spend two hours with you. What would you do?

6. Someone gives you an airplane ticket with which you can travel to any place in the world. Where would you go?

7. The principal just called your name over the intercom and asked you to come to the office. Why?

8. You are on a picnic. Watermelon is served for dessert. The only problem is that you forgot the knife. How will you divide it?

9. You are on a vacation in Hawaii today. What fun things will you do?

10. Write two paragraphs about yourself.

Listing Prompts. Several variations exist for these prompts. Here are initial samples:

1. List five foods you like best.

2. List five foods you dislike.

3. List the attributes that make a person a good friend.

4. List five reasons why you are not watching TV.

5. Today it is very cold. List five ways you can get warm.

6. How do you make a peanut butter sandwich? List each step in the process.

7. List five of the best things that have happened to you this year.

8. List five of the worst things that have happened to you this year.

9. Your alarm clock just went off. List the things you do before you go out the door on your way to an appointment.

10. List your favorite movies of all time.

Seasonal Prompts. Descriptive entries pertaining to seasonal changes draw attention to the outdoors and playing outside for students withdrawn, isolated or reclusive from daily social interaction. Here are useful prompts along these lines:

1. Describe a place you visited during the summer.

2. Tell about your most interesting experience during summer.

3. Tell how you feel about returning to school.

4. You are a jack-o-lantern left over from Halloween. How do you feel?

5. You are a turkey. Thanksgiving is coming. What tricks will you play on the farmer to keep from getting fat?

6. Describe what a turkey looks like.

7. Make a list of all the things you are thankful for.

8. Write ten adjectives to describe winter weather.

9. Make a list of all the Christmas words you can think of.

10. Today is the last day of school. What one thing will you remember about your year in this grade?

Conclusion

It has been our purpose in this chapter to give some idea of the diversity and flexibility of options available to homebound instructors who struggle to adjust lessson plans for students. When grade levels for each student also vary, further adjustments must compensate for skill deficits, while preserving enough excitement in the material. Motivation sustains the student's interest and acceptance of homework that must be completed under a very strange teaching environment.

In many ways these alterations establish individualized lesson plans for more expedient learning. But more importantly the student realizes his teacher is a caring, respectful friend, willing to accommodate his special needs during difficult times.

4. Psychological Implications

Earlier chapters have stressed the importance of teacher flexibility when designing and administering lesson plans for the homebound student. In part flexibility allows for unexpected surprises regarding the student's health, the location of the lesson, and academic materials. One further surprise for homebound teachers is when students fail to participate.

Reluctant students who refuse assignments or simply neglect to complete them will not benefit fully from services offered to them. Many teachers recognize that confinement at home can be unpleasant for students, that classwork is done under irregular circumstances, and thus noncompliance to a degree is predictable.

Pure cases of noncompliance unfortunately represent one among several potential behavior disorders likely to confront the teacher in the course of homebound instruction. Disorders ranging from poor study habits and crying to tantrums and physical aggression not only disrupt teaching sessions, but may catch teachers off guard, with no strategies at the ready.

This chapter provides a necessary reference guide in methods of behavior management for those difficult, sometimes miserable days when nothing seems to go right. Technical assistance in effective, straightforward strategies becomes crucial for teachers to maintain their own composure, let alone control of the teaching session. In college, teachers may have had two or three courses on behavior modification and applied techniques. Background in uses of reinforcers and punishers certainly is a plus, but the complexity of disruptive disorders frequently calls upon more sophisticated interventions that are beyond the scope of many introductory college courses.

In this chapter we will present a directory of possible interventions. We begin, however, with some general recommendations for coping with the stress of disruptive behaviors. Simply applying one or two methods as outlined in the directory of interventions may not be enough to overcome heightened levels of personal frustration, sometimes directed toward the student, his family, or the primary teacher. Judgments on which behavioral methods to use, how to use them, and how to share this methodology with family members can be extremely stressful. Teachers made aware of their increasing stress, before it explodes, stand a better chance of solving behavior problems on the spot.

Coping with Homebound Teaching Stress

A good motto for coping with homebound stress is "Your success is not measured by how much you achieve, but rather by the number of obstacles you overcome." In other words, experienced teachers realize up front the array of potential mishaps facing them with each visit to the student's house. Inadequate teaching conditions, inadequate materials, inadequate cooperation — all are negative events directly eroding the physical and emotional stamina of good teachers. The rate of wear and tear on the body creates actual biological tension. Muscles tighten as teachers withhold their anger and irritation. When biological tension runs rampant it can stir enormous feelings of personal futility, to the point that motivation in teaching, in dealing with severe behavior, decays at a rapid pace.

These changes signal the symptoms of stress. Table 4.1 lists common stressors among homebound teachers. When these stressors are overlooked, serious hazards not only plague the teacher's health, but can also interfere with the necessary supportive learning for students.

For example, take "feeling powerless." Essentially this means there is minimal or virtually no control over required tasks in your job as homebound teacher. When detail after detail must be reported to supervisors, when curriculum decisions or behavioral strategies all first require higher level approval, then flexibility is eliminated and the teacher is at the mercy of another decision-maker. Limitations on flexibility disrupt the natural flow of instruction and will severely undermine the integrity of teachers. Teachers will feel their decisions are worthless, that teaching is boring, and that exerting efforts beyond their job profile is wasteful.

Another common cause of stress is avoidance of behavior problems for fear of parental retaliation or a lawsuit. Teachers might deliberately overlook annoying disturbances such as profanity, yelling and even physical attacks over worrying about threat of litigation. Ignored behaviors thus become worse, compelling teachers to internalize their absolute helplessness.

Side-effects of unmanaged stress in these situations can be disastrous. Teachers who abandon difficult students may have destroyed confidence among other teachers that this student is reachable. Yet if teachers stick it out quality of instruction nearly always deteriorates. Sessions are shorter; few to no incentives are offered; and tolerance to repeated disruptions is lower. All in all, teachers minimize their aggravation by reducing their response effort and removing their feelings from the foreground of student interaction.

Signs of Distress

Signs of distress trigger a natural tendency in human beings to avoid

Table 4.1.
Common Stressors Among
Homebound Teachers

- Trying to reach students who do not learn
- Managing difficult-to-reach students
- Handling discipline problems
- Coping with lesson interruptions
- Surviving parent interactions
- Experiencing racial prejudice from students and parents
- Living with a rigid curriculum
- Having too many things to do
- Having others (administrators, teachers) not listen to you
- Dealing with increased caseload
- Having too much paper work, busy work
- Lacking equipment or proper supplies
- Having too many meetings
- Coping with bad weather or icy, dangerous roads
- Feeling isolated in the job
- Feeling powerless
- Assuming a rescuer role
- Experiencing self-doubts
- Having to interact constantly with other health providers
- Always having to explain what a homebound teacher is
- Worrying about threat of lawsuit
- Experiencing lack of fairness in teacher evaluations
- Not liking your job
- Finding no room for advancement
- Being criticized
- Having your opinion challenged
- Not being assertive

---

and escape the unpleasant situation. Avoidance of aversive events relieves the building pressure in the body. When a teacher experiences signs of distress, numerous positive alternatives to avoidance and escape are available. First, of course, is sharpening the teacher's sensitivity to even the slightest symptom of stress. Check below the signs of stress that affect you most.

Emotional Signs
_____ I become overexcited
_____ I worry too much
_____ I feel insecure
_____ I have difficulty sleeping at night
_____ I become easily confused and forgetful
_____ I become very uncomfortable and ill at ease
_____ I become nervous
_____ I blame others for my mistakes

Visceral Signs
_____ My stomach becomes upset
_____ I feel my heart pounding
_____ I sweat profusely
_____ My hands become moist
_____ I feel light-headed or faint
_____ I experience "cold chills"
_____ My face becomes "hot"
_____ I begin to breathe harder (hyperventilate)

Musculoskeletal Signs
_____ My fingers and hands shake
_____ I can't sit or stand still
_____ I develop twitches
_____ My head begins to ache
_____ I feel my muscles become tense or stiff
_____ I stutter or stammer when I speak
_____ My neck becomes stiff

Biological stressors mobilize teachers to doubt their performance capability too quickly and regret tedious hours spent on remediation of particular students. Many self-doubts arise when overly eager teachers accept myths of the "perfect teacher" as guidelines against which to judge their own "mistakes." Table 4.2 gives a brief list of these myths, as well as a list of common self-defeating inferences that result from myths (cf. Ruben & Ruben, 1985, for extensive review of inferences).

Coping with Stressors

Several prescriptions for coping with stress are readily available in common literature. Solutions vary from general to specific, such as "having a positive attitude" (general) to progressive relaxation and constructive perceptions of self-potential (specific). Among the more effective strategies is a three-part, ABC model for immediate tension reduction. Parts of the model include the following:

Assessment -------⟩ Behavioral Methods -------⟩ Confrontation

Assessment. Clearly identify all physical, emotional and cognitive variables operating upon your behavior either before, during or after instruction with a student.

Behavioral Methods. (a) Decide upon a personal stress-reduction method for immediate use, selected from a wide variety of self-help resources (e.g. Benson, 1975; DeShong, 1981; Ellis & Harper, 1974; Ruben

Table 4.2.
Myths of the Perfect Teacher
and
Self-defeating Inferences

Myths of the Perfect Teacher	Self-defeating Inferences
• I should be able to reach every student	• If you can work hard enough, you can do it
• I always put students' needs ahead of mine	• Nobody appreciates all the work I do. I'm a darn fool
• All students are warm human beings	• Nobody understands me
• I love every student	• I have got to correct every paper students turn in
• I can withstand almost any frustration	• I should watch myself since I'm in the public eye
• I never lose my temper	• I have to be always thinking of new and creative things
• I never make a mistake	• I never feel like I am done
• I can get along with everybody— parents and administrators	• I feel disorganized in my thinking
• I should accomplish a definite amount of work in a given period of time	• I feel guilty about bettering myself financially
	• I admit it; I can't control the kids
	• The principal never supports me
	• The kids are getting worse each year
	• He/she shouldn't even be on my homebound list
	• He/she shouldn't be allowed to get away with that
	• He/she didn't even hear what I said

& Ruben, in press). (b) Decide upon a behavioral strategy that is applicable to targeted problems during sessions with the student.

Confrontation. Put your selections into immediate action and overcome the temptation to avoid and escape problems. Healthy, nonstressful views, for example (see Table 4.3) can reinvigorate feelings of perseverance, toward a commitment of at least trying to improve a bad situation. Likewise, practical application of one, two or multiple behavioral procedures may rapidly ameliorate the stress involved with misbehavior.

Achieving relatively good control over personal stress does not come naturally and may at first seem too calibrated. So, too, applying stress-reduction techniques may feel mechanical and awkward. This is unfortunate, but very common. With practice, onset of stress will be quickly spotted and just as quickly trigger whatever procedures have been found to offer the most relief.

Table 4.3.
Healthy, Nonstressful Statements

- Five years from now, I won't give a darn
- Thirty years from now, I will not remember it
- Only 27 more days until vacation
- Tomorrow night at this time, it will be over
- I can handle it
- I'm tough, I can take it
- I am relaxed
- Relax — take a deep breath
- Take one step at a time
- Chalk it up to experience
- The principal got the job because he was the coach
- Consider the source!
- Leave it be; cool it. Spend your time doing other things
- Stop feeling sorry for yourself
- When the going gets tough, the tough get going
- I don't have a magic wand
- Nobody is going to hold my hand
- I'm still alive
- Better luck next time
- Don't fret, plan!
- Don't be obsessive. Don't be compulsive.
- It's not worth it
- Not every day has to be a record breaker
- I'm really glad that I was honest with myself
- I'm really glad that I was honest with them
- I'm still a little shaky, but I did it
- I'll go at my own pace
- I can back off if it gets to be too much
- It's okay to feel nervous

The same can be said for techniques of behavior management. At first there is thoughtful deliberation on the order of procedural steps, on potential limitations and contraindications, and whether one procedure alone is sufficient. Over time there will be less deliberation as teachers feel more confident in their management efforts.

Directory of Behavioral Interventions

The following directory of behavioral interventions provides technical assistance in deciding the best method to use based on your assessment of the problem. It is a catalog of frequently applied methods, numerically organized and designed for rapid referencing and decision-making. First read "How to Use the Directory." Then read through the descriptive entries for each intervention, which contain key information on the operation, indication, contraindication and limitations of the behavioral procedure.

How to Use the Directory

First, make an assessment or diagnosis of classroom misbehavior. Codes used in psychological diagnosis derive from the nosology of DSM-IIIR (American Psychiatric Association, 1980) and probably are not relevant here. Instead, look for the operational typology of behavior disorder, such as aggressive behavior, crying, and so forth. Locate the disorder, or terms most relevant to the problem, in the section titled "Homebound Problems."

Once you have located the disorder, read the adjacent list of numbers. These represent recommended interventions found in the section titled "Interventions."

Now locate those numbers and their corresponding behavioral interventions. Each entry of intervention contains the following items in sequential order:

Operation: How the procedure works.

Indications: Conditions of the student or environment appropriate for proper application.

Contraindications: Conditions of the student or environment inappropriate for application or which may cause adverse side-effects.

Limitations: Shortcomings and potential problems of the procedure even when applied properly under appropriate conditions.

Homebound Problems

The following list of behavior disorders and other problems draws from two main sources: (a) established systems of taxonomy (DSM-III, DSM-IIIR, ICD-9-CM, etc.), and (b) compilations of major classroom disorders treated by behavior modification and behavior therapy (see also Bellack & Herson, 1985; Bellack, Herson & Kazdin, 1982; Sulzer-Azaroff & Mayer, 1972, 1977). By no means is this an exhaustive list, since there are several other overlapping categories into which homebound problems might be placed (e.g., family problems, anxiety, habits, etc.). However, it is certain to be a starting point for neophyte users of behavioral methods.

Academic Problems: 1, 2, 5, 8, 10, 13, 14, 16, 17, 18, 23, 24, 25, 27, 37, 39, 47, 50, 53, 54, 63, 69

Aggressive Behavior: 3, 9, 14, 15, 16, 20, 22, 24, 26, 29, 41, 46, 48, 52, 56, 57, 59, 62, 66, 70, 71, 75, 76

Assignment noncompletion: 4, 8, 13, 16, 17, 18, 19, 23, 31, 36, 38, 48, 50, 51, 59, 60, 64

Attention problems: 5, 8, 17, 19, 21, 22, 23, 24, 26, 32, 38, 42, 47, 48, 53, 54, 71

Cheating: 8, 14, 15, 22, 24, 25, 31, 35, 43, 44, 49, 52, 76

Crying: 13, 14, 20, 22, 24, 26, 29, 35, 44

Disrupting: 3, 7, 8, 13, 14, 15, 16, 18, 21, 22, 24, 26, 29, 35, 41, 43, 44, 48, 49, 52, 57, 66, 70, 75, 76, 77

Following instructions: 1, 2, 5, 6, 11, 13, 14, 16, 17, 18, 19, 21, 22, 23, 24, 28, 30, 31, 32, 33, 34, 37, 40, 47, 56, 57, 61, 63, 64, 65, 67, 77

Household Rules: 6, 8, 12, 16, 17, 18, 19, 22, 23, 24, 30, 31, 34, 42, 45, 46, 53, 59, 63, 67, 71, 74

Independent play: 5, 6, 7, 8, 11, 12, 15, 16, 17, 18, 20, 22, 23, 26, 31, 32, 33, 42, 45, 46, 53, 54, 55, 56, 63, 64, 65, 67, 71, 72, 73

Nagging: 22, 24, 25, 26, 29, 48, 57, 75, 76

Obscenity: 22, 24, 25, 26, 29, 48, 57, 75, 76

Reading: 1, 2, 5, 6, 10, 13, 14, 15, 17, 18, 19, 27, 28, 36, 37, 38, 47, 50, 55, 63, 64

Study habits: 1, 8, 10, 12, 13, 14, 16, 17, 23, 24, 27, 31, 32, 33, 35, 36, 48, 50, 63, 64

Temper tantrums: 3, 7, 8, 15, 21, 22, 24, 26, 29, 41, 48, 57, 66, 75, 76, 77

Truancy: 8, 13, 14, 16, 17, 23, 31, 35, 42, 48, 49, 50, 53, 54, 57, 59, 60, 65, 67, 71, 76, 77

Writer's block: 2, 4, 9, 10, 11, 13, 14, 17, 22, 37, 47, 51, 53, 59, 62, 63, 64, 65, 67, 74, 75, 77

Writer's cramp: 2, 4, 11, 17, 25, 50, 53, 66, 67, 77

Interventions

Following is a list of behavioral interventions annotated in this section:

1. Acquisitional learning
2. Analogues
3. Anger Control Training
4. Anxiety Management Training
5. Auto-shaping
6. Backward Chaining
7. Behavioral Contrast
8. Behavior Management
9. Behavioral Rehearsal
10. Bibliotherapy
11. Classical Conditioning
12. Coaching
13. Cognitive Conditioning
14. Cognitive Restructuring
15. Constructional Approach
16. Contingency Contracting
17. Continuous Reinforcement
18. Corrective Feedback
19. Cueing
20. Delayed Reinforcement
21. Differential Reinforcement
22. Differential Reinforcement of Alternative Behaviors
23. Differential Reinforcement of Higher Rates of Behavior
24. Differential Reinforcement of Incompatible Behavior
25. Differential Reinforcement of Lower Rates of Behavior
26. Differential Reinforcement of Other Behaviors

27. Educational Programming
28. Errorless Discrimination
29. Extinction
30. Fading
31. Feedback
32. Fixed-Interval Schedule
33. Fixed-Ratio Schedule
34. Forward Chaining
35. Group Contingencies
36. Homework
37. Imitation/Modeling
38. Maintenance
39. Match-to-Sample
40. Mediation Training
41. Movement (Deprivation) Suppression
42. Natural Reinforcement
43. Negative Practice
44. Negative Punishment
45. Negative Reinforcement
46. Noncontingent Reinforcement
47. Observational Learning
48. Opportunities for Desirable Behavior
49. Overcorrection
50. Personalized System of Instruction
51. Physical Guidance
52. Positive Punishment
53. Positive Reinforcement
54. Premack Principle
55. Programming Generalization
56. Reinforcer Sampling
57. Response Cost
58. Response Delay
59. Response Deprivation
60. Response Induction
61. Response Priming
62. Role-play
63. Self-instructional Training
64. Self-reinforcement
65. Self-reporting
66. Sensitization
67. Stimulus Control
68. Stimulus Substitution
69. Task Analysis
70. Time-out
71. Token Economy
72. Variable Interval Schedule
73. Variable Ratio Schedule
74. Verbal Conditioning
75. Vicarious Extinction
76. Vicarious Punishment
77. Vicarious Reinforcement

1. Acquisitional Learning.

Operation: Teachers should provide single or multiple training opportunities consisting of a learning (discriminative) stimulus, a nonrelevant stimulus, and contingent reinforcement. Acquisition takes place as the target behavior occurs in the presence of the discriminative stimulus, followed by a reinforcer.

Indications: The procedure is best for teaching both simple and complex tasks. It facilitates perceptual-motor and social development when used in a systematic routine, with ascending criteria, and assortment of reinforcers, and clear definitions of the target behavior and discriminative and nonrelevant stimuli.

Contraindications: Such training is upset by inconsistent, inaccurate and unreliable administrations. The procedure is too slow for learners with strong discrimination (object identification, decision-making) skills.

Limitations: There are three concerns. First, training stimuli that do not resemble naturalistic (classroom) stimuli may weaken generalization. Second, contrived reinforcers, while initially potent, lose effectiveness in maintenance steps. And third, maintenance depends on properly thinning out reinforcers from a continuous schedule down to an intermittent (delayed) schedule. (For further review, see O'Connor, 1969.)

2. Analogues.

Operation: Educational simulations that frequently vary along three different dimensions. These dimensions include (a) paper-pencil, (b) role-play and enactment, and (c) audio-visual tape.

2A. PAPER-PENCIL ANALOGUES. These include questionnaires, checklists, biographical histories, and various survey forms designed to stimulate authentic replies about disorders. Frequently analogues attempt to quantify general parameters of behavior which are then translated into educational goals and objectives.

2B. ROLE-PLAY AND ENACTMENT. Such analogues involve simulations where the behaver, usually the student, performs the task or instruction under setting events approximately similar to the actual classroom. Role-plays usually take place between teacher and student, whereas in enactments, one of the role-players might be a classmate or primary teacher. Enactments involve role-rehearsal but also include objects serving as "cues" that are brought in from the natural environment.

2C. AUDIO-VISUAL TAPE. Analogues increase in reliability when they include feedback systems. Audio-visual feedback provides immediate and permanent products of target behavior. Replays of acted scenes help identify the verbal and nonverbal responses in an instruction. Such feedback also functions as a "prompt" to which the student might be instructed to reply (e.g., pronunciation of words, object identification, etc.).

Indications: Analogues provide training in the house or hospital or wherever there is a closed environment. They facilitate sensitivity to realistic antecedents, behavior, and consequences, though simulated, and simplify generalization training. Paper-pencil analogues can be administered to large numbers of respondents. Role-play and enactment analogues evoke verbal and physical behaviors related to interpersonal dysfunction.

Contraindications: All three analogues are inadvisable under specific conditions. First, without authorized consent, audio-visual products of behavior may implicate students who already are at legal risk. Consent with delinquents and substance abusers additionally should adhere to state and federal confidentiality laws. Similar protection laws apply for suspected adult and child abusers (molesters). Second, because objects and persons are brought in from the natural environment, monitoring of this selection can prevent the inadvertent regression of a disorder.

Limitations: There are several pitfalls with analogues. First, the "simulation" may lack valid similarity to naturalistic stimuli and be ineffective in prompting realistic replies. Second, the cost of purchasing, storage, and maintenance of audio-visual equipment may be high. Technical errors such as input impedance, mode rejection, unrechargeable batteries, operation complexity, lack of portability, and impaired circuitry further restrict the devices. Fourth, validation of role-play, enactment and audio-visual analogues are still questionable, although more acceptable than paper-pencil analogues. (For further review, see Borkovec, Stone, O'Brien & Kaloupek, 1974; McFall, 1977; Nay, 1977; Ruben, 1984; Ruben, 1988.)

3. Anger Control Training.

Operation: This is a comprehensive package of behavior therapy methods for management of emotional arousal and aggressive responses to aversive and stressful situations. Methods include (a) relaxation, (b) problem-solving, (c) assertion skills, (d) self-monitoring, (e) self-reinforcement and (f) self-instructions under simulated and naturalistic provocations.

Indications: Research evidence shows excellent progress of this package with adolescents, subclassified into groups who display persistent aggression, disobedience, negativity, and provocative opposition to authority figures. Training methods are additionally effective when analogues are employed.

Contraindications: Certain demonstrated forms of behavior may interfere with the training program. These include adolescents who (a) are extremely depressed or suicidal, (b) are substance abusers, and (c) have thought disorders or delusions.

Limitations: Several factors limit success of this training program. First, failures may result when there are competing "contingencies," that is, when factors beyond the control of the teacher directly influence the adolescent's behavior. Examples include severe behavior problems in other areas and parents and peers who are aggressive. Second, lack of generality or maintenance may relate to poor or inexperienced trainers. Third, lack of motivation and resistance to change can sabotage the program even in early stages. Fourth, instructors may adhere rigidly to the session-by-session guides, using "canned procedures." Teaching sessions verbatim from a manual looks mechanical and reduces the needed spontaneous excitement. (For further review, see Feindler, 1987; Feindler & Ecton, 1986; and Kaufman & Wagner, 1972.)

4. Anxiety Management Training.

Operation: The purpose of training is to reduce anxiety by restructuring reinforcers that maintain anxiety self-talk and physiological arousal. Positive self-statements about control and coping will selectively be reinforced, whereas other statements are ignored.

Indications: This procedure is appropriate for all types of simple anxiety or emotional responses related to instruction or school. Variations include assertiveness, desensitization, and cognitive conditioning.

Contraindications: Procedure is insufficient for specific, defined phobias (e.g., agoraphobia) or when anxiety is complicated by an extensive history of a stressful environment: familial, vocational, financial, marital, medical, legal, chemical, and so forth. Problems also arise if the student lacks average social skills.

Limitations: This procedure accidentally promotes an insularity effect; the design restricts training to just the student rather than between student and other people. (For further review, see Suinn, 1977.)

5. Auto-shaping.

Operation: New responses are brought under "stimulus control" through associations between antecedents and consequences. Unlike ordinary operant shaping, here antecedent cues occur, followed within seconds or minutes by some (noncontingent) reinforcer (positive auto-shaping), or followed by the withholding of reinforcers (negative auto-shaping). In both cases the result is slow to gradual rate of responding.

Indications: Procedures are for students who adapt poorly to new situations. Procedure facilitates simple and complex discriminations and chaining, and works best with learning disabled, emotionally impaired and educable retarded.

Contraindications: Associability is a key feature. Delayed associations between antecedents and consequences may lose the effects of training.

Limitations: Application of auto-shaping is primarily for simple acquisitional tasks. (For further review, see Brown & Jenkins, 1968; Siegel, 1977.)

6. Backward Chaining.

Operation: Divide a complex target behavior into sequential parts. Teach the entire series of parts by beginning with the last step plus reinforcement. Then, teach the next to last step, and so on, working backwards. Make verbal prompts along the way. After successful mastery of a new step, repeat all learned steps from finish to start followed by reinforcement.

Indications: Chaining offers advantages for advanced discrimination for tasks with many sequential parts. Appropriate for following long instructions, for adaptive living skills (dressing, grooming, etc.) and with students with a history of noncompliance.

Contraindications: Few, if any, contraindications are known other than the confusion that this procedure is "backwards."

Limitations: It is crucial that the order of "stimulus-response" chains be maintained for each step. Use of probes which test the responses out of sequence are one way to determine the strength of this chain. Chaining also begins with the assumption that simple behaviors *already* are in the student's repertoire. (For further review, see Kelleher, 1966; Martin, England & England, 1971.)

7. Behavioral Contrast.

Operation: This is the alternation of two or more reinforcement schedules with a clear discriminative stimulus associated with each. Cues clearly signal a switch in what students need to perform for reinforcers, and at what pace. Alternating schedules produce differential rates of responding.

Indications: Contrast procedures are fairly new for educational problems. They are appropriate for highly deviant classroom disruption and for cooperative play among family.

Contraindications: Use of contrast procedures with low-functioning students is inadvisable because of the complex discrimination tasks involved.

Limitations: Evidence of generalization from contrast procedures is weak. That is, well-behaved students under lights-off conditions at home may not transfer their good behavior to the classroom if the teacher turns the light off. Another problem is the qualitative aspects of the reinforcer. For example, those students trained by contrasts might inadvertently prefer to behave where their rate of reinforcement is highest. A student who finishes his schoolwork accurately and rapidly at home may prefer this setting over the classroom. (For further review, see Gross & Drabman, 1981.)

8. Behavior Management.

Operation: Apply this approach in three parts. First, determine the preinstruction or "baseline" level of some behavior prior to the start of a program. It is necessary to demonstrate that this behavior occurs at a fairly stable rate. Changes in behavior, during instruction, can be measured later against the baseline. Second, introduce some procedure for that behavior until the behavior reaches a desired level of criteria. Third, maintain this behavioral change by programming generalization (see #55).

Indications: Applications of this procedure are effective for all classroom disruptions. Additional tactics for enhanced results include (a) use reinforcers, (b) select a valid procedure, (c) use graphs to record progress, (d) properly train all participants of the program, (e) provide the least restricted conditions, (f) exercise ethical safeguards against use of punishment practices, (g) be flexibile to alter goals and the procedure, and (h) obtain, when necessary, informed consents.

Contraindications: Large-scale behavioral management may not be feasible in the natural environment for the following reasons: insufficient space, poorly trained parents, no support for program, competing punishers, and irregularity of application.

Limitations: Assigned "contingency managers" take charge of implementing and monitoring procedures. Monitoring these managers can increase costs, time commitments, and extensive labor for the teacher.

Second, behavior management alone may be insufficient for cognitive and affective disorders. (For further review, see Fagan, Long & Stevens, 1975; Sajawaj, 1977; Thorpe & Wezel, 1969.)

9. Behavioral Rehearsal.

Indication: This procedure modifies inappropriate behavior in a progressive step-by-step fashion by role-playing the new behavior. Basic steps involve guidance and modeling. Guidance is given by the teacher on how to engage in the behavior. Then, modeling the behavior best illustrates the form ("topography") and purpose ("function") of behavior. Following this, student tries out the behavior. Combinations of imaginal rehearsal, overt desensitization and a written script may ease the performance. Audiovisual analogues also provide excellent sources of feedback.

Indications: This procedure is typically used for anxiety reduction and for development of prosocial skills.

Contraindications: Behavioral rehearsal poses hardly any complications as long as the student feels comfortable acting out new behaviors.

Limitations: Basic drawbacks include (a) poor reproduction of naturalistic events in the house or hospital, (b) inaccurate rehearsals overlooked in training that have resulted in later maladaptive reactions, and (c) poor control over anticipatory anxiety prior to rehearsals. (For further review, see Ascher & Phillips, 1975; Lazarus, 1966.)

10. Bibliotherapy.

Operation: This intervention provides self-help manuals to assist students in altering dimensions of their behavior. It is also used for enhanced acquisition of skills. Basic requisite includes reading skills that match the required reading level. Manuals should sufficiently teach practical skills ranging from anger control to writing skills. Contingent bibliotherapy involves (a) reinforcement for completed homework (readings), (b) demonstration of the skills (information) read, and (c) development of these skills via other behavioral techniques.

Indications: Bibliotherapy is valuable when instructional sessions are frequent, or when students can move at their own pace.

Contraindications: Restricted use is advised for students who are illiterate, functionally low readers, or enrolled in "English as a second language" course. Also, target behaviors such as addictive behavior where there is a psychophysiological problem will require more extensive self-management training.

Limitations: Frequent shortcomings involve the instructor's lack of familiarity with the assigned books, and the overreliance on bibliotherapy. In the first case, only those manuals thoroughly reviewed are recommended for assignment. In the second, students may feel awkward about making behavior changes without at least intermittent expert guidance. (For further review, see Glasgow & Rosen, 1978, 1979; Ruben, 1985; Ruben, 1989.)

11. Classical Conditioning.

Operation: A reflex consists of a stimulus and a response, when the response is elicited by the stimulus. The stimulus part is called "unconditioned stimulus" (US) and the elicited response the "unconditioned response" (UR). Repeated pairings between the US and some neutral (i.e., never elicited the target behavior) stimulus produce a change in the neutral stimulus, where it acquires elicitive properties and functions like the US. This new stimulus, called a "conditioned stimulus" (CS), alone can cause unconditioned responses to occur. That response no longer occurs as a reflex but is due to *learning,* and becomes a "conditioned response" (CR). Basic techniques of classical conditioning for educators include:

I IA. CONDITIONED EMOTIONAL RESPONSE. In this case, continuous pairings of US and CS produce suppression of some behavior. Usually the CS occurs first (warning sound or stimulus) and is followed by a US (aversive stimulus), establishing avoidance, escape, or fear-induced reactions.

I IB. SIMULTANEOUS CONDITIONING. The US usually occurs slightly after the onset of CS. A longer delay weakens conditioning while shorter delays strengthen it. In "delay conditioning," the CS is left on during the delay. In "trace conditioning," the CS is turned on briefly and then turned off during the delay.

I IC. HIGHER-ORDER CONDITIONING. This is when the CS pairs with a neutral stimulus, turning the latter into another CS (CS2).

Indications: Suggested for inhibition of (school) phobias and anxiety and for increasing comfort in homework situations. Compound uses form techniques of systematic desensitization and various "cognitive conditioning techniques."

Contraindications: Toward "making stimuli less aversive," minimize the number of consecutive trials for strained involuntary responses. In other words, increasing attention-span by avoidance conditioning should employ learning trials that are spaced apart by several minutes.

Limitations: The basic problem is that the strength of CR depends on intermittent pairings of CS with US. Irregular schedules will weaken the CR. A higher order CS is even more susceptible to loss of control. A second problem is unclear effects upon behavior between classically conditioned responses and those same responses under operant conditioning. Strength of the response is probably due to "intermingling effects." (For further review, see Rescorla, 1967.)

12. Coaching.

Operation: Coaching provides feedback from another, independent person (teacher) on performance of the student. This second person functions as objective expert, observing, guiding and correcting responses during behavior rehearsal.

Indications: It provides best results when combined with role-reversal;

that is, when teacher models the skill and then has student repeat it (see #37). Effective for students having social skills deficits, and problem-solving problems. Coaching is enhanced by audio-videotape feedback.

Contraindications: Designated coaches should be properly trained if they are teacher assistants. Also, repeated remediation of the student's behavior will inadvertently suppress appropriate responses, thereby increasing avoidance and escape responses (anxiety, truancy, etc.). Corrections regarding verbal and nonverbal behavior should "fit" the student's manner of responding to prevent resistance. Finally, keep the frequency of coaching trials to a minimum to prevent response fatigue ("ratio strain").

Limitations: Coaching is effective only until the student achieves some criterion of acceptability. Added complications such as overtraining and the dependency upon coaches for advice may disrupt procedures. (For further review, see Allison & Ayllon, 1980; McFall & Twentyman, 1973.)

13. Cognitive Conditioning.

Operation: This is a method of altering thought patterns, beliefs, attitudes and opinions to achieve desirable changes in overt behavior. Modifications deal with the student's private verbal behavior and images relating to himself and the world around him. Conditioning typically includes cognitive restructuring, covert extinction, covert reinforcement, covert punishment, self-instructional methods, problem-solving and imitation/modeling.

Indications: The procedure is appropriate for highly verbal and educated students; usually the target behavior is mild to moderate. Cognitive methods for depression, anxiety and phobias relieve symptoms when the student verbally reports to himself (self-talk) the problem rather than experiences or consequences of actual events.

Contraindications: Inappropriate for mentally retarded and those with social skills deficits or poor imagery skills.

Limitations: Whether self-imagery or self-talk actually corresponds to overt responses is uncertain. Cognitive changes usually require direct contact with explicit contingencies before the student's performance can occur at certain levels. (For further review, see Moheny, 1974.)

14. Cognitive Restructuring.

Operation: General approach draws from "rational emotive therapy," of changing maladaptive emotional reactions and behaviors mediated by the student's attitudes and beliefs about the world. Common variations include rational structuring and attribution.

14A. RATIONAL RESTRUCTURING. First, present counter assumptions underlying the student's beliefs. Second, analyze the student's problem using more rational, adaptive (cogent) beliefs. Third, teach the student to modify internal self-talk. Fourth, conduct imaginal role-play and actual exercises combined with bibliotherapy.

14B. ATTRIBUTION. Here, students are taught the center of control and learn their recovery results from their own efforts rather than from external reasons. Self-control attribution begins with disputing the student's external causes of action, only to replace them with contingencies shaped by the student himself.

Indications: Applications are best with highly verbal and educated students whose cognitive, emotional or behavioral disorders are more episodic than continuous. Educationally advisable for generalized anxiety, work motivation, depression, poor self-reinforcement, poor self-efficacy, and a variety of speech and interpersonal deviations.

Contraindications: There are no serious contraindications in the literature. However, therapeutic gains may vacillate according to how developed the rapport is between teacher and student.

Limitations: Important problems include, for rational restructuring, prematurely or aggressively confronting the student's irrational beliefs; replacing illogical beliefs with ones that are equally unrealistic or prejudicial; and misjudging the rationality of beliefs. For attribution, typical obstacles include the dismissal of certain external causes which present realistic threats. (For further review, see Ellis & Grieger, 1977; Walen, Digiuseppe & Wessler, 1980.)

15. Constructional Approach.

Operation: Training acceptable behavior that substitutes or replaces unacceptable behavior as one component of #22, Differential Reinforcement of Alternative Behaviors (DRA). Follow the procedure of DRO (#26) or DRA but in addition use a conditioning technique to increase rates of some new response. This invokes alternative behaviors. Also needed are reinforcing opportunities to develop and maintain the new responses. Make the opportunities for these new responses very distinct from stimulus conditions for inappropriate behavior.

Indications: Procedure overcomes the side-effects of aggression and recovery suppression of DRO, and is frequently effective for childhood social skills deficits, and prevocational weakness. It is also a nice alternative to positive and negative punishment.

Contraindications: Constructional interventions are contraindicated where the side-effects include negative behavior contrasts, or when new responses actually prompt recurrence of bad behavior.

Limitations: Common to all deceleration procedures is a periodical resistance from students who poorly discriminate between reinforcement and extinction conditions. Another problem results from the teacher's choice of unrealistic, complex alternative behaviors for students to learn. (For further review, see Delprato, 1981; Stevenson, Kaiser & Ruben, 1984.)

16. Contingency Contracting.

Operation: A contract simply states what behaviors of what individuals will produce what reinforcers (or punishers), and who will deliver these consequences. Contracts established between two or more persons (teacher, student, parent, etc.) or for oneself (self-control), typically contain the following parts: (a) clear statement of the target behaviors, (b) method of data collection, (c) reinforcer (or punisher) to be used, their schedules of delivery, and who will deliver them, (d) potential problems and their resolutions, (e) bonus or penalty clauses, (f) a schedule for review of progress, and (g) signatures of all involved and dates of the agreement. The design and negotiation of a contract ensures that (a) all parties involved agree to the goal and procedure, (b) the parties will agree on how close they are to reaching certain goals, and (c) the student has a realistic estimate of time, effort and (in some cases) money involved. Effective contracts are not legally binding, but rather are open to renegotiation in a series of many contracts used to gradually shape behavior.

Indications: Majority of contracts appear for two or more individuals and primarily for family interactions and homework completion.

Contraindications: Negative side-effects are likely for delinquents or children with severely deficient compliance skills. Another problem is failure to establish mutual reinforcement exchange between student and contingency manager (teacher, parent). Consistency and accuracy of behavioral contracts thus depend on the motivation on the part of all parties to follow their defined strategies.

Limitations: Mastery of contracts typically circumvents the need for outside experts. While this can be beneficial, troubleshooting application problems may require the expertise of behavioral specialists. Secondly, management of the contracts may be inaccurate; teachers to an extent might rely on external agents (parents) for proper implementation as well as the agents' reports of failures. (For further review, see DeRisi & Butz, 1975; Homme, Csangi, Gonzales & Rechs, 1969; Sundel & Sundel, 1975.)

17. Continuous Reinforcement.

Operation: Present the reinforcer contingently upon each instance of the desirable (target) behavior. Reinforcers should be of identical nature and amount, unless a schedule of delivery is to change. Continuous reinforcement (CRF) schedules enable acquisition of minimal rates of responding. The decision about quantity and quality of reinforcement depends on (a) the type of reinforcer used (conditioned, unconditioned), (b) deprivation and satiation conditions, (c) the effort required to make the response, and (d) the past history of reinforcement or punishment for that response (for that person).

Indications: Continuous Reinforcement provides powerful shaping results for most adaptive living skills, classroom skills, vocational and educational skills, and for teaching compliance. Transition to intermittent schedules will be an efficient way to maintain these behaviors.

Contraindications: Under CRF schedules, satiation effects occur fairly rapidly, especially when the reinforcers are unconditioned (food, drink). With conditioned reinforcers, satiation effects are somewhat delayed, but acquisition is minimized. Also, extinction effects are more severe if reinforcement density during CRF is thinned out too rapidly. One way to avoid extinction effects is by adding discriminative stimuli, like reminders (prompts, probes) and occasional supplemental reinforcers as well. Continuous Reinforcement is cautioned for behaviors which have "sequential relationships" (are collateral to) with self-injurious and socially harmful behaviors.

Limitations: Because behaviors are maintained better on intermittent schedules, CRF is limited to acquisition phases only. (For further review, see Bijou, Orlando, 1961; Thompson & Grabowski, 1972.)

18. Corrective Feedback.

Operation: This intervention provides students with information about how to do a response, plus requires active correction for the error. Corrective feedback also specifies returning to earlier steps in the instructional procedure, and branching out to supplementary steps when repeated or additional errors are made. Major elements include prompting, reinforcement, and offering several learning trials. Simple commands such as "right" and "wrong" lack controlling properties and are replaced by gestural prompts including modeling of appropriate behavior. Also, descriptive comments strengthen repetition of correct performance. To prevent inadvertent reinforcement of incorrect responses, pause before the correction commences. This way, the word or gesture (feedback) will signal onset of a correction. Finally, have student rehearse the correct response several times before beginning a new trial.

Indications: Suggested for academic and classroom problems.

Contraindications: The amount of effort and time in a series of repeated trials may render the procedure slightly aversive, thus possibly increasing errors. One result of this is the teacher becoming a conditioned aversive stimulus, or the target skill inadvertently being punished. Caution should be exercised when giving corrective feedback to students having a history of severe escape and avoidance responses.

Limitations: Training is sufficient for relatively simple discriminations and responses, but should be supplemented with other behavioral programs. Another limitation is the absence of training support from the natural environment (parents), which may delay or disrupt generalization of skills. (For further review, see Cossairt, Hall & Hopkins, 1973; Drabman & Lagey, 1974; Leach & Dolan, 1985; Peterson, 1982.)

19. Cueing.

Operation: A stimulus signals the availability of reinforcers contingent upon some target behavior. Signals actually function as discriminative or antecedent stimuli which have acquired an evocative effect on the target behavior. Cueing may take the form of visual, auditory or tactile stimuli.

Indications: The frequent use of cueing has been with deep muscle and sensory-induced relaxation, or in communication skills training.

Contraindications: Like any discrimination task, selected antecedent cues for behavior must be clearly distinct from cues for maladaptive behaviors. Secondly, lack of extension to events in the natural environment will weaken generalization.

Limitations: One minor limitation is that cueing will frequently enhance antecedent-response connections only, regardless of the consequences for the behavior. (For further review, see Russell & Sipich, 1973.)

20. Delayed Reinforcement.

Operation: Reinforcement can be scheduled so that consequences are delayed. Temporal delays vary by the amount or quantity of reinforcement, quality or type of response, and state of deprivation. Delay schedules are different from interval and ratio schedules in that the behavior-shaping reinforcer is given instead of interim reinforcers. In other words, recess may be "given" to students who usually receive points for completed assignments minutes or hours before the recess.

Indications: Suggested for classroom use or as part of a token economy system.

Contraindications: Delayed reinforcement risks other (undesirable) behaviors occurring between the target response and delivery of consequences. Another risk is shifting from CRF to delay reinforcement; extinction effects (aggression, etc.) may lead to disintegration of target behavior.

Limitations: One minor problem is the misuse of delay schedules as a form of discipline rather than to thin out CRF schedules. Teachers might lengthen the delay, thinking it will motivate students to work harder or might discourage misbehavior. Unfortunately, all this does is condition the student to delay the desirable behaviors until shortly before reinforcement (i.e., procrastination). (For further review, see Schwarz & Hawkins, 1970.)

21. Differential Reinforcement.

Operation: Reinforce selected responses only in the presence of a discriminative stimulus, and withhold reinforcers for responses in the presence of nonrelevant stimuli. Efficient practice includes the following guidelines: (a) identify relevant stimulus properties, (b) apply reinforcement and extinction procedures, (c) focus student's attention on relevant stimulus properties, (d) introduce an irrelevant stimulus that is clearly different from the discriminative stimulus, (e) introduce the irrelevant stimulus only briefly and at weak intensities, (f) pause following an incorrect response, and (g) provide correct practice trials following incorrect responses. Discriminative stimuli may include different people, settings, and objects.

Indications: Procedure is appropriate for most tasks between concepts. Proper discrimination will last longer if the target behavior is reinforced intermittently in the presence of the discriminative stimulus.

Contraindications: Advanced steps involving use of aversive consequences for responses may produce "generalized inhibitory responses." That is, rather than inhibit unreinforced responses, effects of inhibition may also reduce rates of responding under the discriminative stimulus.

Limitations: Standard forms of discrimination training take many trials and errors before the student achieves some degree of mastery. Another problem is that while appropriate behavior increases, suppression of the inappropriate behavior may be temporary, especially when competing discriminative stimuli and (bootleg) reinforcers are in the environment. (For further review, see Striefel & Wetherby, 1983.)

22. Differential Reinforcement of Alternative Behaviors (DRA).

Operation: This procedure involves selectively reinforcing alternatives to behaviors targeted for reduction. Procedure is gradual or can be long-lasting when combined with aversive (punishment) procedures. Steps to follow include: (a) select an incompatible or discriminated response from student's repertoire, (b) select a behavior also easily maintained by the environment (natural contingencies), (c) use effective reinforcers, and (d) combine this procedure with other procedures, particularly modeling.

Indications: Assuming optimal use, procedure is recommended for classroom and childhood disruptions.

Contraindications: When combined with punishment, procedure is no longer entirely positive and may result in avoidance and escape responding.

Limitations. Desirable responses that are not incompatible or poorly discriminated may be inadvertently put on extinction, and undesirable behaviors may gain strength. Schedules for alternative behavior should ensure clear stimulus control for each response class increased or decreased. (For further review, see Vukelich & Hake, 1971.)

23. Differential Reinforcement of High Rates of Behavior (DRH).

Operation: Selectively reinforce only bursts or specified increased rates of responses emitted with less than some "t" (designated time) between each response. Results are gradual and progressive rate increases.

Indications: Procedure is effective in dealing with speech and reading disorders and classroom disruption, and in teaching general adaptive skills for mentally retarded and the disabled.

Contraindications: Ethical caution is advised if the target behavior under DRH corresponds or is sequentially related to self-injurious behavior.

Limitations: One drawback is the "transitory effect" of high rates of responding. Responses gradually weaken as programmed contingencies are faded. This may be a problem for response generalization. (For further review, see Wilson & McReynolds, 1973.)

24. Differential Reinforcement of Incompatible Behavior (DRI).

Operation: This involves selectively reinforcing responses that are "temporally and spatially" opposite to some undesirable, target behavior. Consider the form (topography) of the behavior to be eliminated, and the relationship it maintains with local antecedent and consequences. As one behavior undergoes extinction, systematically increase another behavior using the same reinforcers. This helps the student discriminate which behaviors are appropriate for reinforcement.

Indications: Classroom uses of DRI are generally the same as those of (#22) DRA.

Contraindications: Caution should be exercised when selecting incompatible responses, and using differential attention. Alternative responses which still enable the student to be disruptive will inadvertently aggravate the problem. Likewise, the withholding of contingent attention for inappropriate behavior may risk a sudden rate increase in that behavior. A last problem, while infrequent, is spontaneous recovery of ignored behaviors.

Limitations: A serious limitation is that DRI requires that the inappropriate behavior be present for extinction. Behaviors which should not occur (self-injurious) or are already infrequent are unnecessarily encouraged to occur. (For further review, see Hall, Lund & Jackson, 1968.)

25. Differential Reinforcement of Lower Rates of Behavior (DRL).

Operation: This involves selectively reinforcing responses only at low rates that are spaced relatively far apart from each other. Choose the response expected within some time interval. If the response is finished before termination of the interval, reinforcement is withheld at the end of the interval. If the response(s) is not finished by the end of the interval, present the reinforcers, whether or not the target behavior occurs at that moment. Variations of DRL (spaced responding, interval, and full session) effectively diminish, without eliminating, undesirable behaviors. Procedures allow for progressive reduction in the response rate. Teacher may wish to use timing devices to determine accurately which reinforcers are effective.

Indications: Appropriate uses include for speech disorders, vocational and educational training, and generally whenever undesirable behavior is tolerable at minimal rates.

Contraindications: Scheduled discriminations become crucial to avoid students learning desirable behaviors at low rates for reinforcement. Also, DRL is inadvisable for reducing behaviors requiring immediate cessation (violent, self-injurious, etc.).

Limitations: Apart from the slow process, one potential problem is ignoring desirable behaviors. A solution is to combine DRL with other behavioral procedures. (For further review, see Deitz, 1977; Poole & Yates, 1975.)

26. Differential Reinforcement of Other Behavior (DRO).

Operation: Selectively reinforce any behavior the student shows except the undesirable one. Program the reinforcement schedule so that the student receives reinforcers contingent upon the "omission" rather than "emission" of a behavior. This explains why DRO is called "omission training." Look for the target response at a specific moment. If the target response is absent, present the reinforcer; if the target response is present, withhold reinforcement. One variation is the delivery of reinforcers if no response occurs during a time interval. Careful scheduling of reinforcement will rapidly reduce behavior and concurrently strengthen an infinite variety of other behaviors.

Indications: Frequently used in classrooms, DRO is effective to reduce speech disorders, aggression, self-stimulatory behaviors, seizures, and a host of delinquency tasks.

Contraindications: Negative side-effects arise from the inaccurate timing of implementation. Since all behaviors other than the target one receive reinforcers, there is the possibility of symptoms substitution and "superstitious conditioning," i.e., when other inappropriate, yet untargeted, behaviors are strengthened inadvertently. So, too, idiosyncratic, habitual response patterns might be reinforced.

Limitations: For all its effectiveness, DRO still entails extinction. If used with students who have many problem behaviors, DRO may produce substantial changes over baseline rates, but maintenance will be weak. Use of additional reinforcement interventions minimizes this problem. (For further review, see Barton, Andrew & Repp, 1986; Goetz, Holmberg & LeBlanc, 1975; Wehner & Harmon, 1975.)

27. Educational Programming.

Operation: Programming basically involves two arrangements: "concurrent" and "serial." In concurrent training, trials on two (or more) different tasks alternate within a single session (time period) before either task reaches criterion levels. In serial training, skill mastery occurs before initiating a second task. Task definitions and training procedures frequently require learning objectives, imitation and modeling, prompting, reinforcement schedules, and repeated trials.

Indications: Programs assist the acquisition and retention of academic performance on multiple tasks.

Contraindications: Possible side-effects such as response decay and aggression can be expected from temporarily disrupting the training process.

Limitations: Generalization often requires concurrent, over serial, training and this differs from the established instructional practices of most classrooms. Also, in switching tasks (concurrent), time is needed to reorient the student to the current task. (For further review, see Panyan & Hall, 1978; Schroeder & Baer, 1972.)

28. Errorless Discrimination.

Operation: Discrimination task that involves carefully manipulating characteristics of the discriminative (relevant) stimulus. Divide the discriminative stimulus into smaller parts. Then, present the student with only one part of the stimulus, in the presence of which responding is reinforced. As responses continue, gradually fade in an alternate (nonrelevant) stimulus which signals nonreinforcement. This avoids using extinction for incorrect responses and also minimizes errors. The method also enables mastery of relatively difficult discriminations.

Indications: Errorless training is for instructional purposes, used with retarded and nonretarded (school-age) children. Tasks vary from subtle geometric shapes to objects contained within other objects, e.g. water inside a glass.

Contraindications: Since the use of punishment and extinction are unnecessary, negative side-effects are rare. However, pairing the relevant with nonrelevant stimuli too rapidly may inhibit discriminations, cause response fatigue, or increase response errors.

Limitations: One drawback is that teachers who use artificial prompts in training may forget to fade them out. This risks that the student will learn to differentiate only on the basis of artificial prompts, not realistic ones. (For further review, see Sidman & Stoddard, 1967; Terrace, 1966.)

29. Extinction.

Operation: Two common forms of extinction appear for respondent and operant conditioning.

29A. OPERANT. This refers to the consistent withholding of reinforcers in the presence of undesirable target behavior, usually until the behavior decreases or returns to low (baseline) levels. Defining features include (a) observing the consequences of maintaining target behavior, (b) arranging for the withdrawal of those reinforcers, and (c) observing behavior decrements. Once a response weakens, it remains weak unless there is lack of discrimination. That is, sudden or inconsistent changes in new stimuli may increase response variability.

29B. RESPONDENT. The inconsistent or eliminated pairings between "CS" and "US" result in a decreased power (or elicitive function) of the CS. This also decreases the rate of the CR. Re-pairing CS with US (and increasing CR) is called "disinhibition." Without this reconditioning, the sudden resurgence of the CR at a later date is called "spontaneous recovery."

Indications: Operant extinction decreases major classroom behaviors, combined reinforcement procedures.

Contraindications: Several problems arise for extinction. First, resistance to extinction may be due to improper or incomplete removal of reinforcement. Second, behaviors on extinction eventually elevate ("extinction burst") for a relatively short period, followed by lower rates. The duration of high rates depends on prior uses of extinction for that behavior. Failures with extinction will likely extend duration. Third, extinction usually prevents reinforcement for targeted *and* nontargeted responses, sequentially related to the target response. In respondent extinction, one side-effect is "ritualistic" or habitual responding. Another problem, from improper discriminations, is excessive escape and avoidance behaviors.

Limitations: One mistake is that users of extinction usually ignore the "behaver" and not the "behavior." Ethically, a long extinction phase may threaten the student or people around him. Teachers should remain in relative promixity around students during extinction. Another mistake is when extinction competes with unknown ("bootleg") reinforcers. Behaviors put on extinction but later reinforced by uninformed parents will sabotage results. For respondent extinction, control over certain US and CS pairings may be impossible in the natural environment. (For further review, see Bijou, 1958; Sajwaj, Twardosz & Burke, 1972.)

30. Fading.

Operation: The gradual removal of discriminative stimuli or prompts from the original training situation. Use enough prompts to barely signal the response, while avoiding abrupt reductions in verbal or physical guidance. Components of the procedure include:

GRADUAL-GUIDANCE. Begin training with extensive physical assistance; then, minimize the physical gestures to only that necessary for the student's motions to begin. Step by step, reduce physical guidance.

TRANSFERRING CONTROL: DEMONSTRATION TO INSTRUCTION. First, model the target behavior and little by little fade it into more subtle gestures, eventually eliminating it altogether. In the process, gradually and concurrently increase verbal (spoken) prompts. Then, allow verbal prompts to serve alone.

TRANSFERRING CONTROL: IRRELEVANT TO RELEVANT STIMULI. Systematically program responses to occur under new, relevant, naturalistic stimuli; i.e., gradually introduce relevant stimuli into the discrimination.

Indications: Fading is common in the home and at school. Frequently the procedure develops strong academic and conversational skills.

Contraindications and Limitations: Reduced physical guidance is inadvisable for students with severe social deficits. Second, abruptly or rapidly faded stimuli will disrupt the discrimination and possibly weaken response rates. Consequently, carefully programmed fading is time-consuming. (For further review, see Becker, Engelmann & Thomas, 1975; Timm, Strain & Eller, 1979.)

31. Feedback.

Operation: Presentation of verbal or nonverbal information following some target response so the student can correct and repeat that response in the future. Modified variations of feedback as a procedure are numerous and include group versus individual, private versus public, personal versus mechanical, and the schedule of feedback.

31A. GROUP VERSUS INDIVIDUAL. Group feedback is provided on student performance by all group members, either by consensus or on a one-to-one basis. In nongroup situations, individual feedback is provided directly by teachers of some target behavior.

31B. PRIVATE VERSUS PUBLIC. Private feedback is given by oneself (thoughts, images), or by another observer through inconspicuous outlets (secret envelope). Public feedback usually involves bulletin-board announcements, graphic displays, program reports, or information carried over the media.

31C. PERSONAL VERSUS MECHANICAL. Personal feedback includes information from another person, whereas it is mechanical when the product of some perfomance is measured (counted, timed, etc.) automatically by preset devices, triggered by the onset or completion of behavior.

31D. SCHEDULE OF FEEDBACK. This involves providing feedback cumulatively on ratio or interval schedules, or on CRF (see #17) schedules.

Indications: Feedback generally applies to all training situations.

Contraindications: Side-effects from inconsistent, inaccurate or delayed feedback usually include fluctuating rates in performance or failure to acquire or master new skills. Feedback as punishment invokes the same emotional (escape and avoidance) responses found in aversive conditioning.

Limitations: Debate continues on whether "feedback" refers to a specific procedure, is a new principle of behavior, or simply has become professional slang from terminology of cybernetics. This question further asks whether all functions of feedback are by nature reinforcers or conditioned stimuli. (For further review, see Ford, 1980; Leitenberg, Agras, Thompson & Wright, 1968.)

32. Fixed-Interval Schedule.

Operation: Delivery of reinforcers dependent upon the passage of a specific (fixed) period of time. Fixed-interval (FI) schedules specify that reinforcers are available only when (a) a particular response occurs, (b) following the passage of specific time. FI schedules are abbreviated with the number of minutes printed next to the FI (e.g., FI5 = FI of 5 mn.).

Indications: The kind of behavior observed with FI schedules is a pause after reinforcement and then an increase in rate of responding until a high rate is reached as the interval ends (called "scalloping"). Changes from pausing to rapid responding can be quite sudden. Such schedules appear on a regular basis in classrooms (weekly quizzes, report cards, lunch periods, recess, etc.), and at home.

Contraindications: FI is inadvisable for acquisitional learning or even as the first or second step in fading from CRF (see #17). Responding on a fixed-interval schedule before the rate is stable may result in fatigue, resistance and anger.

Limitations: First, this schedule indirectly encourages low rates of responding since responses must occur at least once after the interval for reinforcement. Also, students are not penalized by the postponement of reinforcement if they fail to respond for a while during the interval. (For further review, see Weiner, 1964, 1969.)

33. Fixed-Ratio Schedule.

Operation: Delivery of reinforcers contingent upon a given number of responses. The number of responses required prior to reinforcement is "fixed" at a specific amount. Fixed-ratio (FR) schedules usually follow in sequence from CRF (see #17) schedules.

Indications: General performance characteristics under a fixed-ratio schedule include high and fairly consistent rates while the schedule is in effect. This rate continues in early phases of extinction. Rapid responding also allows the student to accumulate more reinforcers within a given period. One finding, then, is that the longer the response requirement (e.g. FR50, FR100), the more rapid the response rate. Another pattern is that after each reinforcement the student pauses before trying to respond again. This rapid burst and pause is called "post-reinforcement pause." FR schedules apply to educational and institutional training programs, while phasing out CRF schedules.

Contraindications: High and strenuous ratios (e.g. FR400) can create pauses at various and unpredictable times, or simply suppress behavior to pre-baseline levels. Another concern is how students will respond during these pauses—engaging in off-task or inappropriate behaviors. For instance, this may entail doodling, leaving the classroom, or daydreaming. Further, inappropriate behaviors may be maintained accidentally with FR schedules.

Limitations: One drawback is that the strength of responses on FR renders that response resistant to extinction (especially in cases of unwanted responses). (For further review, see Bijou & Orlando, 1961; Hutchinson & Azrin, 1961.)

34. Forward Chaining.

Operation: Forward chaining proceeds in a fashion opposite to that of backward chaining. First, divide a target (cluster of) behavior into small steps using a task analysis. Second, reinforce the initial step in the sequence until mastery of some criterion is achieved. Third, reinforce the initial step followed by the second step in the sequence, and so forth until the entire sequence occurs prior to reinforcement. Prompt the student through all the steps in a chain on each trial. For example, in a 15-step training sequence, help the student to perform all 15 steps in proper order. When performance improves, begin fading out manual or instructional guidance.

Indications: Procedure is an alternative to backward chaining (see #6) in basic acquisition task for classroom students.

Contraindications: Negative side-effects of forward chaining are rare, other than those discussed for backward chaining.

Limitations: One major limitation is that acquisition of the chained sequence requires more numbers of trials. This risks reinforcing an inappropriate response which precedes an appropriate response and thus producing an undesirable chain of behavior. (For further review, see Martin, Kehoe, Bird, Jensen & Darbyshire, 1971.)

35. Group Contingencies.

Operation: Group contingencies refer to a criterion of reinforcement based upon the performance of the group as a whole, in contrast to individual contingencies which treat all group members as individuals. The entire group unit agrees upon appropriate consequences for certain behaviors. Contingencies are self-administered by each group member, or administered to one another by selected members, or by teacher. Programming contingencies combines with contingency contracts, self-reinforcement, different schedules of reinforcement, and token systems, and imitation and modeling.

Indications: Group contingencies work more effectively in child and adolescent groups than in adult clinical groups. Suggested behaviors for a contingency include late arrivals, disclosures, on-task behaviors, assertiveness, exchange of compliments, insight, and homework completion. Peer-administered contingencies generally facilitate maintenance and generalization of target behavior.

Contraindications: Contingencies must be developed as a group activity, so that each member equally has opportunities to earn or lose certain reinforcers. If not, members will feel other members take unfair advantage of reinforcement, and this disrupts both the group procedure and positive treatment outcomes. Teachers should thus teach each member how to reinforce another member or themselves.

Limitations: While closer to natural contingencies, group contingencies are less controlled for initially shaping behavior. Secondary effects include the accidental shaping of inappropriate or competing behavior such as students finishing their homework "only" so they have access to reinforcers. (For further review, see Litow & Pumroy, 1975; Wodarski, Feldman & Flax, 1973.)

36. Homework.

Operation: Tasks involving self-recording, self-modification, or completion of questionnaires and surveys that are an extension of instructional sessions. Assignments specify the manner in which procedures, techniques and contingencies should be carried out by the student with or without teacher supervision. Weekly homework enables the practice of skills in the natural environment, and thus facilitates generalization earlier in lessons. Contingent assignments are ones that must be completed according to certain criteria for reinforcement, whereas noncontingent assignments generally are for student motivation.

Indications: Uses of homework are favorable in most self-management (acceleration and deceleration) programs. Students should be familiar with the tasks or have demonstrated them prior to the assignment.

Contraindications: Homework is inadvisable for students with extreme maladaptive or deficient behaviors or for whom the assignment involves embarrassing, anxious, or risky situations (going alone to a movie at night). Homework may also produce untoward effects if the task engenders aversive consequences from family, friends, and co-workers.

Limitations: Serious problems result from misapplication. One problem is that support systems do not exist to follow through with the homework. Second, teachers replace the duration or intensity of lessons with longer and more involved homework assignments. Third, homework may ask for skills that the student lacks, needs remediation on, or resists because of naturalistic (aversive) consequences. (For further review, see Ruben, 1985; Shelton & Levy, 1981.)

37. Imitation/Modeling.

Operation: Modeling occurs by demonstrating a given behavior in proper form (topography) and function by another person (the model). Following this, the student imitates the behaviors observed. Correct imitation receives reinforcement, whereas incorrect imitative trials result in a variety of remedial procedures. Modeling specifies behaviors and contingencies and should be broken down into realistic, easy-to-follow steps (task analysis). Procedural considerations include:

PEER MODELING. Having the student observe a peer performing the target behavior.

IMITATIVE PROMPTS. Verbal and nonverbal discriminative stimuli facilitating the student's correct imitation, although they are later faded out.

GENERALIZED IMITATION. Extensively reinforcing imitation under many circumstances. Each situation contains the relevant defining features for maintenance of the target (imitative) response.

SELECTION OF MODELS. Appropriate selection relates to models having (a) similar characteristics, and (b) prestige or leadership, such as youths seen as "popular."

PREVIOUS OBSERVER EXPERIENCES. Students are more amenable to imitations if they (a) experienced failure in prior tasks, (b) observe the model's competence, and (c) have participated in cooperative experiences with the model.

Indications: Modeling and imitation appear in procedures for children for classroom uses. Best results are achieved with students with highly developed verbal and nonverbal repertoires. Symbolic modeling, a variation, simply occurs through film, videotape, and other media.

Contraindications: One problem results from inconsistency among the models, thus producing unstable rates of imitation. Secondly, unrealistic modeling scenes are difficult to generalize to natural situations. Third, rapid fading of imitative prompts may weaken those imitations not yet under stimulus control. Fourth, instructions alone are inadequate as effective substitutes for modeling plus instruction in imitation trials.

Limitations: Shaping, physical guidance and instructions usually combine with this procedure or else there is slower acquisition of imitation. (For further review, see Baer, Peterson & Sherman, 1967; Lovaas, Berberich, Perloff & Schaeffer, 1966; Odom, Hoyson & Strain, 1985.)

38. Maintenance.

Operation: Maintenance of new responses includes, first, increasing similarity between training and natural settings by (a) fading of reinforcement during training, (b) training students to self-reinforce, and (c) by use of isolated, followed by simultaneous, presentation of situations, rather than simple isolated presentations. Second, training further enhances self-reinforcement and expands parameters of stimulus control (i.e., generalization).

Indications: Maintenance issues are particularly relevant for community and classrooms for children who are asocial. Multifaceted behavioral programs usually contain phases that assess maintenance and generalization.

Contraindications: Maintenance is contraindicated in cases where the strength of target responses (e.g. independent study) correlates to increasing strengths of undesirable behavior (e.g. poor study habits).

Limitations: Skills on maintenance remain strong even if suppressed by actual punishing conditions. Second, establishing maintenance requires skill rehearsal and reinforcement in a variety of training settings. (For further review, see Haney & Jones, 1982; Guevremont, Osnes & Stokes, 1986; Jones & Kazdin, 1975.)

39. Match-to-Sample.

Operation: Selecting from a number of alternatives an object that corresponds to, or matches, a particular sample. Present sample stimulus and one or more choice stimuli; reinforce the correct match. Trials contain relevant stimulus properties of the sample, prompting, and effective reinforcement and extinction procedures.

Indications: Frequently used to teach concepts, alphabet letters, and for discrimination of hygienic or food-related behaviors. Effective for infants, children, and school populations, programmed for "errorless training."

Contraindications: While efficient and long-lasting, responding may be restricted to specific stimuli (e.g., alphabet letters on index cards), unless properties of that stimulus are trained under a variety of naturalistic conditions.

Limitations: Basic problem deals with stimulus presentation and consequences. Relevant and nonrelevant properties of the stimulus (cue) may be unclear. Second, transferring training discrimination to, for example, classroom worksheets may be difficult. Third, incorrect choices by the student sometimes are either too subtle or too numerous for immediate remediation. (For further review, see Egeland, 1975; Salmon, Pear & Kuhn, 1986; Tweeney, 1972.)

40. Mediation Training.

Operation: In mediation (correspondence) training, students are instructed to verbalize (itemize) expected consequences of some behaviors at the time of their emission. Itemization of consequences includes (a) the aversive consequences of behavior, (b) describing the appropriate (alternative) responses, and (c) describing the consequences of those responses. Gains and losses can be oral (spoken), written (as essays), or communicated contingent upon reinforcement.

Indications: Mediation applies to classroom situations (e.g. pupil misbehavior), in conjunction with more direct (acceleration and deceleration) operant techniques.

Contraindications and Limitations: Modifications of classroom behavior by mediation alone do not guarantee an automatic relationship between saying (expecting) and doing. A second consideration is whether mediation for children is more effective than for adults or special disabled populations. (For further review, see Blackwood, 1972; Israel, 1978; Karlan & Rusch, 1982; Matthews, Schimoff & Catania, 1987; Risley & Hart, 1968.)

41. Movement (Deprivation) Suppression.

Operation: Variation of time-out (#70) involving the physical guidance of the student to a nearby corner, where he assumes a "police-frisk" position. Another position is the student facing the corner with his arms crossed behind him. The therapist places one hand on the base of the student's neck and the other on the student's wrists. Verbal and motor movements receive instant reprimands ("Don't move," "get back in the corner," etc.). Duration is 2 to 5 minutes. Fading of physical prompts is gradual, although patient may constantly require suppression.

Indications: Effective applications appear for behaviors that are self-injurious, self-stimulatory, hazardous to others, classroom disruption. Procedure is shown more effective than physical guidance (#51), overcorrection (#49), DRO (#26), contingent exercise, or corner-time-out.

Contraindications: Basic questions surround the rapidity of deceleration and reinforcing side-effects of the procedure. The suppression of undesirable responses also eliminates any related movements, appropriate or inappropriate. Children having poor balance or already disabled could be at risk of injury. Also, physical guidance plus the verbal reprimands for 2 to 5 minutes may function as reinforcers, thereby increasing disruptive behavior.

Limitations: Procedural logistics are unclear for larger students or for restricted classroom conditions as when staff-patient ratio is small. Since, inititally, students in time-out are supervised, consistency among teacher-supervisors adds the cost and time to training. (For further review, see Rolider & Van Houten, 1985.)

42. Natural Reinforcement.

Operation: Selection of reinforcer from an array of already existing options in the student's "natural" environment. Guiding this selection are basic nonintrusive reinforcement categories including (a) edibles, (b) tangibles, (c) exchangeable reinforcers, (d) activity reinforcers, (e) social reinforcers, (f) group contingencies, (see #35), and (g) counter-control.

EDIBLES. Various foods and drinks presented during mealtime are scheduled into daily routines and are contingent upon appropriate behaviors.

TANGIBLES. Various products available in the student's life are asystematic; rearrangement of them so that they prime or encourage proper responding can efficiently increase behavior.

EXCHANGEABLE REINFORCERS. These are token economies, lotteries, and systems wherein there is some intermediate consequence before the terminal reinforcer is delivered. For example, stars awarded contingent upon a task can be exchanged that evening for some wanted activity.

ACTIVITY REINFORCERS. Opportunities for pleasant activities (without tokens) can be made contingent upon completion of assigned tasks (behaviors). When such activities follow unpleasant tasks, the latter are increased due to the Premack principle (see #54).

SOCIAL REINFORCERS. Reinforcers are presented by other people within a social context, but only contingently. Attention, praise, approval, communication in front of others, touching, and the like increase aspects of appropriate behavior.

GROUP CONTINGENCIES. Collective or group reinforcement is where peers acknowledge or encourage the student's performance. Peer counseling programs specifically gear toward the "popular" or "well-liked" students to teach them how to compliment their cohorts only when these cohorts exhibit preferred behaviors (e.g. drug refusals, homework completion, etc.). (See also #35.)

COUNTER-CONTROLS. While an unusual procedure at first, the opportunity for students to directly modify the teacher's behavior can be contingent upon their acceptable rates of certain behaviors.

Indications: Natural reinforcement enhances skill generalization and maintenance especially for programs in the classroom and home.

Contraindications: Initially, it may be useful to select artificial or contrived reinforcers until acquired rates of responding reach a level of criteria. One admonishment is that the gradual return to natural reinforcers should be supported by others (parents, monitors) in the program; otherwise, rates of behavior may return to pre-baseline rates.

Limitations: One disadvantage with natural reinforcement is its frequent availability and large amounts of it. This could diminish value from the restricted use of a "contingency." Contingent presentations thus need to be monitored. (For further review, see Skinner, 1982; Tharp & Wetzel, 1969.)

43. Negative Practice
(Massed Practice, Reactive Extinction, Instructional Repetition).

Operation: The repeated performance of some problem behavior with little rest, resulting in a reduced frequency of its occurrence. The student engages in repeated trials for a predetermined duration, gradually minimizing the length if rest builds up in between trials.

Indications: Most applications involve motor behavior that is involuntary (tics, habits), yet extended treatments have eliminated typing and other recurrent academic errors.

Contraindications: Research evidence produces ambivalent results about overall effectiveness. One side-effect is an exacerbation of the problem. Because guidelines for use are ambiguous, another problem may be overexertion of "practice," not only suppressing unwanted behaviors, but also angering the student.

Limitations: Major drawbacks of utilization include the procedure (a) being aversive to both teacher and student, (b) requiring extensive amount of time, and (c) requiring extensive staff training for accurate use by different teachers. (For further review, see Lahey, McNees & McNees, 1973; Yates, 1958.)

44. Negative Punishment.

Operation: A procedure where the response is followed by the delay (prevention), reduction or removal of usually pleasant (reinforcing) stimuli, thus decreasing the undesirable response on future occasions. Increased latency (time between response and consequence) generally conditions responses that are incompatible to the undesirable behavior so that the student can receive pleasant outcomes (without delay or interruption).

Indications: Applications range in population, setting, and among different operant and respondent techniques. Largely because it is a form of "punishment," this procedure is less preferred than reinforcement procedure.

Contraindications: Caution should be exercised in all uses of punishment. Shaping of incompatible responses that are functionally similar to any escape and avoidance behaviors may accidentally result in heightened anxiety (or phobias) and a peculiar resistance to previous reinforcers in the student's life.

Limitations: Because negative punishment is usually "automatic" in the culture, abuses in practice abound unless efforts to monitor interventions remain consistent. (For further review, see Knight, M.F. & McKenzie, 1974; Ruben & Ruben, 1985.)

45. Negative Reinforcement.

Operation: Negative reinforcement involves the immediate removal or delay of an aversive stimulus following the emission of some behavior. It is unlike extinction, which is the discontinuation of reinforcement, and recovery. Behaviors usually are strengthened by reinforcement contingent upon escape and avoidance.

Indications: Applications typically appear in home, school and the community.

Contraindications: Negative side-effects include aggressive behaviors or inappropriate escape and avoidance tendencies (e.g. truancy). Incorrect or increased practice of negative reinforcement also may inadvertently aggravate treated disorders. The procedure is inadvisable for students having extended histories of punishment.

Limitations: Definitions of negative reinforcement, as distinct from "punishment," are very unclear. The potential evocative effects, clinically, also raise ethical concerns for field interventions. (For further review, see Azrin & Holz, 1966; Michael, 1975.)

46. Noncontingent Reinforcement.

Operation: Presentation of reinforcers at random during a specific or nonspecific interval, and regardless of whether it is preceded by the target behavior.

Indications: Practical use is primarily for methodological reasons. It appears in baseline or reversal phases where because of the serious or harmful risks of behavior, programming must remain (to an extent) in effect. Experimental exigencies for validity are met, while preventing a total return of behavior to pre-baseline rates.

Contraindications: Behaviors that are severe or physically injurious are inappropriate for noncontingent reinforcement, especially if on a random schedule the behavior strengthens.

Limitations: One drawback is the chance that trainers (caretakers, parents, teachers, etc.) will resort to pretraining habits of consequation. Another is that, where the natural environment is already orderly, shifting to noncontingent reinforcement may itself invoke desirable changes unplanned for by the program. (For further review, see Allyon & Azrin, 1965.)

47. Observational Learning.

Operation: A higher order of modeling where the modeled response indicates a "rule" about the performance and consequences expected to follow, although students never witness the model's behavior in particular operant situations. (Procedure is also referred to as "rule-governed behavior.") As discriminated learning, the procedure incorporates covert rehearsal, imaginal and verbal conditioning, and behavioral rehearsal. The derived rule guides the imitator's reproduction of the response under real situations. Imitation and modeling are implemented in a graduated series of trials.

Indications: Procedure is appropriate for young children among peers (peer training). Procedure may vary from reduction of anxiety disorders and disruptive behaviors, to increases in social communication skills.

Contraindications: Vicarious, symbolic and observational learning systems risk developing "rules" about behavior independent of their consequences and thus encouraging interpersonally inappropriate, irrational or maladaptive responses.

Limitations: One obvious pitfall is a low degree of monitored control over what exactly the student "observes" (and hence creates "rules" for). Second, research is unclear about whether learning occurs from operant-modeled responses or also from respondent-modeled responses. (For further review, see Bandura, Grusec & Menlove, 1966; Maccoby & Wilson, 1957; Ollendick, Dailey & Shapiro, 1983.)

48. Opportunities for Desirable Behavior (ODB).

Operation: Contingent presentation of opportunities either for reinforcement or for engaging in behavior leading to reinforcement, following desired (target) behavior. An example is a student who for smiling (instead of crying) can call his sister (behavior) who will invite him for dinner (reinforcer). Procedure employs intermediate reinforcers like a token economy, but unlike the tokens these reinforcers usually are naturalistic. Procedure develops multiple responses in a sequence.

Indications: Research in reinforcement theory and response patterning indicates uses for acceleration and deceleration of behavior, primarily for school-age children.

Contraindications: Prolonged duration of the opportunity to behave without allowing target behavior to occur may cause the same effects as being under a "limited hold"; aggression, increasing bursts of responding, and superstitious responding.

Limitations: Unclear opportunities do not encourage proper responding. Teachers should be descriptive when offering a reinforcement opportunity. Another concern is that preferred reponses cannot be performed for different reasons despite offered opportunities (physical disability, academic deficits, etc.). (For further review, see Krumboltz & Krumboltz, 1972.)

49. Overcorrection.

Operation: Specific type of punishment involving the (a) over-restitution of environmental effects of an inappropriate act, and (b) the intensive practice of correct forms of (appropriate) behavior. The first component is called "restitutional overcorrection," where the student restores the environment (bedroom, family room, etc.) to a state much improved over its condition before the disruption. The second component is called "positive-practice overcorrection," wherein the student engages in correct behavior taken to extremes. When there is no environmental disruption, positive practice occurs alone. Basic guidelines include (a) both components should be topographically and functionally related to the misbehavior, (b) both components should be applied immediately following the misbehavior, (c) both components should be extended in duration, (d) both components should be actively performed by student, and (e) both components should include minimal physical guidance, later faded out.

Indications: Effective procedure for behaviors that are self-injurious, self-stimulatory, aggressive-disruptive, as well as for habits, poor oral reading and other academic responses. The procedure minimizes punishment, is educative, and allows for rapid and long-lasting reduction.

Contraindications: Incorrect use of physical guidance producing extreme force, or harm to the student, may produce resistance, aggression, and increased rates of disruptive responses. The expediency and generality of overcorrection also raises concern for the teacher; it may be ineffective for the student with a poor history of following instructions.

Limitations: Reported problems encompass (a) difficulty in selecting the restitutional activity, (b) the degree to which both restitution and positive practice are necessary for positive outcomes, (c) the development of punishment side-effects not closely monitored, and (d) whether similarity of the corrective behavior matters as much as the functional similarity. (For further review, see Carey & Bucher, 1986; Epstein, Doke, Sajwaj, Sorrell & Rimmer, 1974; Foxx & Azrin, 1972; Ollendick & Matson, 1978; Singh, 1987.)

50. Personalized System of Instruction (PSI).

Operation: System of instruction involving proctors, assistants and instructors, all of whom establish a series of units completed at the student's own pace, by study questions, frequent and alternate tests (remediation), and by demonstration of mastery per unit assigned. Optimally, in a well-programmed course, every student should earn an "A". Variations of PSI employ a programmed text, teaching machines, closed-circuit television, or computers. Grading and answers to questions are immediate and handled by proctors and assistants, whereas the instructor primarily organizes brief lectures, curricula, and final examinations.

Indications: Use of PSI reportedly enhances student motivation, performance, completion of assignments, and information retention far more than traditional lecture formats.

Contraindications: Frequent criticisms of PSI include its simplification of teaching to the point of student control and loss of academics. The outpour of grade "A's" raises political questions among unsympathetic faculty, and thus introduction of PSI in more orthodox educational systems may require preliminary demonstration of its advantages.

Limitations: The problems in running PSI are numerous and range from inter-staff inconsistency to the repeated production of needed (alternate) test forms. Contingencies need to be arranged for all individuals (students and staff) in the system following the principles of organizational behavior management. (For further review, see Keller, 1968; Skinner, 1968.)

51. Physical Guidance.

Operation: Applying physical contact to induce students to go through the motions of the target behavior. Guidance represents one component of any acquisitional procedure (task analysis), usually supplemented by instructions, modeling and imitation, differential reinforcement and fading.

Indications: Used in procedures which teach instructions of simple or complex imitative skills in school-age children.

Contraindications: Rapid or forceful use of guidance may provoke aggressive responses or increase latency in compliance. Performance requirements of training should be realistic and enable students eventually to take control over their behaviors.

Limitations: One major drawback is that "tactile" (physical) control of any sort may act as reinforcement, accidentally strengthening unwanted responses. A second problem is the absence of defined and consistent guidelines for application. (For further review, see Kazdin & Erickson, 1975.)

52. Positive Punishment.

Operation: Presenting an unpleasant (aversive) stimulus contingent upon an undesirable response, which rapidly decreases that behavior. Major guidelines include: (a) apply consistently and immediately following the response, (b) combine it with extinction and reinforcement of alternative behaviors, (c) arrange environment to prevent escape and avoidance opportunities, except for acceptable alternative behaviors (which may be a type of escape or avoidance), (d) maximize the intensity of the punishing stimulus, and (e) utilize safety and ethical precautions. Procedures vary but they all facilitate discrimination. Among techniques employed are: time-out ribbon, lemon juice, water spray, contingent exercise, icing, response cost, spraying aromatic ammonia, overcorrection, negative practice, response satiation, stimulus satiation, and on rare occasion, electric shock.

Indications: Effective results are shown for autistic behavior, self-injurious and self-stimulatory behaviors, delinquency, noncompliance and academic failures.

Contraindications: Negative or untoward effects of punishment (aversive control) include elicited or emotional anger and aggression, escape and avoidance, poor generalization, response induction, transient effects, imitation, negative self-statements, and the suppression of responses that are appropriate to prevent (avoid) punishment. Finally, associations of the punisher with the person using punishment (teacher) can jeopardize lesson plans.

Limitations: The extent of side-effects should not entirely discourage practice of punishment but instead support its cautious usage. Practice should accompany informed consent of student, parent, advocate or human rights committee. Another important consideration is that effects are rapid but not long-lasting; alternative programming is necessary for maintenance. (For further review, see Azrin, 1958; Balsam & Bondy, 1983; Church, 1963; Risley, 1968.)

53. Positive Reinforcement.

Operation: Presentation of some event (pleasant or unpleasant) following target behavior which strengthens the future occurrence of that behavior. Guidelines for reinforcement include: (a) reinforce immediately following target behavior, (b) specify stimulus conditions (opportunities) for reinforcement, (c) deliver sufficient density of reinforcers to generate or maintain behavior without satiation, (d) select appropriate reinforcers for that student (reinforcer sampling), (e) use a variety of reinforcers, (f) eliminate competing (reinforcing and punishing) contingencies, (g) begin on CRF, and (h) shift to intermittent schedules after response rate is stable or at desired levels. Selection of unconditioned, conditioned or (social) generalized conditioned reinforcers depends on the student's history and the behavior in question. Categories of reinforcement include (a) consumables (candy, cakes, etc.), (b) activity (opportunities for television), (c) possessional (wearing a favorite shirt), (d) manipulative (play with tape-recorder), and (e) social (affectionate hugs, social attention).

Indications: Factors affecting reinforcement potential include (a) deprivation and satiation, (b) immediacy, and (c) schedule of delivery. Procedure is superior to deceleration techniques in altering or increasing IQ scores, sport behaviors, hyperactivity, driving, verbal and nonverbal tasks.

Contraindications: Negative side-effects of reinforcement range from suppression of the target response to emotional and ritualistic patterns. Accidentally, inappropriate behaviors occur in between reinforcement intervals, for example, during recess, or, on a larger scale, between homebound and return to school. Reinforcing events also fluctuate in value and function depending on contingent and noncontingent (hence, inconsistent) applications. The effects of accidental extinction during noncontingent reinforcement will depend on the response strength, and student's past history of reinforcement (schedules). However, this counter-control may sufficiently strengthen incompatible (inappropriate) responses. A last consideration is that altering one response on reinforcement may influence related or concurrent responses not under reinforcement.

Limitations: Consider that reinforced responses represent one, among an array of events, directly and multiply affecting response outcome. Positive reinforcement, while necessary, will of course exclude many of these factors adding to response strength. (For further review, see Kazdin, 1982; Leitenberg, Agras, Thompson, & Wright, 1968.)

54. Premack Principle.

Operation: High frequency behaviors are made contingent upon low frequency behaviors to increase the performance of the low frequency behavior. Reinforcers usually are already available in the student's natural environment. Reinforcing behaviors (larger activities) should be selected on the basis of formal observation (e.g. reinforcer sampling). Guidelines for use include: (a) select at least two responses and define them based on their duration, and (b) establish operant contingencies by designating the higher-probability behavior as the contingent response. Advantages of the procedure include providing (a) an independent method of conditioning and measurement, (b) an easy means to identify and utilize reinforcing events, and (c) a natural use of reinforcers.

Indications: Exemplary support for the principle appears for classroom populations.

Contraindications: No major contraindications are reported.

Limitations: Considerable drawbacks are known. First, proper operant-baseline assessments are rare. Second, unsystematic observations during training subjectify the results. Third, duration as a measure is subject to artifact error (variation, observer bias, etc.). (For further review, see Knapp, 1976; Premack, 1965.)

55. Programming Generalization.

Operation: Procedure to programming generalization focuses on training across settings, over time, across persons, and to similar interactions. Techniques employed follow nine basic guidelines: (a) teach behaviors that will produce reinforcement in everyday settings, (b) verify if persons in contact with the student while he emits behavior will reinforce him, (c) use many and varied trainers, (d) diversify the training program using single and discriminable units, (e) engineer delayed reinforcement in later stages, (f) introduce new stimuli similar to training situations, (g) reinforce student's generalization of newly acquired skills, (h) phase out treatment gradually and undetectably following stabilized rates, and (i) plan a follow-up assessment of generalization to refresh training if necessary.

Indications: All applied behavioral analysis and behavior therapy programs must incorporate a defined generalization component either during or after skill acquisition stages. Operant generalization does not occur spontaneously, and training may focus on "response" or "stimulus" generalization.

Contraindications: Relapses after training result from unsuccessful generalization or improper mastery of some target behavior. Even if it is programmed, generalization may produce untoward effects in part or none of the relevant skills transfer.

Limitations: Generalization is limited by two basic problems. First, it assumes that students keep the skills on them, like clothing, and retrieve the skills in different settings. Opponents argue that this implies internal hypothetical principles, since no settings are that distinct, and that performance develops over time in a continuous manner. A second problem is that, however it is defined, certain actions such as self-talk and self-reinforcement (of incompatible behavior) may confound generalization effects. (For further review, see Pigott, Fantuzzo & Gorsuch, 1987; Ruben & Ruben, 1987; Stokes & Baer, 1977; Wahler, Breland & Car, 1979.)

56. Reinforcer Sampling.

Operation: The procedure is to briefly present (potential) reinforcers before a response to increase the probability of that response occurring; and then to present the remainder of that reinforcer following the response. Once the student responds to it as a reinforcer (i.e., target behavior increases), it becomes a reinforcer and is made contingent upon performance of specific behaviors.

Indications: Sampling facilitates the introduction and effective use of reinforcers and thus enables more rapid acquisition of behavior. Adoption of it as a standard procedure appears to simplify difficult lesson plans.

Contraindications: Relatively few problems result from sampling. Access to the reinforcer after 5 minutes may accidentally shape avoidance responses; delay in time encourages distraction. At the other extreme, too short a presentation risks a misrepresentative sample, from which incorrect decisions about reinforcement might be derived. In both cases, caution is advised if students are unable to delay gratification.

Limitations: Access to the reinforcer for prolonged durations, before or after the response, causes satiation. Another pitfall is that, in practice, sampling occurs hours and weeks before the time of its utilization; proper use requires sampling in close proximity to the actual training period. Third, reinforcers sampled in one setting, while effective there, may be ineffective as functioning reinforcers in other similar or dissimilar settings. (For further review, see Allyon & Azrin, 1968.)

57. Response Cost.

Operation: The response-contingent withdrawal of specified amounts of reinforcers. Partial removal of tokens, money, opportunities for engaging in desired behavior, or the imposition of fines contingent upon emission of inappropriate behavior are all examples of response cost. Procedure operates functionally similar to negative punishment. Guidelines for use include: (a) build up a reinforcer reserve before imposing a cost system, (b) establish whether the chosen reinforcers (to be withdrawn) are powerful, (c) communicate specific instructions on how response cost works, and (d) combine response cost with other reinforcement interventions.

Indications: Appropriate use is for classrooms or home use. Results generally include (a) strong and rapid behavioral changes, (b) possibly long-lasting effects (given maintenance and generalization), and (c) clerically, a convenience for teachers.

Contraindications: Withdrawal of reinforcers initially fosters escape and aggressive behaviors (tantrums, resistance, rebellion, etc.). Another problem is imposing penalties that are too large and, using tokens, too quickly exhaust the student's reserve of reinforcers.

Limitations: Aversive properties of response cost will pair with the implementers of the system. Procedurally, the goal of response reduction does not stress increasing incompatible or alternative behaviors. (For further review, see Burchard & Barrera, 1972; Duty, McInnis & Paul, 1974; Weiner, 1964b.)

58. Response Delay.

Operation: After the student is attentive, instructions are presented about the behavior. Three to 5 seconds must pass before the student responds. Correct responses receive reinforcers, whereas off-task or inappropriate responding is followed by verbal reprimands (or additional deceleration methods).

Indications: Response delay training over repeated trials strengthens "waiting" behavior, and facilitates acquisition of discrimination tasks, especially in autistic and impulsive children. Results also support effectiveness for mentally retarded and socio-economically deprived children and adults.

Contraindications: Requiring autistic (or other) to delay responding causes side-effects similar to delayed reinforcement (#20) and extinction (#29) – i.e., aggression, increased impulsivity, before a leveling effect. Side-effects are also due to errors in the time interval (too long or too short). Since the delay allows patients to attend to cues, unclear stimulus presentations (cues) might signal the wrong response.

Limitations: One consideration is that reducing impulsivity also requires that concurrent attention and orientation skills be strengthened. Support for this concurrency is weak. A second problem is lacking a defined procedure for maintenance and generalization of response delays. (See Dyer, Christian & Luce, 1982.)

59. Response Deprivation.

Operation: Based in part on the response deprivation hypothesis, this procedure stipulates that reinforcement effects occur only when the child increases responding to eliminate the deprivation of the contingent response. This means any response already in the student's repertoire is a potential reinforcer, given the presence of response deprivation. In practice, stimulus cues prompting opportunities for behavior are made visible, but no reinforcers are presented. Next is an allotted time during which responses can occur. Variations of the time schedule mix with the Premack principle, and response satiation, producing higher-probability behaviors.

Indications: Recent, but limited use in applied setting has been for classroom disruptions and selected clinical disorders.

Contraindications: A practical caution is that scheduled requirements not be so small as to prohibit appropriate responding. Access to a desirable response for only 25 seconds, for example, may discourage efforts producing that response.

Limitations: Procedural factors are still highly theoretical, and much of the data derives from animal laboratory research. Instructional applications generally are limited to situations where there are only two clearly defined responses. (See Dougher, 1983; Konarski, Johnson, Crowell & Whitman, 1980; Michael, 1982; Timberlake & Allison, 1982.)

60. Response Induction.

Operation: A conditioning procedure of increasing one or several responses from a response class in a short time by differential reinforcement. Imitation and modeling usually serve as prompts for correct behavior, followed by reinforcers. Conditioning of single or multiple responses depends on the arrangement of contingent and noncontingent schedules, and the level of criterion set for target responses.

Indications: Because of the similarity to acquisitional learning, response induction is considered more an extension than an alternative to successive approximations (shaping). Particular uses are for conditioning generalized responses sequences of children.

Contraindications and Limitations: Topographically varied responses are difficult to strengthen independently. As a unit, these responses give rise to questions about the defined features of a response class and whether responses are best conditioned in pairs, rather than separately. (See Hefferline & Keenan, 1961; Peterson, 1968.)

61. Response Priming.

Operation: Presenting partial or entire stimulus cues (verbal, nonverbal) for a sequence of target behaviors. The response "primed" is the second from last response in a sequence, based on the rationale that the strength of the final response in the sequence depends on earlier responses being reinforced. Guidelines include: (a) divide responses into a sequence, (b) prompt responses near the end of the sequence, and (c) provide reinforcers after the patient performs the "primed" response, plus the remainder of responses in the sequence.

Indications: Extensive uses have been for communication skills, medication compliance, in token economies, and for general discrimination tasks for widely diverse populations.

Contraindications: Caution is suggested for trainers who confuse priming with coaxing and inadvertently shape avoidance behaviors.

Limitations: The assumption that reinforcement of earlier responses increases the terminal response in a sequence is also open to question. Other reasons also suffice. For example, discriminative stimuli (primes) may also function as conditioned reinforcement. (For further review, see Azrin & Powell, 1969; O'Brien, Azrin & Henson, 1969.)

62. Role-play.

Operation: The goal of role-play is to simulate interpersonal interactions between student and teacher. Each scene or trial involves the teacher modeling behavior, and then, using role-reversal, the student imitates the response. Teachers play the role of the significant other during practice exercises, reproducing as many stimulus cues as possible to evoke the target performance. Nuances of role-play entail (a) verbal and nonverbal actions of the players, (b) the extent to which inductions match naturalistic conditions, and (c) whether new role behaviors are carried out in real-life situations.

Indications: Numerous studies show validity of role-play for social communication skills, assertiveness, attitudinal changes, catharsis, marital and group therapies, and along with analogues, and fixed-role therapies; in short, with any therapeutically deficient response due primarily to inhibition stemming from expectations or a direct operant history.

Contraindications: Negative side-effects from role-play include the misapplication of new skills, drop-out rates, and minimal cooperation during role-play scenerios. This also may be due to role-plays seeming meaningless to the student.

Limitations: A problem defining "criteria" for role-play performance is that measuring progress requires a powerful data collection system. The precision needed for monitoring is usually unreasonable for routine clinical practice. (For further review, see Bellack, Hersen & Lamparski, 1979; Ruben, 1985.)

63. Self-instructional Training.

Operation: Strategy designed to teach self-management skills by restructuring private speech and mediated skills as cues for problem solving, behavior alternatives, and expected outcomes. General format calls for (a) student becoming aware of his thoughts in specific situations, and (b) altering self-statements made, first, in front of the teacher, and then to himself. Self-instructions frequently are combined with assertiveness, relaxation, and mediation training.

Indications: Comparative results show benefits for impulsive and withdrawn children, social isolates, and children with creative problem-solving deficits.

Contraindications and Limitations: One negative result is lack of correspondence between what patients say and do. Another concern is that language is a weak inducement for behavior change. Additional clinical limitations relate to restricted recording and monitoring of the patient's rule-governed and rule-following instructions. (For further review, see Billings & Wasik, 1985; Bonnstein, 1985; Roberts, Nelson & Olson, 1987.)

64. Self-reinforcement.

Operation: The student adopts a criterion of what constitutes appropriate performance and consistently (or intermittently) reinforces himself for matching or exceeding the adopted standard. Needed is a prior operant reinforcement history of this performance as well as a degree of discrimination between this and other behaviors and between different stimulus conditions. Other considerations include: (a) presence or absence of effective role-model in teaching self-reinforcement, (b) that self-reinforcement be accompanied by verbal self-evaluations, and (c) the child using DRO (or similar procedure) on himself.

Indications: Self-imposed reinforcement (on varying schedules) is direct for speech disfluencies, low self-concept, response inhibition, and social avoidance responses. Children experiencing personal distress, grandiose ideations or antisocial tendencies may require considerable behavioral rehearsal prior to their mastery of "covert-level" (reinforcement) control.

Contraindications: Children having extended histories of low self-imagery and disorderly thinking (self-deprecating thoughts) may set unrealistic criteria for self-reinforcement and thus get discouraged quickly.

Limitations: Theoretical concerns largely stem from self-reinforcement seen as an "intrinsic process." Research shows the connection of response patterns without social or natural reinforcement (support), but what controls this connection is highly ambiguous. (For further review, see Bandura & Parloff, 1967; Goldiamond, 1976.)

65. Self-reporting (Self-recording).

Operation: Self-reporting entails the observing, recording and evaluating of one's own behavior in the context of learning skills. Such approaches take the form of having the student use a golf counter, paperclips, or notepad to record frequency, duration, or some dimension of behaviors. Written records of behavior may elaborate upon antecedent, behaviors, consequences, persons involved, and other setting events. As self-observation occurs, students react to this feedback and consequently may alter their behaviors. These "reactivity effects" enable rapid attainment of goals.

Indications: Self-reporting occurs for study behavior, parental attention, disruptive behaviors, swimming, story-writing, work behavior, social skills, anxiety, and in classroom and home settings.

Contraindications and Limitations: It is not entirely clear why alterations in behavior come about due to self-monitoring, and whether such changes endure. Another problem is low agreement on reliability between self-report measures and measures by independent observers. A third drawback is irreversibility; once self-monitoring commences and the student learns strong observation skills, they continue these skills despite so-called "reversal" phases. (For further review, see Fremouw & Brown, 1980; Kanfer, 1970; Zimmerman & Levitt, 1975.)

66. Sensitization.

Operation: Counter-conditioning procedure of pairings between some unpleasant (aversive) stimulus and the performance of problem behavior, weakening the probability of that behavior. Variations which utilize imaginal aversive stimuli (covert sensitization) and nonimaginal stimuli (overt sensitization) both follow classical and operant conditioning principles. Sensitization exercises require (a) progressive muscle relaxation, (b) awareness of the behavior (contingencies), (c) the establishment of an ascending hierarchy of anxiety scenes, and (d) the ability to escape from aversive scenes by imagining or actually performing appropriate (incompatible) responses.

Indications: Procedure is successful for obsessive anxieties, test phobia and fear of academic failure.

Contraindications: Prolonged imaginal exposure to aversive scenes can produce extreme emotional arousal and possibly this will intensify anxiety or lead to unwanted escape and avoidance images. Second, since nausea is the most common aversive stimulus, caution is advised to prevent illness or physical upset in conditioning trials.

Limitations: Major setbacks result from (a) poor construction or retention of imagery, (b) difficulty in monitoring the transition from aversive imagery to pleasant imagery, (c) inappropriate length of exposure time for either aversive or pleasant imagery, and (d) reliance on the teacher's verbal instructions rather than upon the student's own imagery. (For further review, see Cautela, 1967; Maletzky, 1973.)

67. Stimulus Control.

Operation: Defined as the probability that a particular response will occur in the presence of a particular antecedent stimulus. Stimulus events such as cues, signals, prompts, or instructions set an occasion for responding, followed by a reinforcer. The student learns responding only when relevant dimensions of that particular antecedent are present. Training produces discriminations for a class of responses. Guidelines include: (a) select a response, (b) when the response is emitted under some stimulus, reinforce it, and (c) if the stimulus is absent, do not reinforce the emitted response.

Indications: Stimulus control is a prerequisite in almost all behavior-change procedures, since training essentially is a discrimination process.

Contraindications and Limitations: One common problem is that, realistically, no single response has exclusive relationship to one stimulus. Rather, two or more responses may occur for one stimulus, just as two or more stimuli may evoke one response. (For example, students respond "two" when seeing either the printed arabic number "2," or the printed word "two.") Another drawback is poor control over interfering stimuli. Responses conditioned to the relevant properties of some target stimulus may reappear when some but not all of the relevant properties are present. (For further review, see Becker, Engelmann & Thomas, 1971; Terrace, 1966.)

68. Stimulus Substitution.

Operation: In classical conditioning, where the CS comes to elicit the same response as the US, the UR and CR may differ in strength as conditioning proceeds. Classical conditioning of motor responses is an example. Eyeblink responses under the US may occur at different rates than when under the CS.

Indications: Process of stimulus substitution explains the reason for emotional responding to conditioned stimuli (CS and higher order conditioned stimuli). Procedural implications are also important for auto-shaping (See #5).

Contraindications and Limitations: On the whole, research support for stimulus substitution is ambiguous and the physiological mechanisms behind different levels of UR/CR are still unknown. (For further review, see Martin & Levey, 1971.)

69. Task Analysis.

Operation: Task analysis divides a complex skill into subskills and subcomponents, presented in sufficient detail and relationship among other component skills. This is so that students can achieve mastery at each level until the entire performance is learned. Guidelines include (a) selecting and appropriate behavior or response class, (b) breaking down the skill into distinct and achievable (criteria-related) steps, (c) reinforcing successive approximations to criteria, and (d) progressively moving to different task steps. Behavioral criteria per step usually include frequency, duration, and function of the response. Preparation of the task requires that each step be small, realistic, and involve behaviors to some extent already present in the student's repertoire. Correction of errors may involve returning to earlier steps for repeated mastery.

Indications: Task analysis provides excellent guidelines for acquisitional learning. Applications appear for adaptive living skills (hygiene, feeding, etc.), for language and speech skills, and for social communication skills. Recent use has been for academic and problem-solving tasks.

Contraindications: Optimizing completion of the objective sometimes involves rapid, rather than gradual, movement through each task step. This creates resistance if failures are not remedied in earlier steps. Another concern is that students having major attention deficits may be inappropriate for task analysis training.

Limitations: Task analyses are frequently impractical for complex or multiple-sequential behaviors such as playing the piano, swimming, dancing, and mathematics. Training efforts toward these ends have been optimistic, but each task step still omits important (controlling) variables in the performance. (For further review, see Christ, Wallis & Haught, 1984; Williams & Cuvo, 1986.)

70. Time-out.

Operation: Considerable variations exist for the time-out procedure. In general, it is a method by which access to sources of reinforcement is removed for a particular time period, contingent upon the emission of a response. Removed, specifically, is the opportunity for some behavior which produces social or tangible reinforcers. This differs from extinction in that reinforcement is initially present in the situation. It is different from punishment in that punishment involves the presentation of aversive stimuli rather than the withdrawal of reinforcing consequences. Still, results resemble (negative) punishment in terms of response reduction effects. Considerations essentially entail (a) duration (3 to 10 minutes), (b) explanations (student is told why he is sent to time-out), (c) release (contingent or noncontingent upon incompatible behaviors), (d) cueing (warning signal or stimulus alerting student that continuation of unwanted behavior results in time-out), (e) removal of reinforcers from time-out location, (f) consistent applications, and (g) providing opportunities for alternative behaviors (upon release from time-out). Diverse applications include: time-out room, time-out ribbon, and removal of others.

70A. TIME-OUT ROOM. Traditionally, time-out includes escorting the disruptive student from the reinforcing situation to a secluded room. Variations include any room (another classroom), in the corner, or at the back of a large room. Confinement lasts for a prespecified period of time.

70B. TIME-OUT RIBBON. Students are assigned tangible (decorative) objects that become their own and may symbolize "good behavior." These are removed from the student who is acting out, and returned after a specific time period and contingent upon incompatible responses.

70C. REMOVAL OF OTHERS. In this case, disruption results in the removal of reinforcing events (objects, other people, etc.) in proximity to the student, while the student remains in the same room.

Indications: Support for time-out in applied settings is extensive and has proven effective for autistic behaviors, classroom disruption, and aggression.

Contraindications: Equally researched have been the punishing and untoward effects of time-out. Because time-out can be reinforcing, there is a risk of behavior exacerbation. For this reason, self-stimulatory, self-injurious, and other physically harmful responses are inappropriate for time-out. So, too, are physically aggressive or destructive behaviors which harm property and others. A second problem is the suppression of other behaviors besides the target response. Failure on the part of the student to carefully discriminate between unwanted and wanted responses can affect what few social interaction skills exist. A third problem is pairing the aversive process of time-out with the teacher administering it. A good precaution for this is arranging different teachers to run time-out.

Limitations: Research implies that there can be no "standard" time-out procedure because of nuances in the setting. Another limitation, albeit for the best, is the number of ethical and legal constraints employed to assure safe applications. (For further review, see Benoit & Mayer, 1975; Clark, Rowbury, Baer & Baer, 1973; Foxx & Shapiro, 1978; Solnick, Rincover & Peterson, 1977.)

71. Token Economy.

Operation: A token economy describes an organized system of contingencies that incorporate continuous and intermittent reinforcement in the form of a medium of exchange. Tokens are an object or symbol exchangeable for a back-up reinforcer, usually available some time beyond when the target behavior first occurred. This system effectively requires attention to the following conditions: (a) identification of target behaviors, (b) delay and amount of tokens, (c) possible punishment consequences, (d) supervision of staff and records, and (e) fading out the system.

IDENTIFY TARGET BEHAVIORS. Types of targeted behavior depend on who the students are, their setting, the nature of disorderly behaviors, and the severity of problems based on assessment.

DELIVERY AND AMOUNT OF TOKENS. Tokens established as "privileges" are earned contingently for specific behaviors and should be delivered each time that behavior occurs according to graduated criteria. The amount and frequency of tokens delivered depend on how they are spent. If redeemable for food, then tokens, like money, must add up to a cost in dollars and cents. If redeemable for activities (e.g. watching television, field trips), corresponding values need to be set. Unauthorized access to tokens might result in the loss of either tokens already earned (response cost), or expected to be earned.

POSSIBLE PUNISHMENT CONTINGENCIES. Further use of fines or penalties for undesirable behaviors will require guidelines known to all students on how tokens (and redeemable reinforcers) may be gained or lost.

SUPERVISION OF STAFF AND RECORDS. Token systems operate much like a business in that accounting, staff supervision, monitoring, and reliability are all necessary functions. Contingencies may be necessary for cooperation and compliance among all teachers or parents involved. Managers of token systems also should keep scrupulous records of token reinforcement exchanges among students, and frequently these are evaluated to help improve the overall quality of the program.

FADING OUT TOKENS. Transferring behaviors to the natural environment requires gradual fading out of tokens. One way is to gradually decrease the value of tokens, toward eliminating them. A second way is gradually decreasing the value of back-up reinforcers. A third is to introduce realistic tokens (money) and show the value these have in the community.

Indications: Precisely and effectively planned token economies are generally effective to delay reinforcement for complex behaviors. Uses include for residential homes, classrooms, parent-training groups, teaching of academic skills, teaching of daily-living skills, and enabling difficult populations (e.g. delinquents).

Contraindications: Negative side-effects of a token system derive from shortage of teachers, unauthorized access to tokens, and the tendency by staff to reinforce wrong (non–token related) responses. The latter is the greatest risk of this program; that, through tokens, disruptive behaviors are strengthened accidentally. For example, in job or academic skills, students may try earning tokens for effortless work even though the assignment is completed (meets minimal criteria). Escape and avoidance responses thus are potential hazards.

Limitations: The phasing out of tokens is a necessary step but causes an unfortunate setback in learned skills. Also, the logistic, economic, and legal issues considered even in the smallest of token programs involve a great deal of time and planning, which may be an obstacle to many teachers. Finally, conceptually speaking, the principal idea of token economies is met with resistance from the public, school boards, PTA groups, and frequently from parents who consent for their children's participation. (For further review, see Allyon & Azrin, 1968; Kazdin, 1977; Kazdin & Bootzin, 1972; Walker & Buckley, 1975.)

72. Variable Interval Schedule (VI).

Operation: Presentation of a reinforcer after an average amount of time elapses and also a response occurs. Such schedules begin in short intervals and increase gradually and progressively. If responses decrease, temporarily shorten the intervals until moderate responding occurs. This schedule should more closely approximate contingencies in the natural environment.

Indications: Since variable interval schedules generate lower response rates than ratio schedules, appropriate uses include DRL (see #25) and maintenance schedules (see #38). The result is consistent rates of behavior resistant to extinction (see #29).

Contraindications and Limitations: Errors result when students learn that no matter how "hard" they try (or behave), reinforcement remains variable. The disadvantage of this is that students poorly predict reinforcement and thus lose control over an aspect of their environment. (For further review, see Lippman & Meyer, 1967; Weiner, 1964.)

73. Variable Ratio Schedule (VR).

Operation: Presentation of a reinforcer following an average number of responses. Schedule is set to generate lower rates of responding. Longer (and bursts of) responding may be followed by pauses. Responses put on VR schedules maintain much longer under extinction.

Indications: VR schedules are used to induce higher rates of specific behavior, since reinforcement to a degree is predictable. Training of children and adults under VR also prepares their behaviors for intermittent schedules, without much decay (loss or fluctuation) in the behavior.

Contraindications: Use of VR for depressed students or those with low self-control is discouraged unless the ratio requirement is low and prevents them from relapsing or "quitting" (analogous to "ratio strain").

Limitations: The problem with VR is that between bursts of high responding, periods of nonresponding become longer, thereby increasing undesirable and incompatible (off-task) responses. The inevitability of ratio strain from abrupt and higher shifts in ratio also encourages incompatible responses. (For further review, see Orlando & Bijou, 1960.)

74. Verbal Conditioning.

Operation: Verbal conditioning deals with increasing correspondence between verbal and nonverbal behaviors. Training also covers the content (e.g. relevant and irrelevant) of verbalizations as appropriate or inappropriate for the context (classroom, house, social-interpersonal interaction, etc.). Components include contingent reinforcement for verbal content as a precursor or mediator to "doing" the behavior described. The degree of congruency also depends on the prompts and contingencies employed, and whether language deficits and excesses require more extended conditioning trials.

Indications: The choice of conditioning either verbal or nonverbal behaviors implies that students who are mute or have limited speech can learn from reinforcement of nonverbal behaviors. Likewise, those who are verbal but whose nonverbal responses prohibit contact (self-injurious, aggressive) can learn from reinforcement of verbal behavior.

Contraindications and Limitations: Practical problems arise when statements made either aloud or to oneself do not correspond to the actions performed. For example, students promising to finish homework may never do so. (For further review, see Israel & Brown, 1977; Ruben, 1983.)

75. Vicarious Extinction.

Operation: The student observes models performing the target behavior without that student experiencing adverse consequences for it. This "perceived absence" of aversive stimuli decreases the student's fears and hence his avoidance behaviors. Avoidance responses are extinguished in gradual approximations as the student is exposed to a hierarchy of high stressful events. Besides stimulus exposure trials, the model himself may influence the vicarious effects, and so he must be careful to demonstrate all the relevant features of the fearful stimuli and responses. In addition, exposure to diverse models is encouraged.

Indications: Vicarious extinction reduces or eliminates general phobias and emotional inhibitions by children. Graduated stimulus exposures usually follow with relaxation, systematic desensitization, and symbolic modeling.

Contraindications and Limitations: Findings reveal that extinguished fears depend entirely upon the authenticity of the model (e.g. peer, teacher, etc.). Qualitative and quantitative features about the model generally outweigh the model's confrontive actions toward aversive (fearful) events, which may cause problems for models who enact the scene differently. (For further review, see Bandura, Grusec & Menlove, 1967.)

76. Vicarious Punishment.

Operation: The student observes models performing a target behavior, followed by adverse consequences. The goal is to observationally learn that this response is inappropriate and should be suppressed. Ample evidence for mediated punishment also shows that, given opportunities to imitate the model's punished behavior, students engage in alternative responses.

Indications: Use of this procedure is for aggressive, disruptive, and childhood disorders, combined with other behavioral techniques.

Contraindications and Limitations: While reports of negative side-effects are rare, there is concern that observed punishers in the model's performance may function for the imitator as reinforcers. Another problem is that the schedule of punishment for the model may be unrealistic or nongeneralizable to the imitator's (student's) natural environment. (For further review, see Bandura, 1973; Rosenkrans, Hartup, 1967).

77. Vicarious Reinforcement.

Operation: A procedure wherein the responses of one student are altered by that student observing reinforcement for some (target) behavior of another student (model).

Indications: Applications have been for classroom students, and academic behaviors. In all cases, training via the model is powerful to induce desirable changes.

Contraindications: Important side-effects are to be considered. First, the explicit or direct reinforcement of one student may serve as implicit punishment for the observer. This inadvertent effect may occur for not only one observer, but all observers in proximity to the model. Second, reinforced behaviors of the model may include those not specified as the target response, thereby causing duplication of unwanted behavior.

Limitations: Data are unclear as to whether the reinforcement of another person actually "reinforces" the observer or, instead, whether it functions as a discriminative stimulus. That is, it "suggests" contingent reinforcement for the observer's behavior. As such, the "vicarious" component may be less significant than the simple discrimination made. (For further review, see Bandura, 1971; Kazdin, 1973; Sechrest, 1963.)

Conclusion

Techniques for control and management of unwanted disruptions during a homebound lesson are now at your fingertips. Close attention should be paid to the logistics of each procedure, especially where side-effects risk the reverse or regression of a desired effect. Applying each step carefully, as described, can avoid costly mistakes and collapse of your effort. A typical conclusion, for example, when failures abound with students is that "behavior modification doesn't work all the time." Believable as it sounds, there is a serious fundamental error in this belief: it is not that behavior modification fails, but that the behavior modifiers fail to use it correctly.

Resist temptation to blame failures on the procedure per se; instead, look to your own mistakes and sharpen the consistency and accuracy of each intervention.

5. Society and the Homebound Child

Our society recognizes social problems and appears concerned with solving them. There are numerous problems for homebound children and their families; most concern social stigmas, attitudes of society, and lack of community support. Troubles arise within the character of each homebound student and within the range of his immediate relations with others. He has to deal with himself and with those limited areas of social life of which he is directly and personally aware (Mills, 1959).

This chapter addresses those messages of despair hidden behind the cheerful smiles that greet homebound teachers at the door — fears that are swept under the mat by parents, educators and friends of homebound students. Why hide these emotions? And what can teachers do about it? In this chapter we explore this issue, beginning with the imposition of societal values upon the student as he or she stumbles through a maze of adjustments.

Attitudes

Personal troubles typically start at home, but for the homebound child they are brought home from school, the hospital or another treating facility. Prior to P.L. 94-142, educators and community members believed that the terminally ill child, for instance, should not be bothered with educational pressures. These children and families were concerned enough with medical issues, let alone cluttering their lives with academic issues. The prevailing belief was simple: terminally ill students too sick to be in school no longer need school. Prevent them from becoming cognitively and affectively mature, from worrying about the competitive world, and be assured their lives will remain simple.

Dangerously, these promulgated beliefs conjured up a pitiful image of the terminally ill and orthopedically disabled student as a helpless, unreachable creature waiting for death. Such harsh social judgments feed on an unabating ignorance about what "handicaps" really mean and how they are different in classification. Grouping them into one large clump — "they're handicapped" — is convenient, but it loses precious details that are not only technical but also related to personality adjustment. Considering impairment, disabilities and handicaps as homogeneous also limits the availability of community support.

Let us consider proper distinction among these terms. A disability may restrict the ability to perform in a manner considered normal. Yet this may or may not constitute a handicapping condition. For instance, a mild to moderate cerebral palsied high school student, having improved from corrective surgery and physical therapy, would have opportunity to function in a school setting and through vocational programs. In every capacity, this individual can become a productive citizen in his adult life.

A handicap is an impairment or disability that limits normal activities. "Handicapped" acquires meaning from labeling that is attached to the child's experiences that depart from normative experiences. Inability to ride the bus, to play on the playground, to read fluently — all deviate from peer, family or school expectations of performance. Unspoken inferences concerning how children "should act" and what certain-aged children are capable of distort the facts of illness and inadequate performance. Inferred is that children out on prolonged absence did something terribly wrong, or that variables "beyond their control" have consumed them. Consequently, onlookers regard impairments with suspicion.

Attitudes and Friends

Jimmy told us, "When I try to carry on a conversation with my friends, I keep talking about my problem, and I can't stop myself. I just need someone to listen. My friends get tired of hearing about it, so they stop calling and coming over. They don't understand that I just need to get if off my chest."

Jimmy's dilemma is a common frustration. Should students express their anguish to friends and confidants, or will this disclosure alienate people? Most homebound students are scared that their friends either will be afraid of them or might "pick up" the disease or impairment. Clearly students are victims of an ignorant culture entrenched in primitive views about their handicaps. To replace these fears, educators must seek out a compassionate and knowledgeable community in health organizations or support groups; restoring confidence in the student begins, naturally, with dismantling the stereotyped beliefs about his affliction.

Social Contacts

One assured solution to eliminating stereotypes is through continued social interaction. Disabled students allowed to maintain a relatively routine social contact with friends, relatives, members of their church and peer-support groups, profit in terms of regained acceptance. Removal of their insularity is nearly automatic once they partake in familiar activities. In society, schools are the ideal environment to promote reintegration and restoration of student confidence. Children returning to school rejoin their classmates, or if children are in special education, at least they enjoy more eclectic interactions compared to total isolation at home.

Attitudes and the Family

Children are defeated when they indulge in self-pity. Focusing on one's disabling condition, loss of control and dependency on others destroy motivation and can be a serious threat to homebound instruction. Teachers alert to this common occurrence can overcome it with curriculum modifications. For example, Diane was a thirteen-year-old with muscular dystrophy who was weak and unable to socialize due to obstructed breathing and a low immune system. Changing her focus to an activity she missed that gave her much pleasure — baking — brought immediate results.

Instead of traditional homework, visits were spent on a baking project. Her instant delight outweighed the dread of being attached to her iron lung. Baking became the source of assigned papers and of news headlines, and essentially it earned her school credit. Baking projects were more than a diversion; they reminded Diane that previously enjoyed activities were still possible given some adaptation.

Often homebound families, much like Diane's family, are exhausted by the never-ending routine of physician visits, prescription renewals and related scheduling. Where possible, teachers can encourage more visible participation of the child in daily family decisions. Take, for example, Lori's quadraplegia that initially mobilized her family around her every need. Soon Lori was able to increase her role of helping her family by using a helmet with a pointer to type out the daily grocery list, phone messages, and correspondence.

Rehabilitation

Once homebound children begin phases of rehabilitation, restrictions are lifted from their reclusive lifestyle. Rehabilitation, in principle, should be an interdisciplinary venture, integrating professionals toward a united goal: that of "adjustment." Typically the prelude to rehabilitation is not adjustment but the perfunctory communication established between homebound teacher, family, school and community agencies (Figure 5.1).

Communication is vital because goals and expectations greatly differ among all treatment providers. Goals of the educator are curriculum-based whereas the medical doctor and physical therapist care less about history

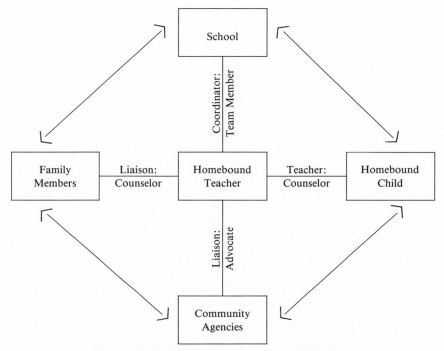

Figure 5.1. Society and the Homebound Teacher.

and English and more about physical recovery. A rapprochement between all concerned parties lies in a central plan, coordinated by the homebound teacher, that includes methods, achievable goals, and movement toward the child's independence. Factors also affecting the team plan are (1) the language used, (2) differences in expectation, (3) degree of mutual support, (4) external and internal influences, (5) community resources, and (6) barriers to networking.

Language Used

Communication requires that there be a common ground for language. Medical jargon, for instance, often escapes the educators and parents, and is unnecessary if physicians are to be team contributors. One solution to "foreign" terminology is for homebound instructors to translate medical explanations or coach parents in a more assertive relationship with their physicians and other providers.

Degree of Support

Homebound students and their families desperately need rehabilitative support. Besides compassion, an obvious quality of showing support, contacts also involve praise to the parents and child for adherence to regimen, for an optimistic prognosis, and for small approximations toward any specified goals. Attention to minor positive details fosters a genuine caring attitude, and professionals are perceived by family members as dependable in cases of emergency.

External and Internal Environment

Changes in the child's field of events are continuous. With serious impediments, disruption in family plans or schedules vary from mild to drastic. Some parents find they must quit their job to nurse children back to health; still others decide on relocation to another city or state that offers direct access to advanced medical technology. Changes in the family ecosystem further diversify when there are mechanical devices to facilitate ambulation or respiration. Rapid adjustment may be necessary, but it weakens parental support and at times creates resentment toward external professionals, viewed as "those who forced this upon us." Externalizing the locus of control so that others are blamed minimizes the family's guilt.

Teachers sensitive to this disintegration of morale are best advised to locate alternative ways the child can receive medical benefits without dramatic life-altering decisions. Home health facilities, hospice programs, and low-cost or volunteer sitters and nurses can replace the monopolizing burden of parents providing 24-hour care. Relief from total absorption of the child's ailments frees parents to work more effectively with the rehabilitative team.

Community Resources

As a result of section 504 of the Rehabilitation Act of 1973 and P.L. 94-142, special education teachers must organize the resources in the community to support the needs of students and their families. One mechanism to document community involvement is on the IEP. Another is by following a systematic series of steps in locating appropriate service agencies. To begin:

1. Take inventory of your region in terms of available resources.

2. Consult national organizations sponsored in the medical discipline related to your student's disability (see Appendix B).

3. Look for referral centers or umbrella agencies such as United Way or Chamber of Commerce, through whom you can locate specific nonprofit or for-profit organizations.

4. Look at state and local services in the following categories:
   a. Department of Education
   b. Department of Social Services
   c. Public Health Department
   d. Legal services

e. Vocational services
f. Bureaus for blind or hearing impaired
g. PTA (Parent-Teacher Association)
h. Mental Health Department
i. Red Cross
j. YMCA/YWCA
k. Jewish Community Centers
l. Salvation Army/Goodwill
m. Boy Scouts/Girl Scouts
n. Churches/Synagogues
o. Hospitals
p. Community service groups (Jaycees, Lions, etc.)
q. Nursing homes

Establishing reliable contact persons within different service agencies is an important step toward effective referrals. But the number of agencies to do this with is manifold. Once agencies or persons are contacted, determine their standards for admitting students into the program. Qualification standards play an important role in the evaluation of agencies for the homebound student. Select an appropriate referral agency based on answers to the following questions:

1. Cost: Is the service fee affordable?
2. Eligibility requirements:
   a. Geographic: Does the client live too far from the agency?
   b. Age, sex, race: Do these factors pose an obstacle?
3. Range of services: To what extent does the agency fulfill the client's needs?
4. Application procedures: Do the forms or interviews make unrealistic demands on your student?
5. Size of program and population served: How individualized is the service?
6. Program attitudes toward handicapped: Do agency personnel feel prejudice toward the handicapped?
7. Agency requirements.
   a. Is there a minimum or maximum length of stay?
   b. What medications, if any, are involved?
   c. What is the agency's treatment philosophy?
8. Attitudes of other agencies toward this agency: Does the agency hold a good reputation in the community?

Barriers to Networking

The major barrier to service integration is the resistance to organizational change. The majority of health and human service systems do not allow for integration with agencies outside of their immediate sphere of service. Thus barriers arise that frustrate the perseverant teacher seeking referrals for the student. Among the most prevalent barriers to organizational change are:

Overcentralization of Authority and Power. This causes long delays in change needed to meet new or changing needs of the student. Information must first be directed through several levels of administration to the policy-making administrator prior to any initial change occurring. When multiple agencies are involved, this is further complicated by the need for complementary change in each affected agency.

Vertical and Horizontal Fragmentation. This is a lack of knowledge between service provider systems. Because most students are involved with multiple services, it is not unusual for two systems to be providing different information to the same student about the same problem.

Agency Territoriality. Each service agency perceives a certain set of territorial boundaries to be in existence. The agency resists intrusion into its territory by other agencies. This inhibits the effective networking of service delivery by all providers attempting to affect the problem.

Peer Pressure to Protect and Expand the Unit. Peers at all levels of an agency tend to protect the agency and move toward expanding that realm of influence, territory and staffing of agency. This pressure also exists in attempting to define any new health and human service problem area either within or outside that agency.

Compulsive Rule-Following. Within the socialization of any agency is the importance placed on following the policies and rules of the agency. Because policies and rules invariably pertain to intra-agency matters, teachers who follow these rules to the letter may discourage or delay interaction with other agencies.

Committee Structure. When new problems present themselves to health and service agencies, many times inter- and intra-agency committees are formed to define the problem and then determine the best service solution. One common result of this committee structure is to delay initial service while the committee debates policy in-house and among other existing agencies.

When this many barriers are involved, one is tempted to pass the buck to somebody else. Homebound teachers need not do this; they can rely on the formed team of professionals for assistance in penetrating obstacles, and can rely on family members for following through with the referral.

In the next chapter we see how an established support network proves indispensable for children with short-term and chronic illnesses.

6. Short-Term and Chronic Illness

Over half of the students in a typical homebound caseload are normal school-aged children that have been in accidents. Injuries vary from mild abrasions to broken bones, torn ligaments, fractures, burns, and head injuries. The most common injuries are either sports-related or due to vehicle or pedestrian accidents.

After the initial impact and hospitalization, there are many sudden limitations families are not prepared to handle. Limitations of mobility affect toileting and bathing. Speech may be limited. Independent feeding and dressing deteriorate, and pain from surgery or accident can intensify as turbulence within the family rises. The synergistic effect of all these factors, coupled with social isolation during recuperative months, is severe.

This chapter prepares homebound instructors for the structure of lesson plans and interventions adaptive to children struck with these short-term and chronic health problems. Different types of injuries are presented, some with case studies, followed by analysis and recommendations for the teacher.

Broken Bones

Most students with fractured femurs or other broken bones are in a body cast. The body cast is made from plaster and actually covers the child's torso; it extends from chest to the pelvic area, leaving a hole in the plaster in front of the genitals and hole in back for toileting. This makes bedpan use more accommodating. The plastered body cast continues down the broken or fractured leg to the ankle, depending on the injury. The other leg, even if undamaged, may be partially plastered with a bar attached from leg to leg to provide stability.

First sessions with these students generally consist of information gathering. It is also a time to set the rules according to their classroom teachers' instructions and requirements. Questions that instantly gain rapport are quite appropriate at this time: "What is your favorite TV show?" "What are your hobbies?" Moments spent in building a rapport can prevent impenetrable trials later when the student's endurance is low and motivation plummets. Inquire about his or her habits, routines, and accept the challenge to exchange basic information about yourself.

With most children in body casts, early morning sessions are inadvisable. Basic hygienic activities now take longer, are more frustrating, and the injured person is dependent on others. A morning session invites disaster as the teacher risks becoming a nursemaid rather than an instructor. To avoid this problem, schedule sessions for later in the morning or early afternoon.

In the case that follows, an early morning session found the student and family unprepared. Perhaps this contributed to the student's emotional outburst. Fortunately, the difficulty of this child's situation allowed him to admit his needs and helped us progress toward meeting them.

CASE FIVE: REGGIE

I walked into Smith Elementary, an inner city school in the South. By 3:30 p.m., all the children had been dismissed and the floors had been just mopped. The 3:30 conference was with Mrs. Anderson, a sixth-grade teacher and contact for my newest student, Reggie.

Reggie had been hit by a car while crossing the street on his way to the store. His right femur was fractured and his left arm broken. Reggie would be confined to bed for the next ten weeks.

Mrs. Anderson was waiting for me at her desk. A huge tower of papers leaned slightly to the left as she reached for one every few minutes, grading them slowly. She stopped when she saw me and I introduced myself. Mrs. Anderson's eyes widened and she smiled. Although she looked tired and ready to retire for the day, she seemed eager to tell me something about this student. "Have you met Reggie yet?"

"No," I answered. "I'll meet him at 8:30 tomorrow morning. I hope the family remembers, since they don't have a phone. But I wrote them a letter."

"Have you read his records?"

"No, I like to meet each teacher and then each student with an open mind . . . is there something I should know about Reggie?"

Mrs. Anderson laughed out loud and put her hands together as if to pray. I knew it was coming.

"He's the baddest boy in school. . . . I don't mean a little restless or mouthy, no sir. He's the school bully, the classroom punk. And the children are plenty scared of him!" Mrs. Anderson took out her record book. "He never hands anything in, you know." She showed me his grades. "He's failing again, but we need to pass him up to seventh grade, now that he's fourteen . . . but he's flunked a few times. Yes, ma'am, if you can teach him anything, anything at all, you will be further ahead than we have been." Mrs. Anderson shook her graying head and handed me a folder with the general areas she would be teaching during the next ten weeks.

After we briefly discussed the papers, she looked me in the eyes and simply said, "Good luck!"

At 8:30 the next morning I pulled up to a small brick duplex on a corner lot. I grabbed my books and went up the stairs to meet the family. I knocked and waited; knocked louder, and had a terrible feeling that I was not expected. I hoped they had received the letter. I politely knocked a third time, and the door was answered by a sleepy young woman with green and orange curlers in her hair.

"Is it 8:30 already?" she said apologetically. "Come on in, but we'll need a few minutes." She led me into her kitchen and I sat patiently while she hurried to awaken Reggie. I noticed the kitchen, hall, and TV room were cluttered with religious literature. There was a framed copy of the Lord's Prayer, a large poster of the Last Supper, and 20 or so quotes from different portions of the Bible tacked on the walls. There was a picture of Reggie and his mother alongside of Jimmy Swaggart with GOD LOVES YOU — 1985 under Swaggart's signature.

Reggie's mother started to raise her voice, telling him, "The Lord has put you in this mess, now you must do what you have to do." Reggie protested in a deep, lethargic drawl, "But Ma, I ain't ready yet. . . . I hurt, and I ain't in no mood for school!"

She screamed, "The teacher is waitin' on you. . . are you ready, mister?"

"Yes, ma'am."

Reggie's mother came out of his room, quite upset, and motioned for me to enter. I walked in to meet a disgruntled, sleepy student. He appeared overly stuffed into a tight-fitting body cast. Plaster encased him from shoulder to arm and from chest to ankle. I held his five school books and searched for somewhere to sit. There was no chair, so I set the books on the floor and went to get a kitchen chair. Reggie's mother was sipping coffee in front of the TV, engrossed in the PTL Club. She didn't seem to notice me carrying the kitchen chair to Reggie's room.

As I sat next to Reggie's bed, he deliberately looked at the wall. I spoke to him.

"It's just you and me, Reggie. You have to have school, and I am your teacher for the next ten weeks. I have had a lot of students in body casts and I know you are not comfortable. There is one important thing to think about. With my help and your effort, you can pass the sixth grade. Do you want to go to junior high next year?"

"Yeah, sure I do, but I have trouble with schoolwork, so I just don't do it," Reggie said, facing the wall.

"Reggie, there is some good that came out of your accident. You now have a private teacher to help you with your work. How many kids do you know with their own, private tutor? We will have no distractions, no pressure. I just have one rule: if you do your homework — and I *will* give you homework — then I will be able to offer you full credit and passing grades. You might even learn something."

"Yes, ma'am."

As I reached to get his English book, I couldn't help remembering Mrs. Anderson warning me about the baddest boy in the school. I held the book up to Reggie's eyes and asked him to read aloud. He looked at the book, glanced at me, and started to sob. I put the book down and just let the meanest boy in Smith Elementary School have his cry. It was refreshing to see a soft, sensitive side to this overgrown sixth grader. I gave him a few minutes to collect himself.

"Reggie, is this book too hard for you to read?"

"It's all too hard, all them books."

"I have something in my car for you. . . . Do you like sports?"

"Yes, ma'am."

"I'll be right back." I got up and went out to my car, where I always keep supplementary workbooks and worksheets. I pulled out *The Superstars of Sports* which featured contemporary sports figures such as Magic Johnson, Jim Palmer, Muhammad Ali and others. Reggie perked up slightly when he saw his new reading book. Since it was written for high interest and low reading level, he was able to read it the first try. He didn't realize it was written on a second grade level. Reggie began to listen to my other directions about learning his times tables and studying the United States map. I explained we would take an imaginary trip, anywhere he wanted to go, and study the states we would drive through. We would count the mileage and approximate costs we would incur. After an hour and a half, Reggie looked at me and asked, "Are you a real teacher?"

"As real as you'll ever have, Reggie."

During the following ten weeks that I worked with Reggie, he was able to complete most of his work. I did not use his sixth-grade books at all. We covered the areas Mrs. Anderson wrote down that first day, yet all work was on an individual level of ability, pace and interest.

When it was time to return to school, Reggie had grown up quite a bit under extremely uncomfortable circumstances. His education had gone smoothly. I saw it as an ideal teaching scenario: Reggie couldn't run away from the situation; in fact, he couldn't move. He couldn't bully anyone, and he had the undivided attention of his homebound teacher.

In the next few weeks, I referred Reggie to the school psychologist, who took the time and interest to qualify Reggie for special education. Perhaps Smith Elementary had seen the last of the meanest boy in school.

Corrective Surgery

Homebound programs for children who have had corrective surgery are usually short-term (4 to 10 weeks). Many times the child is at home awaiting post-surgery placement in a more appropriate facility. Transitional periods raise normal anxiety levels, in addition to the physical pain while recuperating. Injuries or problems that commonly require corrective surgery during the child's first 10 years include spina bifida, burns, cerebral palsy, and osteogenesis imperfecta (brittle bones).

Spina Bifida (Spina Bifida Occulta)

Spina bifida is a defect in the spinal column due to abnormal fetal development. It is a congenital orthopedic handicap. It results from failure of the lower end of the spinal cord to close. Nerve fibers and fluid may protrude from the lower back in the shape of a sac (meningocele), covered by a thin membrane. If the covering bulges out in a sac, surgery is a must to correct the defect.

Associated Disabilities. Hydrocephalus, a condition caused by excess spinal fluid, is a common associated disability. This deformity is prevalent in 90 to 95 percent of children with myelomeningoceles.

Sensory Loss. The nerves are weakened or nonfunctioning, resulting in lack of sensitivity to touch, pain, pressure, heat, or cold in areas of the skin that are normally sensitive. Bowel and bladder weaknesses also are common. Sphincter muscles are usually not able to function properly. This can cause a back-up of urine into the kidneys, which in turn causes serious kidney infection and possibly kidney failure. Bowel problems, making matters worse, can cause constipation and impacted stools. Teachers may wish to encourage a "planned evacuation" program to avoid bathroom problems.

Bone Deformities. Dislocation of the hip, club foot and severe rocker bottom are due to partial paralysis in the lower limbs creating a muscle imbalance. Weakness of the trunk may lead to curvature of the spine (scoliosis), humpback (kyphosis) or swayback (lordosis).

Treaments. Neurosurgery, the usual practice, will result in closure of the myelomeningocele. This surgery avoids a life-threatening infection, but does not reduce paralysis. Hydrocephalus is treated by draining the blocked ventricles. Shunts, or permanent draining devices, are made of plastic and have an interposing valve between the ventricle and the heart. Orthopedic surgery also helps to reduce or prevent dislocation of the hip.

Due to sensory deprivation, lack of bowel and bladder control, surgical pain, ambulation limitations and separation from parents, such children suffer high psychological stressors. Spina bifida children are certified orthopedically handicapped and can be mainstreamed depending on their individual strengths and weaknesses. Such children continue on homebound education throughout their required twelve years of public schooling.

Burns

Burns in childhood usually result from poor supervision and can be a devastating disability. Homebound children with burns face immediate schedule readjustments in routine and, depending on age, may suffer emotional agony. Consider that the child was most likely a normal, healthy individual until the accident. The trauma can range from mild to severe in reactivity, apart from however the child's parents reacted.

Treatment. Treatment for burns has three main stages. First is keeping the patient alive and restoring fluid balance; this stage may last three to four days. Secondly, dead or contaminated skin is removed surgically. The underlayers of epidermis are immediately covered to prevent infection. An emergency tracheotomy might be performed if the face or neck receives severe burns. Severity of the burn determines the length of this stage, from 6 to 10 weeks.

The third stage, of restoration and skin reconstruction, can last for two years or more. This is a difficult and seemingly endless process. As the skin heals, it tightens and scars. Open wounds require constant care to avert infection. Tight skin also causes itching, but scratching would reverse the healing process.

Jobst elastic garments can be worn over burn areas for 23 hours a day. The Jobst garments can create a frightful appearance, especially if worn on the face or hand. Friends and family may be repelled at first by the sight, but they will grow accustomed to the child's appearance. Social acceptance is facilitated by a tape recording of the child's voice sent to school to be heard among his friends; likewise, recorded words of encouragement from his peers can assuage the child's loneliness.

Cerebral Palsy

The term "cerebral palsy" means brain paralysis. This non-progressive disorder occurs during pregnancy or at birth. Cerebral palsied children commonly are placed in a program for the orthopedically handicapped and require homebound services only after receiving corrective surgery.

There are six classifications of cerebral palsy as defined by Bleck and Nagel (1975). Classifications include spasticity, athetosis, rigidity, ataxia, tremor, and mixed.

Spasticity. Spasticity is characterized by tight, sudden movements. Movements may seem exaggerated at times, but as natural growth occurs, spastic muscles contract and deformities appear in the limbs, spine, or pelvis.

Athetosis. Athetosis is characterized by involuntary, purposeless limb movements. Muscles are normal with athetoid children. However, arms and legs might appear twisted, or there will be sporadic jerking motions.

Rigidity. Rigidity is a form of spasticity. Trying to move a rigid limb will not be a successful venture. A limb becomes so tight that it feels like a solid piece of pipe. All four limbs affected this way are usually a quadraplegic condition.

Ataxia. Ataxia is characterized by a lack of balance, lack of position space, and uncoordinated movement. Ataxic children walk as if drunk.

Their feet are apart and they use their arms and hands to balance their stride. Because they frequently fall, these children will wear protective head gear or knee pads.

Tremor. Tremor is a shakiness of the limbs only while the child is awake. Tremors subside or are in remission while the child is asleep.

Mixed. Mixed characteristics usually take a spastic and athetoid form, primarily in quadraplegics.

Children with cerebral palsy also may have impaired speech. This may be a temporary or permanent condition and at times is correctable after surgery. A child undergoing surgery who is nonverbal, or is nonverbal after surgery, is prone to low frustration tolerance. Homebound teachers working with such children can overcome the language barrier by providing an alternative communication system. This was done in the case of Charlie.

CASE SIX: CHARLIE

I met Charlie the day he returned home from the hospital. He was stretched out on the soft, recently vacuumed carpet in the middle of the living room. His schoolbooks were piled neatly on top of the table. On his right side was a Cabbage Patch little boy doll, dressed in a new, matching outfit. He had a name tag taped onto his shirt with "Charlie Jr." printed on the tag. Young, silent Charlie Jr. sat in a miniature wheelchair made especially for him. This cute little doll offered security and comfort to a sorrowful ten-year-old boy.

My student's fragile body was plastered in a white body cast from his chest to his ankles. Everywhere, his thirteen-year-old brother had written, "Get Well, Charlie" and drawn pictures of Garfield the Cat up and down his cast. Two pillows lifted Charlie's freshly washed, brown-haired head, and a blanket covered his bottom half.

All I knew of Charlie's condition was the brief information I had received. Charlie was a nonverbal, quadraplegic fourth grader, with athetoid cerebral palsy. I spoke briefly to his resource room teacher, but she had only known Charlie two weeks, ever since the first day of this school year. Charlie would have to remain confined for nine weeks in his body cast due to corrective surgery.

I kicked off my shoes and sat on the floor, cross-legged. I studied Charlie's eyes, and he studied mine. I picked up his lap board, or "communication board," and examined it. This type of board usually fits over the arms of a wheelchair like a tray. Lap boards can be attached to most wheelchairs and will accompany the child wherever he goes. Emergency words such as bathroom, hungry, tired, water, yes, no, and thank-you will appear on the board. Charlie's board also showed "capital letter," various types of punctuation, numbers 0-10, and the alphabet.

Charlie, like most athetoid cerebral palsied children, had uncontrolled movements. Although Charlie's body was stifled in plaster, his arm movements were free. Typically, it can take many minutes to point to a single signal on the communication board. Charlie would need even more time than usual and also required more of my time than most of my students. The materials and approach to teaching thus were radically different and quite creative to center around his limited communication repertoire.

I talked to Charlie, making sure Charlie knew that I was aware he could hear me and understand what I was saying. I told him that I have many students in body casts and I knew he was not comfortable. I also knew he would need to do schoolwork. I asked him, "Do your arms feel okay?" Charlie nodded.

"Good," I said, "We can begin. First, will you tell me what your favorite TV show is?" I held up the lap board and he began to point. Spelling out the words and symbols: "CAPITAL LETTER – T – H – E – CAPITAL LETTER – P – R – I – C – E – I – S – R – I – G – H – T – CAPITAL LETTER – N – A – N – C – Y, – CAPITAL LETTER – C – O – M – E – O – N – D – O – W – N!"

Spelling the words out took almost ten minutes. Yet, when Charlie finished answering, we both laughed at the words. It was my first glimpse of the Charlie I would come to know for the next nine weeks. I positioned Charlie's lap board in my right hand and leaned on the carpet, on my side, so my head was near the pillows in order to see what Charlie saw. I said, "Which do you want to do first, Charlie, math or spelling?" He turned his head, looked me directly in the eyes, laughed, and spelled out: "CAPITAL LETTER – Y – O – U – T – E – A – C – H – E – R – S – A – R – E – A – L – L – A – L – I – K – E! – CAPITAL LETTER – M – A – T – H."

He gave me another wider smile, as if it had been too long since he felt like showing his pearly white teeth. Even in this severely physically handicapped child were normal feelings, desires and humor.

Chronic Illnesses

Common chronic illnesses of children found in the homebound program are asthma, lupus, osteogenesis imperfecta (brittle bones), diabetes, sickle cell disease, and head injuries. Children suffering these problems or injuries often look healthy to others, until their problems become severe enough to warrant confinement. Signs of severity vary but largely include coughing or wheezing attacks, dizziness, pain, and extreme lethargy.

Asthma

Asthma is the most common chronic disease of childhood. Most children with asthma have a relatively mild form which is controllable via medication. Symptoms include wheezing, a dry hacking cough or obstructed breathing.

Etiology. Asthma affects the lungs in three types of reactions in the air passages of the lungs. First, muscles in the walls of the airways (bronchial tubes) tighten and constrict. Secondly, the inside walls of the airways swell up. Third, the swollen walls give off mucus, which clogs the airways. Consequently the child struggles to breathe.

Asthma is brought on by excessive sensitivity of the lungs to various stimuli. Each child might react differently. Typical stimulatory factors include allergic reactions (commonly to pollen, molds, animal dander, house dust, feathers, or various foods), respiratory infections, common cold, vigorous exercise, sudden temperature changes, air pollution or strong odors, cigarette smoke, or emotional situations.

There are three signs of a more serious episode of asthma. Breathlessness, the most common, may cause the child to talk in one word sentences or not at all. Another sign is when the child's neck muscles tighten with each inhalation. Changes in color in the lips and nails may be a third sign.

Lupus

Lupus, or systematic lupus erythematosus, is usually described as a chronic inflammatory disease of the connective tissues of the body. Studies show that the basic defect involves changes in the tissues found between the body's cells. This tissue connects and supports the cells of the body the way that mortar connects and supports the bricks of a house. It becomes an immunological reaction, often referred to as an auto-immune disease. As part of the body's defense system changes, antibodies begin reacting against the body tissue. Approximately 50,000 new lupus victims are diagnosed each year. The disease can be found in all age groups, but young women are most often afflicted.

Etiology. Although this disease has been known since the 1800s, it continues to baffle the medical field by its puzzling symptoms. Questions still surround the cause of lupus, but it is known that the disease is not contagious. Lupus of the discoid type involves the skin. Sometimes a facial rash takes the form of an open butterfly spread over the bridge of the nose and cheeks, highly sun-sensitive. A second type, systemic lupus, involves the internal organs of the body. Membranes surrounding the heart, lungs and abdominal organs are at risk.

A complex disease, lupus may manifest itself in a variety of symptoms. Common signs include weakness, loss of appetite, loss of weight, a flu-like feeling, shortness of breath, painful breathing, rapid heartbeat, enlarged lymph nodes, and body rashes. Physicians must remember that these symptoms are common to other diseases, so additional data is essential for a differential diagnosis.

Treatment. There are no definite treatments for lupus. Physicians will conduct blood tests, urinalysis, and skin and kidney biopsies. Relief, if any, is of the symptoms rather than of the underlying physical disorder. Strategies preventive of severe lupus attacks are to avoid excess sunshine, get plenty of rest, and eat balanced and nutritious meals. Medications prescribed or bought over the counter likely will include aspirin, steroids, anti-malaria drugs, and drugs to suppress the immune system of the body.

Osteogenesis Imperfecta (Brittle Bones)

Osteogenesis imperfecta (OI) means imperfect bone formation. The common terms used are "brittle bone disease" or "blue sclera," due to the blue tint in the whites of the eyes in most OI children.

Etiology. Causes are still unknown, but there is an inherited dominant trait in most afflicted children. Cases have appeared without any hereditary link of OI and instead trace to gene mutation. Both males and females are equally at risk. The basic defect is in the collagen fibers or protein matrix of the bone. Given this protein deficiency, the total amount of bone salts (e.g. calcium, phosphorus) is reduced. The bone structure becomes weak, and the collagen of the tissues remains immature.

Signs and symptoms. Congenital OI babies are born with shortened, deformed limbs, various broken bones, and an extremely short skull. Skull bones are usually soft at first. The forehead broadens as the child grows, and the temples will bulge. The child's face will have a triangular shape. His chest will seem barrel-shaped and the spine is often curved. When OI is diagnosed in later life, the disease is usually mild. Frequently the blue discoloration of the eyes is the only symptom.

Treatment. Currently, magnesium oxide, taken orally, has proven effective in changing blood chemistry to produce calcification. Consequently, the treatment of choice is surgery. The entire shaft of the bone is removed, cut into pieces, and threaded onto a steel rod inserted between the ends of the long bone. This approach, combined with bracing of the lower limbs, has been the best regimen to date and allows at least partial ambulation. (See Bleck & Nagel, 1975.) The remainder of the time afflicted children will be in a wheelchair.

Children with OI have normal intelligence. They are usually quick learners and maintain fairly positive attitudes about school. Deafness and visual problems may be concomitant to degenerative cases of OI, although usually this condition stabilizes. For this reason, OI children fully participate in mainstreaming.

Diabetes

Diabetes is not an infectious disease, but it does last a lifetime. Diabetes means that the pancreas does not make enough insulin. Without insulin, food cannot be metabolized properly. Diabetic children must take daily injections or tablets of insulin and must maintain a balance of food and exercise. If not, insulin reactions may occur when the blood sugar gets too low, especially before meals or after exercise.

Insulin Reactions: Warning Signs. Insulin reactions occur when the blood sugar level drops too low. Insulin and exercise lower blood sugar, whereas food raises it. There will be controlled sugar levels when food, insulin and exercise are regulated. Too little food, delayed meals, strenuous exercise without extra food, nervous tension or too much insulin is likely to trigger a reaction. Sudden symptoms include pallor, excessive perspiration, hunger, headache, dizziness, blurred vision, irritability, inappropriate responses, crying, confusion, poor concentration, drowsiness, lack of coordination, trembling, abdominal pain, and nausea.

Insulin Reactions: Home Treatments. Give the child two packets or two teaspoons of sugar, immediately. Another treatment that works well is one-half to two-thirds cup of sweetened fruit juice or candy (six or seven lifesavers or jelly beans are easy to carry around). Always repeat the above strategy if the child does not improve in fifteen minutes. Should improvement not occur, call his parents or physician.

Teachers meeting with diabetic children before mealtime (breakfast, lunch, dinner, etc.) should be alert to signs of insulin reactions during the session. Routine meals are essential in the daily regulation of diabetes. Exclusion of the child from certain activities risking insulin reaction should be weighed against the value of that instruction. Diabetic children can and should participate in all activities as long as care is exercised to avoid reactions.

Sickle Cell Disease

Sickle Cell Trait. Sickle cell trait is not a contagious disease. One in twelve blacks in the United States has the sickle cell trait. Sickle cell trait and sickle cell anemia occur mostly in individuals of African descent. Such children are generally healthy and live normal life spans, unaware of being afflicted.

Sickle Cell Anemia. Sickle cell anemia is an inherited disorder of sickle cell hemoglobin from both parents. Children with this disease have a very low blood count and may experience attacks of pain, jaundice, infections, and associated disorders warranting immediate hospitalization.

Etiology. Sickle cell anemia involves the red blood cells. Rather than being round, they form a "sickle" shape when they lose oxygen. This occurs because of the presence of an abnormal hemoglobin. Sickle cells are fragile and break down more rapidly than they are replaced. Anemia is the result.

Associated Problems. Pain attacks are a common manifestation of this disease. Attacks are due to the plugging of blood vessels. Pain may last for a few hours or intermittently spread over several weeks. Other associated problems include pneumonia, gallstones, strokes, leg ulcers, growth retardation and delayed puberty.

Most children with sickle cell anemia have normal intelligence, unless they suffer a secondary stroke. These children may be absent frequently because of pain attacks or related complications. It is also frequent that children are more inattentive by the end of the school day. In severe cases, additional needs to watch for include need to drink more water, need to urinate more frequently, need to lie down, need to avoid long sunshine exposure, and need for support for being teased about their short height.

Head Injuries

In the United States, each year, one million children and youths will sustain head injuries from motor vehicle accidents, falls, sports and physical abuse. Statistically, the largest group of head-injured people is in the 15 to 24 age range, but this frequency is as high for younger children under fifteen years of age (Savage, 1987). Not all head traumas are severe, and some may not involve the loss of functioning or minimal brain injury loss.

Coma Length and Recovery. When children are in a coma less than 24 hours, there is rarely permanent brain damage. Children that remain in coma longer than three days may drop in IQ at least one standard deviation (84 percent of cases). Head-injured individuals remaining in a coma less than six weeks may return to independent functioning of 90 percent over a three-year period of rehabilitation.

Following impact of injury, students enter a series of recovery stages beginning with acute rehabilitation and then step-by-step into different treatment modes. Barrer and Ruben (1984) more fully reviewed later stages of community reentry as a transitional placement combining restored independent living skills and initiation of pre-vocational or pre-educational training. With advances in medical technology, today many chronically head-injured children can have portable mechanical devices or installed devices in their private homes, operated by hired nurses or by the parents. This naturally has reduced the cost and emotional detachment of prolonged hospitalization (see Fig. 6.1).

Levels of Cognitive Functioning. The Rancho Scale, prepared by the Division of Neurological Services at Rancho Los Amigos Hospital, describes eight levels of cognitive functioning. These levels assist a team of professionals in determining the range of student functioning and likely progress thereafter. Following is a brief description of these cognitive levels:

1. Generalized response: The patient appears to be in a deep sleep and is completely unresponsive to any stimulation.

2. Localized response: Patient reacts specifically but inconsistently to stimuli. Responses are directly related to the type of stimulus, such as turning the head toward a sound or focusing on objects presented. Patient may withdraw an extremity or vocalize when presented with painful stimulation. The person might also follow simple commands in an incoherent, inconsistent or delayed manner, such as closing his eyes.

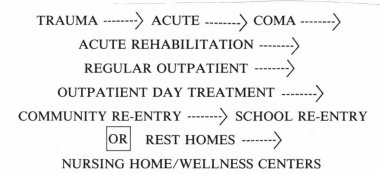

TRAUMA -------〉 ACUTE --------〉 COMA --------〉

ACUTE REHABILITATION --------〉

REGULAR OUTPATIENT --------〉

OUTPATIENT DAY TREATMENT --------〉

COMMUNITY RE-ENTRY --------〉 SCHOOL RE-ENTRY

OR REST HOMES --------〉

NURSING HOME/WELLNESS CENTERS

Figure 6.1. Stages of Head-Injury Recovery.

3. Confused-agitated: Patient is in a heightened state of arousal with severely decreased ability to process information. He is detached from the present and responds primarily to his own internal confusion. Behavior is frequently bizarre and non-purposeful relative to the immediate environment. He may not discriminate among persons or objects and is unable to cooperate directly with treatment. Self-care is also poor and requires assistance.

4. Confused, inappropriate, non-agitated: Patient appears alert and can respond to simple commands fairly consistently. However, with increased complexity of commands, the responses are random, non-purposeful or fragmented. He may show agitated behavior but not due to internal pain. He may seem highly distractible and will require frequent redirection. With structure, students can converse on a social-automatic level for short periods of time. Verbalizations are often inappropriate, and memory remains severely impaired. Confusion of past and present is apparent, as is a lack of initiative of functional tasks.

5. Confused-appropriate: Patient shows goal-directed behavior but is dependent on people for direction. Response to discomfort is appropriate, and he can tolerate unpleasant stimulation. He can follow simple directions consistently and demonstrates transfer of learned tasks. Past memories show more depth and detail than recent memory. He no longer wanders and is clearly oriented to time and place.

6. Automatic-appropriate: Patient appears appropriate and oriented within hospital or home setting. He goes through daily routines automatically, but in a robot-like fashion, with minimal affect or diversion. There is increased awareness of self, body, family, foods, people and general interactions with environment. While still deficient in problem-solving, transfer of learned skills is significantly stronger once he leaves the hospital. One sign of restored awareness and functionality is his interest in social and recreational activities.

7. *Purposeful and appropriate:* Patient is alert and oriented. He can recall and integrate past and present events and is responsive to the environment. Need for supervision is minimal. Physical capability sufficiently enables his independence of personal and functional needs. Although essentially recovered, readjustment in a work or educational setting is still likely to be an emotional experience.

Public school systems give careful consideration to the many questions about head-injured students. Some recent issues facing both legislative and program review include:

1. Are the special education and regular education teachers knowledgeable about traumatic head injury and its associated problems?

2. What services are available when children return to school?

3. What educational interventions (cognitive, behavioral) will make the student's transition to normal instruction more effective in terms of skill acquisition and for re-entry into the classroom?

Recommendations for School Re-entry. For a successful school re-entry experience, teachers, administrators and significant school personnel need proper inservice training. There must be a team approach, sharing information and interventions. Simply placing the head-injured student in a learning disability or language deficit program is an inadequate solution. Such programs lack the specific training components needed for this unique disorder. Secondly, wrong placements may further aggravate adjustment problems for the head-injured student. Table 6.1 reviews compensatory strategies for common cognitive problems.

Naturally it is impossible to predict many problems confronted by the head-injured individual upon return to school. At best, teachers can plan ahead with a temporary guideline of academic skills, realizing that attention span and physical endurance will be inconsistent. Related problems abound for secondary students also concerned with social image and self-esteem. Taken together, we can see the trials and tribulations of adjustment in the case of Richard.

CASE SEVEN: RICHARD

At 10:00 AM, on a rainy Monday in October, I walked into Richard's life. As his mother accompanied me to his bedroom, she said, "We may have to wake him, he sleeps most of the day and night." Richard was stretched out on his rented hospital bed, asleep, an IV in his arm and a tube in his nose. Richard's mother tried to awaken him by saying, "Richard, it's time for school, your new teacher is here." I pulled up a chair and silently recalled how he came to be in this predicament.

Richard had been cruising in a car with his best buddies, drinking a 6-pack (possibly a 12-pack) of beer. They were out looking for some action. The driver, however, was not looking at the road. The accident

Problem	*Strategy*
On task/attending problems	Limit the background noises; limit amount of information on each assigned page; adjust assignments to attention span.
Memory: unable to retain information	Accompany visual cues with oral information, use verbal rehearsal (repeating information by student), limit amount of information presented; provide a log book or journal to record daily work or events.
Retrieving information that has been stored in memory	Role-play situation, include multiple choice cues in daily work
Sequencing — difficulty recognizing, describing, and understanding sequence	Limit number of steps in a task, present the first part of the sequence and have student try the second. Show or discuss one step at a time, and have the student use verbal rehearsal.
Disorientation or confusion	Provide an uncluttered, quiet environment, provide pictorial charts, schedules that clearly define rules and routines. Use a buddy system.
Impulsive responses	Discuss rules each day and role-play appropriate responses. Have **Stop-Action Intervention.** That means to immediately stop student from disruptive behavior; be consistent with rules and consequences. Provide time at end of session for student(s) to tell personal stories or jokes.
Working independently	Review directions or sample items; provide a written sequence to follow and a check-off list as he completes each step. Provide positive reinforcement at various intervals. Point to a posted sign stating **Return to Work** instead of giving verbal reprimands.

Table 6.1. Compensatory Strategies for Cognitive Problems.

action. The driver, however, was not looking at the road. The accident happened quickly, leaving Richard's three buddies with scrapes and bruises. Richard, unfortunately, was not that lucky. He was not wearing a seatbelt and at the time of impact, he flew out of the back seat, breaking through the front panel glass, and was immediately knocked unconscious.

Richard's mother sat next to me and began to tell me it was a miracle that he had lived. The doctors had told her that Richard might not come out of the coma; and if he did, that she should find a suitable nursing facility for the remainder of his life. Yet she felt certain that one day, Richard would return to his normal, 17-year-old self. Richard's mother pointed to his picture on the nightstand. He was the star quarterback in his ninth-grade year. Although not the best student, he was a popular, handsome young man.

The first few weeks Richard was hospitalized, his friends came by in droves, but after a few months, they seemed to lose interest and faith that he would return to their lives. Their active friendship faded as time passed. His mother knew it would be a shock to Richard when he realized his friends were not sympathetic to him now.

I smiled and nodded, looking at Richard as he tried to wake up. I thought, only a mother could have such optimism for a seemingly hopeless situation. Richard's mom, against the doctor's wishes, took Richard home so she could care for him, her youngest son.

He had been home for seven months now, a year since the accident. Some motor skill and verbal skill improvement was evident through continuous therapy. Other than slurred speech, Richard could speak with meaning. His mother now felt he could benefit from school, yet she was not sure what his current abilities were.

As we talked, Richard had opened his eyes and was staring at me. He had a look of anger and confusion. I wasn't sure he knew where he was at that moment. Richard's mother introduced me as his new teacher, and he shut his eyes. He opened them quickly, saw that I had not left, and turned his head away from my gaze, grumbling under his breath. I was sure I recognized a few slurred obscenities. Richard's mother assured me that some things hadn't changed, such as his attitude about school.

I took some preliminary information for my register and told Richard and his mother that I would see them in two days, for our first one-hour session.

On Wednesday morning I came prepared to start a cognitive retraining program with Richard. I helped him sit up straight in bed, putting three pillows behind his back and head, and two pillows on each side to help support his body. I sat next to him and showed him the English tracking books, *Math Mastery,* and *Superstars of Sports* workbooks. Richard looked at me and blurted out, "The Dallas Cowboys are going to beat the hell out of Pittsburgh.... The Cowboys are my favorite team, aren't they the greatest?"

Putting the books down, I asked Richard to explain the rules of football to me. I felt if he could continue talking, I could take the opportunity to observe his speech, memory, and concentration in connection with a subject he enjoyed.

Richard began to describe rules and penalties of the game. He went into a brief description of the responsibilities of each player. His speech was quite slurred, as if he had had a stroke, yet the pace was rapid and enthusiastic. He did repeat phrases three or four times, at one point, so I could understand him. Richard's mother constantly reminded him to slow down and breathe correctly. After she left the room to answer the phone, I asked him to write three sentences about the Dallas Cowboys. He put paper in the clipboard and found his pencil. Richard just stared at the paper. He looked at me, eyes wide as saucers, and stated slowly, "I don't remember how to spell . . . anything."

"Why don't I get you started. Which words do you need help with?"

Richard started screaming, "All of them, *all of them . . . Mom . . . get my mom!*"

Richard's mother dashed into the room, looking surprised. As she tried to calm down Richard, I explained how common it was to have aphasia or a breakdown in communication. I explained receptive breakdowns (not understanding what you hear) and expressive breakdowns (the inability to express oneself orally or in writing, sometimes both).

I asked Richard to try a tracking book. He protested, "That's not a tenth-grade book."

"We won't use your regular high school books for a while. I can give you high school credit for all the work you do for me. The books I have are specifically for those students who have had head injury."

Richard tried the first page in *Cues and Comprehension,* a tracking English series. He was stuck on a few words, but succeeded. His tense face and shoulder muscles seemed to loosen up as he worked through the book. I then introduced the *Math Mastery* and *Visual Transfer Skills* workbooks. Although he had little trouble, he performed at only an 80 percent success rate. Next, I gave him spelling words, taken from his oral information on football. He had five words to study for next session: Dallas, cowboys, football, points, and huddle. Richard relaxed and smiled.

"I'll really get credit for this?"

"Not only will you receive credit, but the more you work, the more information you will relearn and remember."

As the months passed, I added other subjects such as health, science and current events using the newspaper, *TV Guide,* and *Sports Illustrated.* These areas were modified to suit Richard's interests, pace and abilities. Our one-hour sessions turned into two-hour sessions. Richard's mother was thrilled; not only was Richard proving his doctors wrong by gaining physical strength, he also gained a new attitude toward schoolwork.

The end of the first year was quickly approaching. Richard's relearning was slow, but at a steady pace. There was much time spent on review of all information because his short-term memory hampered rapid progress.

The summer passed quickly. In September of the second year, I walked into Richard's house and, to my surprise, he was in a wheelchair, waiting for me at the kitchen table. He had had intense physical, occupational and recreational therapy during the summer months. Richard had gained weight and started to resemble the picture on his nightstand. His speech had also improved, although he still talked too fast, forgetting to breathe correctly.

I saw he had completed every page of the books I had left him over the summer months. Richard was ready for his new school year. Although he was not ready for high school texts, his evaluations on the Woodcock Reading Test and Key Math Test showed an approximate fifth-grade level in reading skills and a sixth-grade level in math skills — a marked improvement.

We sat, side by side, the first few weeks of school. Richard worked diligently on his tracking and subject areas. Yet I could tell he had other things on his mind.

"Richard," I asked one day, "What are you thinking about?"

"My friends," he answered. "I don't know why they don't return my calls."

We just talked the rest of the session. Richard understood that his friends had graduated high school last year. He realized it had been over three years since his accident. Now that he was going to be 19, shouldn't he be driving, working and meeting girls? Richard willingly shared his concerns.

"This will come in time, Richard," I said. "Try to concentrate on your studies."

But soon I found Richard relating all of his assignments either to girls or sex. I knew I had to speak to his mother when Richard handed me a picture of an erupting volcano that more than resembled a fiery erection spurting out of a bulging mountainside; that was one phallus too many.

After I talked with Richard's mother about Richard's current social needs, she decided to enter him into a new five-month rehabilitation program in the foothills of the Appalacian Mountains some 200 miles away. It offered intense therapy, educational services, and social interaction; it was perfect for his need for independence.

Richard's mother contacted me five months later, to let me know Richard would like to have one more year of homebound instruction. It would be his senior year toward graduation.

In September of that year, I drove up Richard's driveway and noticed a tall, stocky, blond-haired young man shooting baskets through a basketball net. I thought, "How nice, a neighbor is visiting Richard." When I got out of the car, this young man turned around, grinned widely, and yelled, "Hey there — Mrs. Macciomei ... *catch!*"

I couldn't even raise my arms to catch the ball that Richard was throwing me. I just stared at him with tears in my eyes.

"Play a little hoop with me, Nancy."

I kicked off my shoes, staring and smiling at Richard. There I was, shooting a few baskets in my stocking feet with a person who only five months ago had been in a wheelchair. Richard's hair had turned blond during his stay in the mountains, and he was extremely muscular from lifting weights and swimming. He was not only walking; he was running. I let him shoot a few more baskets and then told him we should talk about school.

Richard, his mother and I discussed our goals for this year and for graduation. He had had a full educational program in the mountains and received good grades as well as credit for his junior year. I felt Richard was ready for a pre-vocational evaluation through the public schools.

As his senior year continued, we focused on a strict vocational curriculum. Richard began a training program through Goodwill and learned to fix bicycles and other small machinery. His motivation and physical endurance were excellent and his goal seemed closer at hand — to graduate high school.

On June 4, I sat on the bleachers at the local high school with Richard's mother. We cried through the entire graduation ceremony. When Richard's name was called, we jumped up and cheered, as he proudly took his hard-earned steps to the platform.

Perhaps Richard never will regain his full intellectual skills. But he defied the odds; this nursing home candidate was now a healthy, productive high school graduate. I knew that Richard now had a second chance at the life he almost lost.

7. Terminal Illness

Children with terminal illnesses have special problems associated with physical, emotional, social and educational adjustment. During their illness they are entitled to receive the same free and appropriate opportunities for instruction as any other homebound student.

This chapter focuses on terminal illnesses encountered in homebound practice and the many roles of homebound teachers in dealing with terminally ill students. Covered are muscular dystrophy, cystic fibrosis, Friedreich's ataxia, cancer, leukemia, and AIDS. We also examine the experience of death and dying in terms of coping with the family bereavement.

By way of introducing this topic, consider the reality of a normally intelligent student afflicted with a terminal disease. How does she make each day count? How do other people view her situation, including her parents, friends and teachers? We see in the case of Stacy how people treat her differently because she is ill, and the value she places on "thinking healthy."

CASE EIGHT: STACY
by Eleanor Harris, Homebound Teacher,
Charlotte-Mecklenburg (N.C.) Schools.

The day I met Stacy was the same day she was interviewed by a reporter from *The News*. Stacy sat, tied upright in her wheelchair, with her shriveled little legs covered by a thin blanket. Her eyes twinkled in her elongated but not unattractive face. "What do you most dislike people to do when they meet you?" asked the reporter.

"Pat me on the head," was Stacy's quick reply. "It makes me feel like a dog."

"What do you do when they pat you on the head?" the woman continued.

"I bark," Stacy returned with a laugh.

I learned that Stacy had Werdnig-Hoffman muscular dystrophy and had not been expected to live to start school at age 6. Now she was entering high school. I was to be her teacher because she was excellent in math, which was my specialty.

As I got to know Stacy better, I continued to be amazed by her sense of humor and courage. When she was not tied upright in her wheelchair, her head rested on its arm. With her emaciated and twisted little body,

Stacy was more affected physically by her illness than any other student I ever encountered on homebound. Despite this, she showed a strong personality. She also was never afraid to be realistic about her life and her world.

Each summer Stacy went to a camp for children with muscular dystrophy. There was one other girl at the camp with Stacy's type of dystrophy. They would greet each other with the exclamation, "Are you still alive? You were supposed to have died years ago." It delighted Stacy immensely to have outfoxed the doctors. This attitude, I believe, contributed greatly to her comparatively long life.

Stacy also desired to be as much like other people her age as possible. She wanted to visit her classes at school and to know all of her classmates. When she was in the eighth grade, the yearbook was dedicated to her, and when a senior in high school, she attended every special senior activity. For example, she took her father to the prom, where they demonstrated "wheelchair dancing."

Each year Stacy would get so excited about camp that she would get sick while there and have to spend a few days in the hospital. I worried about her health, although she shrugged off these setbacks. Her philosophy was bold: "Nobody can live more than one day at a time."

One summer at muscular dystrophy camp, Stacy met Nick, a young lifeguard who wanted to become a doctor. He and Stacy became fast friends. He began calling Stacy each day and visiting her regularly. He took her out to dinner so often that they became well known at popular night spots. Stacy knew all the waiters and bartenders by name. Nick never attended medical school, but he did become a pharmaceutical salesman and stayed in close contact with Stacy.

When Nick got married, Stacy was in the wedding. Her mother prepared a dress just like that of the other bridesmaids, and Stacy rolled down the aisle in her wheelchair. Her shiny blonde hair was slightly curled. Tied upright in her chair, she held her head high, and was in good spirits. For this young woman, who made the National Honor Society, graduated high school and is still alive today, taking "one day at a time" made sense; it also taught others around her to make the most of every single minute in her presence.

Muscular Dystrophy

There is no single disease called "muscular dystrophy." The term designates a group of muscle-destroying disorders which vary in hereditary pattern, age of onset, initial muscles attacked, and rate of progression. Following are the main disorders under the rubric of muscular dystrophy:
1. Duchenne Muscular Dystrophy (Pseudohypertrophic).
2. Facio-Scapula-Humeral (Landbuzy-Dejerine).
3. Limb-Girdle (Juvenile Dystrophy of erb).
4. Myotonic Dystrophy (Steiners Disease).
5. Friedreich's Ataxia (Spinal Muscular Atrophy).
6. Peroneal Muscular Atrophy (Charcot-Marie-Tooth Disease).

7. Infantile Progressive Spinal Muscular Atrophy (Werdnig-Hoffman Disease).

Etiology

Causes of Duchenne muscular dystrophy, the most common type, are unknown. However, research shows it to be an inherited disease affecting mostly males. As muscles are replaced by fatty tissue, the child's walk will resemble a duck's, and he will have difficulty rising from a lying down position. The child may "walk-up" his body with his hands. This "walking-up" is called *Gower's sign*. Pain, especially in the legs, is common.

Muscle weakness typically is evident as the disease progresses, and affected children first use a wheelchair by early adolescence. Because this disease affects all muscles, including those of the heart and diaphragm, control over body functions and of respiration remain at constant risk.

Prognosis

Over a period of time, dystrophic individuals become weaker and less mobile. Elevated levels of creatine phosphokinase (CPK) are found in the blood. This enzyme is released by weakened muscle cells. A biopsy determines the severity of overall muscular condition.

The course of muscular dystrophy is predicted by stages of functional ability. Stages range from ambulation with lordosis (stage 1), to independence in a wheelchair (stage 5), to confinement in bed and complete dependency (stage 8) (Bleck & Nagel, 1975). Death usually occurs in the final stage from respiratory or cardiac failure, between ages 17 and 25.

The loss of muscular control over basic motor functions is highly distressing to patient and family. Consequently, interim treatment attempts to ensure the student's mobility and independence for as long as possible.

The homebound program is interwoven in the fabric of these life circumstances, providing at best a curriculum for cognitive stimulation. But this is only one among many concurrent tasks of teaching. Dystrophic children desperately need reminders of their independence. For example, let the children try to accomplish tasks by themselves, even if it is easier and quicker for you to do the tasks. It is also important that the student get out of the wheelchair, lying on the carpet, blanket or floor to stretch out.

When weakness is severe, try pairing up the dystrophic child with other children for a peer-learning experience. Intelligence of dystrophic students is unaffected, and curriculum planning, with or without other peers, basically follows regular grade-level work. Another important rule is to judge the quality of work rather than quantity.

Curriculum modifications no doubt are inevitable and depend upon the teacher's creativity in helping the student deal with unpleasant and restrictive physical circumstances. In the case of Diane, creativity stimulated the otherwise painful existence of a dystrophic child connected to an iron lung.

CASE NINE: DIANE

It was a hot September day. The black interior of my Camaro intensified the humid 92 degrees outside. As I drove up the street that led to my first student of the year, I couldn't help wishing school were postponed until this heat wave ended. I pulled into their driveway and tried to repair my appearance. If my new student would see me as a large, sweaty teacher, at least I might look large, sweaty and *neat*. I knocked on the front door.

The door opened. I looked down to find a chubby little black boy with ice cream all over his face. I tried to contain my chuckle, but it slipped out. He asked me if I was Diane's teacher. I asked where his mother was. "She's workin', sombody's got to make some money!" With that he took me to meet Diane.

As we approached her room I could hear a loud, continuous "whoosh," as if air were slowly being sucked in and let out with one big push. We entered Diane's room, and her brother introduced me. I greeted Diane with a smile as I gazed around her room, inch by inch. It looked like many thirteen-year-old girls' rooms, with pictures of movie stars, stuffed soft animals, and a television. What was unusual was the huge, silver, oblong machine that stood on four legs above the floor. The "Whoosh" sound came from inside this machine. All that stuck out was Diane's small head, eyes facing the ceiling, and a type of rear view mirror that reflected images in the room and on the television.

No doubt about it: Diane was in the later stages of progressive muscular dystrophy. Her tiny, extremely frail body was wasting away as her disease became more pronounced. It was obvious that without this iron lung, Diane could not survive.

Diane welcomed me with a bright smile. She asked me to stand on her right side so she could get a good look at me. As I moved, I noticed the little window partition at the side of the iron lung. Although scarcely larger than a playing card, one quick glance through it disclosed Diane's devastating physical limitations. Her slender arms lay dormant next to her body. Her legs were stretched out, covered with a small blanket. The only evidence of movement was the slight upward and downward motion of her chest to the "Whoosh" sound of the iron lung. One thing became instantly clear: normal academic study was not for her. She needed simple day-to-day activities.

We talked about school, television shows, and her favorite hobby, which was baking cookies and cakes. Although she had been unable to help her mother in the last few months, she still enjoyed watching her mix up the ingredients and tasting the results. Baking was definitely Diane's favorite pastime. We decided that after some minor academic learning, we, too, might try baking a bit.

At first, our sessions were done orally; I stood on Diane's right side, directly behind her head, holding a book. As weeks progressed, we did less academics and spent more time discussing television shows and her family. This was an important decision for me; her emotional needs came first. Finally, my promise to start baking with her came true. We baked once a week, and this hobby soon became an obsession. Every session was a new experiment in the art of baking.

It was the session before Christmas break. I had a table set up on Diane's right side with all the ingredients for chocolate chip cookies. My favorite recipe was ready to be taught. In her high, squeaky voice, Diane pleaded with me to let her try to mix the soft ingredients. She told me of the door on the left side of the iron lung that could be quickly opened and shut. The bowl would just fit through it. I thought a moment and decided to try it. I realized just how quickly she meant when I opened the latch and the "whoosh" sound came to a dead halt.

Diane yelled, "Hurry, hurry shut the door!" I felt my heart beating a mile a minute; how could I let this happen to her? In my jerking motions to shut the door I spilled the cookie ingredients all over Diane's legs, the blanket, and the iron lung. It all happened so quickly. But I had to shut that latch. Then the chaos really began. True, the "whoosh" started up again, but Diane panicked and was crying hysterically. I didn't know what to do first, console Diane—or clean up the mess?

I came around to Diane's head, apologized and kissed her on the cheek. I spent the next hour cleaning the mixture of eggs, Crisco, and sugar off her legs, blanket and iron lung, quickly shutting the door between each wipe so the "whoosh" could continue. After the mess was finally cleaned and a new blanket placed over her frail body, we both knew the session was over.

I gathered my things, turned on the television and began to leave. Diane asked me to turn the light off. Without a moment's thought I reached for the nearest switch and shut if off. As I stepped into the hallway, I realized something was wrong. It dawned on me that the "whoosh" had stopped. My books, bowls, and utensils spilled to the ground with a crash as I made a mad dash back to Diane's room. I immediately turned her light on and restored electrical power to her iron lung. Diane sighed with relief and smiled as if to say, "It's the thought that counts."

Maybe. But what really counted was her affinity for enjoyment. I hoped I had helped to provide that enjoyment even with all of our mishaps that day.

Friedreich's Ataxia

Friedreich's ataxia is an inherited condition. It is progressive degeneration of the sensory cells in the dorsal ganglia and nerves to the limbs and trunk (peripheral nerves) (see Koehler, 1975). It affects both males and females equally. Symptoms are multiple but most surface during a person's teenage years or early twenties. Among the most common symptoms are gradual muscular discoordination (ataxia), involuntary movement of the eyeball (nystagmus), speech disorders, and eventual spinal deformities.

Associated problems arising include falling, clumsiness, and a shaky, sloppy handwriting. Curvature of the spine (scoliosis okyphosis) usually is present in teenagers and early adults.

Prognosis
Although causes are unknown, current research suggests a metabolic disorder. Progression of Friedreich's ataxia can be extremely rapid or quite slow. There may be seizures, inability to control blood sugar level, diminished visual acuity, and cognitive deterioration. Afflicted students resort to wheelchairs by their late teens. Death strikes them between their mid-twenties and late thirties.

Treatment
Physical and occupational therapy are a must. Therapy usually focuses on the orthopedic deformities developing as the disease enters into its later stages.

Most often, special education services for these children are readily available in every school district. They remain in regular classes as long as possible. Diminished muscular capacity slows their pace of learning, but through adaptations they can be more productive. For example, ataxic students can usually use an electric typewriter or computer to assist with daily homework. When adaptive means are no longer useful, homebound services commence.

Part of homebound addresses the emotional crisis present in the family. Family members may at first resent the child's increased dependency and be unprepared to reevaluate their own needs relative to a dying sibling or child. Physical decay in speech and mobility may alienate the adolescent, not only from family, but from peers as well, adding to the helplessness and depression.

Cystic Fibrosis

Cystic fibrosis is an hereditary disease affecting lung changes with a major presence of thick mucus. It involves all the secreting glands (except those that channel into the bloodstream). The mucus does not flow normally, leaving the lungs clogged. As time passes, mucus accumulation eventually blocks the lungs, preventing the passage of air. This results in infection or lung collapse.

Symptoms
Cystic fibrosis may be evident at birth or early childhood. Lung disease may manifest earlier due to serious respiratory infections. Even a simple

cold will turn into a persistent cough for several months, many times developing into pneumonia or bronchitis. Given this rapid pace, symptoms of cystic fibrosis may mimic symptoms of asthma. Examined to ascertain the diagnosis are internal organs such as the stomach, intestines, and pancreas. Other definite signs include a barrel-shaped chest. The extremities may be thin with rounded fingertips and toes.

Treatment
Emphasis in treatment is upon the lungs. Postural drainage and aerosolized treatments are common methods to clear the lungs. The child will have to sit in various positions to drain different areas of the lungs. Use of antibiotics also helps to prevent lung infection.

Prognosis
Even with early detection and treatment, the disease is progressive. What causes death is lack of oxygen, which almost immediately produces lung damage. Death usually occurs when the child is around 14 years old.

Educators aware of this progressive course of illness are in a better position to intervene. Fibrotic children generally have normal to high intelligence and in many cases are "brighter" than their healthy counterparts largely because their daily focus is on cognitive success rather than on physical success. When weakness prevails, homebound services commence. While at home, students should be encouraged to cough out all their mucus rather than stifling the cough. Place a bag and Kleenex box next to the working area for more convenience, so that the child will not have to run to the bathroom every few minutes. Also, permit the child to eat or drink during the session.

Cancer

Cancer can grow in any tissue or organ of the human body. The term "cancer" refers to a group of diseases. Shimken (1980) describes cancer as the abnormal, unrestricted growth of body cells, with the resultant mass compressing, invading and destroying contiguous normal tissues. Cancer cells then break off or leave the original mass and are carried by the blood or lymph to distant sites of the body. Cancers are classified by their appearance under the microscope, and by site of the body from which they arise. Let us consider a main type of cancer, solid tumors.

Solid Tumors

Solid tumors usually arise in one or many organs of the body. They are due to excessive, abnormal cell growth. Tumors that are benign are dangerous only if they interfere with bodily functions. Benign tumors can be removed surgically. By contrast, malignant tumors pose serious life-threatening risks. If not removed or treated, the malignancy may spread to various parts of the body through the lympathic system or bloodstream. Malignant tumors further give rise to secondary tumors.

Three areas in the body that commonly house solid tumors are the brain, kidneys and the bones. With solid tumors, particularly brain tumors, surgery is a precarious but needed procedure. One obvious danger with neurosurgery is the agitation or near-destruction of contiguous brain tissue. When tumors are inoperable, children might receive radiation therapy.

Leukemia

Leukemia is a cancer of the body tissues that produce blood, found in the bone marrow, spleen, and lymph nodes. This type of cancer arises from the overproduction of white blood cells.

Lack of normal cells causes various physical symptoms such as fatigue, anemia, bruising, fever and discomfort. Since newly produced cells are not mature, they cannot fight infection in the body. This is why children with leukemia become very sick from otherwise normal illnesses; the immune system is weak.

Leukemia in almost all children is acute. Rarely is the disease in chronic form. In chronic leukemia, blood cells progress very slowly; in acute leukemia, blood cells progress rapidly, and life expectancy can be short.

Types of Leukemia

There are two main types of leukemia: lymphocytic and granulocytic. Lymphocytic is an increased number of white blood cells produced in lymph nodes. Granulocytic is an increase of the number of white blood cells produced in the bone marrow. Normal granulocytes are essential to the body's defense against infection; persons with abnormal granulocytes lack this defense capability.

There is a third type, monocytic leukemia, but it accounts for less than five percent of cases. It involves white blood cells called monocytes and has acute phases.

Treatment

The goal of treatment is to suppress symptoms into remission. Chemical therapy attempts to interfere with reproduction of leukemic cells. Drugs may cause an initial remission, but they are toxic and have adverse side-effects. Among common side-effects are pain, nausea, hair loss, swelling, loss of appetite, and occasional kidney damage. As with any cancer, radiation treatment is available; radiation is applied to the head and spinal cord to prevent further nervous system damage.

Prognosis

Prognosis can differ depending on certain factors. Miller (1980) suggests that white cell count, platelet count, hemoglobin, age, sex and enlargement of glands predict a good or poor prognosis. Interestingly, the outlook on leukemic children has been quite optimistic over the last three decades. Prior to 1950, most affected children died in a matter of a few months. By 1977, more than half of the common type of leukemia cases had survival rates over five years. Treated leukemia also delays death and can generate 50 to 70 percent long-term remissions lasting at least five years. The most favorable prognosis occurs in females over the age of three and under the age of ten.

Remission and Relapse

Children with acute leukemia enter treatment with remission as the goal. Complete remission refers to the disappearance of leukemic cells from the bone marrow and blood. Bone marrow then resumes production of normal red blood cells, white blood cells, and platelets. Completed remission usually is the result of intensive chemotherapy. More than 90 percent of all children with acute lymphoblastic leukemia achieve remission within a matter of weeks after diagnosis and initiation of chemotherapy.

The remainder of leukemic children risk a remanifestation of the disease after weeks and months. This is due to the fact that not all of the leukemic cells are entirely destroyed. Even in remission, small numbers of leukemic cells lie dormant. Children who take medication while in remission can significantly reduce this risk of relapse, even after a seemingly complete remission occurs.

Relapse symptoms should be detected immediately. They include signs such as extreme fatigue, pallor, increased bruising, prolonged fevers, or infections. Treatment is repeated with the same goal of achieving remission.

Families who bravely hope and pray for a remission are devastated by signs of relapse. Again the family must face the undesirable prospects of pain and death. For some children, death comes after the first relapse, while for others death is after many vicious cycles of remissions and relapses.

Despair can ruin the child's belief in recovery and should be counterbalanced by a stimulating atmosphere of school. Leukemic children desperately need to feel a part of normal activities, with normal expectations. Homebound provides this normalization process. Children continue to develop despite their decaying condition. Each session should be a challenge and should include socialization, leisure and academics. Sometimes against parents' wishes that their children be spared of school stress, it is important that homebound remove the boredom and anxiety of children besieged by helplessness.

Parents who take an active role in their chilren's temporary healing want to be very close to them. When children are hospitalized, extra beds for parents are now a standard option; parents can spend the night near the bedside of their loved ones. Another familial activity for leukemic children is special camps, organizations and retreats especially designed with medical accommodations. An option of enormous popularity is the Ronald McDonald Houses. There are three dozen cities in the United States that offer accommodations in Ronald McDonald houses, with extensions in Canada and Australia.

AIDS

Acquired Immune Deficiency Syndrome, or AIDS, is a serious, highly communicable disease that eliminates the body's ability to fight infection. The world today is unfortunately in the midst of an AIDS epidemic about which educators and consumers alike are in varying degrees of ignorance. Fear, perhaps, is the greatest cause for the spread of rumors, stereotypes and misrepresentative information. The public's fear of AIDS trickles down to the student afflicted by this disease and biases the professionals upon whom students depend.

The two diseases most often associated with AIDS are a lung infection called pneumocystis carinii pneumonia, and a rare form of cancer called Kaposi's sarcoma. It is these diseases, not the AIDS virus itself, that can lead to death.

Etiology

The cause of AIDS is a virus called Human T-Cell Lymphotropic Virus (HTLV-III). This virus alters the structure of the cell it attacks. Infection with the virus can produce AIDS or a less severe condition known as AIDS-Related Complex (ARC). "Acquired" means the disease is passed from one person to another. It is not hereditary. "Immune deficiency" means the body's defense system is defective.

The first stage of AIDS is the Human Immunodeficiency Virus (HIV) infection. Spread of this virus to the brain invades the nucleus of the neurons and changes RNA to DNA. Consequently the person develops a propensity toward an HIV infection. Transmission of the infection occurs in one of three ways: through blood-to-blood contact (e.g. transfusion), through sexual intercourse, and through the birth canal. Variations of sexual transmission do occur, and educators are advised to read available research or governmental booklets for an update on facts.

Symptoms

Following are common signs of the AIDS virus, though this is certainly not an exhaustive list:

1. Unexplained, persistent fatigue.
2. Unexplained fever, night sweating, and chills for several weeks.
3. Sudden and unexplained weight loss of ten pounds or more.
4. Diarrhea that persists for several weeks.
5. A dry persistent cough.
6. Purple or pink spots and bumps on or under the skin, inside the mouth, nose or around the eyes.
7. White spots around or in the mouth that persist for weeks.
8. Subtle changes in thinking, becoming easily distractible.
9. Motor disturbances.
10. Behavioral disturbance in the form of social withdrawal, extreme apathy, agitation, or paranoid delusions.

Diagnosis

Prominent forms of the AIDS virus are detectable through an AIDS virus antibody test. Antibodies, again, fight off bacteria or anything else that is not supposed to be in the bloodstream. Test results *only* indicate if the person is infected with the AIDS virus. Positive results do not automatically mean that person will develop AIDS. Positive results nonetheless are a cue that preventive action should be considered. Recommendations by the Harris County Medical Society (1987) for delaying onset of AIDS include:

1. Eat a well balanced diet.
2. Avoid drug abuse which can damage immune system.
3. Get plenty of rest and exercise.
4. Avoid or reduce stress.
5. Think positively.
6. Contact a physician who can provide follow-up care and regular check-ups.
7. Consider joining a peer-support group or seeking professional counseling.

Individuals with AIDS may display acute sensitivity to any social reminder of their incapacitation. Hearing news of AIDS on the radio or in conversation with friends may arouse self-doubt and depression. Families informed of their children's condition are at first baffled. Was my six-year-old child having sex with somebody? In teenagers or early adults there is talk of suicide, of refusal to suffer the pain and humiliation ahead of them. At these times the teacher's best direction is twofold. Either refer the child, adult or family to counseling, *or* try to dismantle the moral questions of the situation, focusing more on the facts.

Prognosis

At present there is no vaccine to prevent AIDS. There is also no cure. At high risk according to United States surgeon general reports are three broad categories of individuals: male homosexuals, intravenous drug users, and newborn offspring of IV drug users. Moderate-risk groups are hemophiliacs, and health care workers in direct contact with the HIV infection.

Strategies and Prevention

Knowing the facts can overcome the many irrational and debilitating fears. One solution, mentioned earlier, was counseling. But this is after learning of the contracted virus. Early prevention is another alternative, by identifying high- and moderate-risk groups and their involvement in educational awareness. Properly informing students, parents and professionals among the referral network begins with a no-nonsense dismissal of myths about AIDS. Consider, for example, the following three myths and facts that dispute them:

Myth: Aids can be transmitted by casual contact with an infected person: such as a handshake, a cough, or a sneeze. AIDS can be transmitted, also, by sharing food, dishes, bathrooms, and swimming pools.

Fact: All evidence indicates that the AIDS virus cannot be transmitted by air, food, or water. Evidence shows that it cannot penetrate intact human skin. It is spread by unprotected sexual intercourse, by sharing intravenous needles and syringes, and by an infected mother to her unborn child. There is not a single documented case of AIDS transmitted by routine contact at home, work or school. In numerous studies of families caring for AIDS patients at home, AIDS has never occurred in a family member who was not the sexual partner of an infected person or the newborn child of an infected woman.

Myth: Children with AIDS should be barred from schools to protect other children.

Fact: AIDS is not transmitted by casual contact in any setting and scientists know of no case of AIDS ever transmitted from one child to another at school. Certain circumstances may require

            special education or homebound arrangements for a child with
            AIDS, but the vast majority of children infected with AIDS
            virus can attend school without posing any risk to their
            classmates or teachers.

    Myth: Kissing is very dangerous and can pass the virus that causes
            AIDS.
    Fact: Of the 41,000 cases of AIDS in the United States, not one has
            been traced to kissing or saliva transmission. The AIDS virus
            rarely appears in the saliva of infected persons and then in
            very tiny amounts. In studies of people living with AIDS pa-
            tients, no one became infected after sharing food, dishes or
            glasses.

The serious stigma attached to an AIDS victim clearly, then, is owing to ignorance. Because the psychological stress is almost as severe as the disease itself, homebound education and teacher support become crucial in the student's transition welcoming students back into the classroom. Lack of support, coupled with suspicion of AIDS children, forces repression of the angry child's feelings and eventual alienation from his peer group. Under pressure from the federal government, public school systems now are mandated to respond to these needs. Legislation must be established that secures educational opportunities and protects the rights of infected students.

Regulations such as those in Table 7.1, from Charlotte-Mecklenburg schools in North Carolina, specifically address committee formation, dissemination of AIDS information, and proper steps to ensure appropriate education.

Clearly, AIDS is no longer the concern of just a few groups in society. In 1988, AIDS became a national health priority proportional to the rising number of reported cases. This medical exigency is responsible for advanced efforts to isolate, evaluate and administer a cure. In the meantime, students infected by AIDS are entitled to compassion, understanding and the positive outlook teachers give to other terminally ill students.

Death and Dying

The idea of death is still a taboo in our society. Death seems more acceptable when an aged person dies of natural causes after a long and fruitful life. When a terminally ill child is dying, that's "not the way it's supposed to be." Parents grow up expecting to witness deaths of their elders, and themselves to die before their offspring. Reversal of this process is more than a shock; it strikes people as unnatural.

Hope seems an essential component for living. When there is little

Education of Students with the Communicable Disease Acquired Immune Deficiency Syndrome (AIDS) or AIDS Related Complex (ARC)

The process for each principal to follow in best determining on an individual basis whether a student with AIDS/ARC needs a more restrictive educational placement is as follows:

(1) Each case will be evaluated by an interdisciplinary committee comprised of the student's personal physician, teacher, school principal (or designee), school nurse, and the local health director (or designee). Consultation may also be obtained from other sources, such as a physician with expertise in managing communicable disease cases and the Head of the Communicable Disease Control Branch of the North Carolina Division of Health Services.

(2) Parents will be informed of the entire procedure at the outset of the review process. They will be given the right to bring any person(s) they wish to the interdisciplinary committee meeting. They will be informed of their right to appeal the committee's decision to the Board of Education.

(3) The committee will make recommendations to the principal concerning the placement of the student and will conduct periodic reevaluation of the case, since the student's condition may either improve or worsen over time. The deliberations and recommendations of this committee are to be confidential.

It is the responsibility of the principal to ensure that appropriate and periodic reevaluations are conducted and current medical reports are maintained and filed in the school office. The student's records will be kept confidential.

(4) If deemed appropriate by the committee, a student in a high risk situation may be temporarily removed from the classroom until a school program adjustment can be made, an alternative education program can be established or until it is determined that the risk has abated and the student can return to the classroom. Alternative educational programs shall approximate as much as possible the instruction the student would receive in the regular classroom.

(5) All cases of AIDS/ARC are to be reported to the superintendent. In addition, school officials are required to report certain diseases, including AIDS, to the local Health Department.[1] Confidentiality of such reports is protected by law,[2] and officials cannot be held liable for reporting.[3]

[1]See G.S.130A-136
[2]See G.S.130A-143
[3]See G.S.130A-142

Table 7.1. Charlotte-Mecklenburg (N.C.) regulations for the education of students with AIDS.

hope for a terminally ill child, families must recognize that death may occur at any time. Making plans, and explaining death to the child and parents, is not an honor. But sometimes it is as much a homebound teacher's duty as selecting the right curriculum.

Telling the Child

One of the most difficult questions teachers have to answer for the parent is, "What do I tell my child?" Parents wonder whether to tell the truth and how to explain the disease. Decisions usually vary with the child's age, religion, and parents' coping skills. There is no one right way to do it. Where divulging this information might aggravate the physical condition, parents often choose to delay or be evasive about details.

Teachers should not take for granted that children are informed. But at times, in fact quite frequently, the most knowledgeable persons are the children, who withhold details from their parents so as not to scare them. In years past, parents rarely told the children the diagnosis and prognosis. With the current trend toward open parent-child communication, however, discussions about death, fears of loss, and the demands of family recovery are more frequent.

Death of a Classmate

Most often the dying child at one time was at one time part of a normal classroom. A mainstreamed child naturally draws attention to his or her sudden or prolonged absence. Classmates who inquire about the absence are at the mercy of teachers who decide when and how to discuss death. One solution is leading a discussion about death, perhaps with an invited speaker; still another is creating a project of papers, movies and field trips concerning terminal illness or the concept of death.

One such project begins with the following personal questionnaire concerning the reactions to loss and grief. Breaking the students into two groups, teachers then lead a discussion based on replies to the survey. It is important not to force students to reveal their survey replies.

Questionnaire:
Dying, Death, and Grief

Please circle one answer for each question.

1. To the best of your memory, at what age were you first aware of death?
   a. under three   b. three to five   c. five to ten   d. ten or older

2. What was your own first personal involvement with death or grief?
   a. grandparents   b. parent   c. brother or sister   d. pet

3. When was your last personal involvement with death or grief?
   a. within the past six months   b. within the last year   c. two years   d. more than five years

4. When you were a child, how was death talked about in your family?
   a. openly   b. with some sense of discomfort   c. only when necessary   d. as though it were a taboo subject, or not at all

5. Which best describes your childhood conceptions of death?
   a. heaven and hell concept   b. after-life   c. death as sleep
   d. mysterious

6. Which of the following most influenced your present attitudes toward death?
   a. death of someone close   b. specific reading   c. religious
   upbringing   d. introspection and meditation   e. rituals

Give your honest reaction to the following four statements:

7. The fear of death never bothers me.
   a. very strongly agree   b. agree   c. neutral   d. disagree
   e. strongly disagree

8. I fear dying a painful death.
   a. strongly agree   b. agree   c. neutral   d. disagree
   e. strongly disagree

9. I often think about how short life really is.
   a. strongly agree   b. agree   c. neutral   d. disagree
   e. strongly disagree

10. I shudder when I hear people talking about nuclear destruction or World War III.
    a. strongly agree   b. agree   c. neutral   d. disagree
    e. strongly disagree

11. To what extent has the possibility of human destruction by nuclear war influenced your present attitudes toward death or life?
    a. enormously   b. moderately   c. somewhat   d. very little

12. How often do you think about your own death?
    a. very frequently   b. occasionally   c. rarely   d. never

13. If you could choose, when would you die?
    a. in youth   b. in the middle or "prime" of life   c. after the "prime" of life   d. old age

14. When do you believe that, in fact, you will die?
    a. in youth   b. in the middle or "prime" of life   c. after the "prime" of life   d. old age

15. Has there been a time in your life when you wanted to die?
    a. yes, due to physical pain   b. yes, due to emotional upset
    c. yes, due to an intolerable social situation   d. yes, due to great embarrassment

16. What does death mean to you?
    a. the end; the final process of life   b. the beginning of a life after death   c. a joining of the spirit with a universal cosmic consciousness   d. termination yet with survival of the spirit   e. other (explain) _____

17. What aspect of your own death is the most distasteful to you?
    a. I could no longer have any experiences   b. I am afraid of what
    might happen to my body after death   c. I am uncertain as to
    what might happen to me if there is a life after death   d. I could
    no longer provide for my family   e. it would cause grief to
    my relatives and friends

18. In your opinion, at what age are people most afraid of death?
    a. up to 12 years   b. 13 to 19 years   c. 20 to 29 years
    d. 30 to 39 years   e. 40 to 49 years   f. 50 to 59 years
    g. 60 and up

19. How often have you been in a situation in which you seriously
    thought you might die?
    a. many times   b. several times   c. once or twice   d. never

20. If you had a choice, what kind of death would you prefer?
    a. tragic, violent death   b. sudden but not violent death
    c. quiet, dignified death

21. If it were possible, would you want to know the exact date on which
    you are going to die?
    a. yes   b. no

22. If you were told that you had a terminal disease and a limited time
    to live, how would you want to spend your time until you died?
    a. I would make a marked change in my life-style   b. I would
    become more withdrawn   c. I would shift from my own needs to
    a concern for others   d. I would attempt to complete projects; tie
    up loose ends   e. I would make little or no change in my life-style

23. How do you feel about having an autopsy done on your body?
    a. approve   b. don't care   c. disapprove

24. Was this survey difficult to react to?
    a. yes   b. no   c. on a few questions

Next, have each student find current, relevant articles from any
newspaper that depict a loss, grief or death and instruct them to write or
verbally describe their opinions. News-clippings and pictures then are
posted so each student can react to them.

Beyond a cognitive appreciation, actual experience puts peers in touch
with their feelings immediately. Adolescents, for instance, may find attending the funeral or memorial service a valued expression of their sorrow.
Gifts, attendance to the household and visits to the cemetery border on
strong reality exposure but are far from morbid.

Affected classmates eagerly see resolution of their emotions from the
teacher's outlook on death. At times, though, the person most affected is
the teacher.

Homebound teachers can grow closely attached to their students. Like the passing of a friend, the death of a student touches a sensitive nerve ending for the teacher who has become part of the family.

CASE TEN: URLENE

Spring came early in the South that year. The few mild winter months seemed to surrender to stifling heat and humidity. I could taste the dust while driving along a winding country road. As I approached the driveway of the church, the cars crowding the parking lot seemed to raise the temperature another ten degrees. Men in three-piece, dark suits directed the traffic. I reflected on how many people must have known and been touched by one strong-willed, fourteen-year-old girl.

Urlene was a typical teenager. She loved romance novels, soap operas, and stuffed animals. She dreamed of being a model, a teacher, or just a girl in love. Most of the time, Urlene would argue with her mother, which she secretly enjoyed, or get an attitude that would make the most patient person angry and frustrated.

I began to teach Urlene when she was no longer able to go to school. As her homebound teacher, I came to her house every other day, for two years, and tutored her in each subject area required for school. We talked about everything that enters a teenager's mind — even about her cancer, which became increasingly worse. Becoming familiar with her mother, brother, stepfather and grandparents, I was able to understand Urlene's world through her eyes.

During most sessions, I could smell the evening meal being prepared. Urlene's mother was a great cook. Throughout the two years I tasted a lot of her Southern cooking. I remember tasting the bouncing pigs' feet that were boiling in her large, black pot; Urlene and her family always teased me about that day.

I parked my car and walked toward the church. To the right of the church was a farmer plowing his acres. On my left, across the parking lot, cows were enjoying their lunch in the sunshine. The Carolina skies were blue, the grass thick and green. It was a hot spring day to most, but to me it was the final day of a very special teacher-student relationship.

I sat, sweaty and nervous, on the pew between two large, perspiring elderly women. The index card I was clutching became ragged and wet as I anticipated the next few minutes. I had memorized my one-minute speech, but felt insecure about delivering it on this solemn occasion. I had never done this before.

I remembered when Urlene's mother had asked me to say a few words at the funeral. I had mixed feelings. Was it all right for a Jewish Midwestern teacher to speak at a Southern Baptist funeral? I was assured it was what Urlene would have wanted.

Slowly, I looked around the crowded wooden church. Friends, family, school children and community members stood against the walls of the undersized, sweltering sanctuary. The young children, in their Sunday best, held onto flowers while their older siblings and parents were openly displaying their grief.

Gradually, I made contact with the saddened eyes of the congregation. The nurses from the local hospice noticed my gaze and offered me a sad smile. I was sure they knew that Urlene loved to work with her hands and had made many toys for the neighborhood children. She even made a Christmas tape for my own son, with Alvin and the Chipmunks singing favorite seasonal songs. Urlene's original commentary made each song special. My son and I will always treasure that tape.

Soon, the organ began playing and the procession of flower girls entered the church. Each girl carried delicate flowers and laid them carefully on Urlene's casket. The five female members of the choir, all portly women, sang euphonious praises as the congregation wept. These spirited women moved their hips and arms to the music they made while the congregation shouted, "Amen," and "Praise the Lord."

I sat on the edge of my seat, aware that my turn to speak was next on the agenda. The minister, with his shiny slicked-back hair and flowing black robe, came forward and introduced me to the mourners. My knees felt weak and my throat was dry. As I began to rise, the two ladies on each side gave me a supportive smile, and I walked to the front of the congregation. I stood next to the casket in which Urlene lay peacefully. Her struggle was over. I noticed she was wearing the necklace I had bought for her birthday. We had shared a lot in the recent past.

My eulogy was brief, yet I was moved by the bond all of us shared — the loss of this teenager. I no longer felt the ethnic and religious differences. I never looked at the crushed index card. When I finished, I kissed the surviving parents and younger brother, and then found my seat. I glanced up to see teachers, principals, and young friends from the elementary and junior high school that Urlene had attended. The community, young and old, had gathered to bid a final farewell to Urlene.

Out of the forty students I had that year, I took pride in knowing just one very special teenager; I hope that memory never fades.

This chapter explored the hidden reality of homebound students with terminal illness. Coping with infected students as they progress in and out of remission takes a toll on the family, the friends and teachers. Reviewed were common diseases confronted including muscular dystrophy, cystic fibrosis, Friedreich's ataxia, cancer, leukemia and AIDS. Topics covered besides prognosis and treatment were the experiential hardship of death and dying and the role of homebound instruction.

Moved by these guidelines, educators considering a homebound caseload face the most spectacular challenge of being in a family teaching environment. Out of the classroom and into the natural learning setting is not like "out of the frying pan and into the fire." Quite the contrary. There is an inherently rewarding experience not available in regular teaching. It is the experience of knowing *you really make a difference*. Teachers act in multiple capacities, in multiple settings, for the ultimate victory of curing a disabled student of a disabled mind. Stimulated education preserves the thinking, feeling and behaving side of students so they will remember how to be strong in their years ahead.

Appendix A: State Legislation on Homebound Teaching

The following is a compilation of each state's special education rules and regulations concerning the Homebound Program. We hope to display, through a comparative review, that there is much that is noteworthy in the homebound/hospital programs across the country. There is a definite population that requires fully developed programs serviced by professionals certified in special education.

Our reserach showed that each state adheres at least to the minimum legislation of P.L. 94-142. Surprisingly, many states have expanded their regulations beyond the federal requirements. Further, most states combine homebound programs with hospital programs. A few states, such as Michigan, have separate booklets on their homebound programs.

Entries for each state contain the following categories: departmental office address, legislative package title, date legislation was effective, and teacher certification requirements. Interesting features in state legislation are also discussed where appropriate.

ALABAMA

State of Alabama, Department of Education, Montgomery, Alabama 36130. Package Title: Alabama State Department of Education Division of Student Instructional Services Program for Exceptional Children and Youth Administrative Policy Manual, Bulletin Number 36. Date Effective: 1986.

State Definition. Homebound/hospital services: Special education students whose special education needs cannot be met within a school facility program may be served within the home or other non-school environment if the IEP committee determines that it is the student's least restrictive environment. There will be two contact sessions per week for a total of at least 180 minutes per week. If pursuing the diploma option, students must receive the coursework required to earn the appropriate number of units in grades 9–12.

Teacher Certification. The public education agency superintendent is responsible for appointing a qualified person to provide the services specified by the student's IEP committee.

Interesting Features in State Legislation. Regular education students who are performing satisfactorily in a regular school program do not become eligible for special education services just because they may have a temporary health or medical problem which requires a temporary recuperative period. These students are best served by the regular education program.

147

ALASKA

Department of Education, P.O. Box F, Juneau, Alaska 99811. Package Title: Title IV Education Regulations, Chapter 52: Education for Exceptional Children. Date Effective: April 1987.

State Definition. Homebound/hospital instruction means an individualized special education program provided to a child with a handicap that prevents the child from attending a regular or special education program even with the aid of special transportation when the multidisciplinary evaluation and the resultant individualized education program indicate this program alternative as appropriate for meeting the child's needs; to fall within this definition, a child receiving homebound/hospital instruction must be provided for each day the child is unable to attend school. There must be a minimum of two hours of homebound/hospital instruction provided for each day the child is unable to attend school.

Teacher Certification. An Alaska teacher's certificate is required.

ARIZONA

Arizona Department of Education, C. Diane Bishop, Superintendent, 1535 West Jefferson Street, Phoenix, Arizona 85007. (602) 255-3183. Package Title: Administrative Rules and Regulations of the State Board of Education (R7-2-401-405). Date Effective: 1986.

State Definition: Homebound or hospitalized means a student who is capable of profiting from academic instruction but is unable to attend school due to illness, disease, accident, pregnancy, or handicapping condition who has been examined by a competent medical doctor and who is certified by that doctor as being unable to attend regular classes for a period of not less than three school months or a student who is capable of profiting from academic instruction but is unable to attend school regularly due to chronic or acute health problems who has been examined by a competent medical doctor and who is certified by that doctor as being unable to attend regular classes for intermittent periods of time totaling three school months during a school year.

Teacher Certification. A special education certificate is required.

ARKANSAS

Arkansas Department of Education, 4 State Capitol Mall, Little Rock, Arkansas 72201-1071. (501) 371-1461. Dr. Ruth Steele, Director. Package Title: Program Standards and Eligibility Criteria for Special Education. Date Effective: 1987.

State Definition. Hospital and/or homebound instruction is the instructional setting which is considered to be the most restrictive within the continuum of services in the least restrictive environment. For students receiving instruction within the hospital or homebound setting, the IEP and subsequent placement must be reviewed every three months. To assist in determining that any student 5 to 21 years of age, who, because of the severity of or the nature and/or extent of his handicapping condition, requires homebound or hospital instruction shall have his IEP implemented within his facility of confinement for as long as the handicapping condition prevents the student from safely and adequately attending school.

Teacher Certification. A homebound/hospital teacher must have an Arkansas Teacher Certificate and must be certified in at least one area of special education.

Interesting Features in State Legislation. The Arkansas Program Standards and Eligibility Criteria were well developed into easily identified information and outstanding programs. The package, in general, was very impressive.

CALIFORNIA

California State Department of Education, 721 Capitol Mall, Sacramento, California 95814; Bill Honig. Superintendent of Public Instruction. Package Title: California Special Education Programs: A composite of laws. Date Effective: 1988.

State Definition. Any student that is of our school for a designated period of time, for a medical reason, is eligible for the homebound program. As of this year, 1988, each county in California handles their own Home and Hospital Program. It is no longer a function of the special needs division.

Teacher Certification. A California teacher's certificate is required. Each county may request additional endorsements according to their specific stipulations for the Homebound program.

COLORADO

Colorado Department of Education, 201 E. Colfax Avenue, Denver, Colorado 80203. Package Title: Colorado Code of Regulations: 301-8. Date Effective: April 1987.

State Definition. When the child is not attending a private school or institutional program and his condition precludes him from attending a public school facility, then his educational needs may be served through the use of communication equipment linking his home to the regular classroom and/or the assignment of an itinerant homebound teacher.

Teacher Certification. Properly assigned home/hospital teachers are provided as needed to satisfy student needs, but they are not required to be endorsed in special education.

CONNECTICUT

Connecticut State Department of Education, Division of Education Support Services, Bureau of Special Education and Pupil Personnel Services. Packet Title: Regulations Concerning Children Requiring Special Education, Section 10-76a to 10-761, Inclusive of the General Statutes. Date Effective: September 1980.

State Definition. Homebound/hospitalized instruction shall be provided when a child's condition will cause an absence of at least three weeks' duration. Homebound instruction shall be provided for at least one hour per day or five hours per week for children in grades kindergarten through sixth grade; and at least two hours per day, or ten hours a week for children in grades seven through twelve.

Teacher Certification. Connecticut teacher's certificate is required.

DELAWARE

Department of Public Instruction, Townsend Building, Dover, Delaware 19901. Package Title: Administrative Manual: Programs for Exceptional Children. Date Effective: March 1987.

State Definition. Level VI is an alternative educational program provided at home, hospital, or related site. However, for those children hospitalized or at home for a sudden illness or accident considered to be of a temporary nature, procedures for placement shall be limited to medical certification that the child cannot attend school. The following weekly schedule of hours of instruction will be supported by state funds to the extent that appropriation allow: GRADES 1-5, three to five hours of instruction; GRADES 6-8, five to seven hours a week of instruction; GRADES 9-12, six to ten hours of instruction a week.

Teacher Certification. A teacher certificate in special education is required.

Interesting Features in State Legislation. A home to school telephone instructional system may be provided when economically feasible and educationally advisable as determined by the local district administration. When this system is provided, the teachers may be authorized to visit the home for one hour per week to give assistance. Also, summer instruction may be provided with state funds, subject to the availability of funds and approval by the department of public instruction.

FLORIDA

State of Florida, Department of Education, Tallahassee, Florida 32399; Betty Castor, Commissioner of Education. Package Title: A Resource Manual for the Development and Evaluation of Special Programs for Exceptional Students, Volume 1-B, Florida Statutes and State Board of Education Rules, Excerpts for Programs for Exceptional Students. Date Effective: September 1986.

State Definition. Special programs for students who are homebound or hospitalized: a homebound or hospitalized student is a student who has a medically diagnosed physical or mental condition which confines the student to home or hospital and whose activities are restricted for an extended period of time. A student is eligible when given a certificate by a licensed physician that the student is expected to be absent from school for at least 15 consecutive school days, or due to a chronic condition for at least 15 school days which need not run consecutively. Also, a student is eligible when under care for illness or injury which is acute or catastrophic in nature.

Teacher Certification. A Florida certificate in subject area or area of special education is required.

Interesting Features in State Legislation. When instruction is by telephone, the parent, guardian, or primary care-giver shall provide an open, uninterrupted telephone line during the instructional period and shall ensure that the student is prepared to actively participate in learning.

GEORGIA

Georgia Department of Education, Program for Exceptional Children, Twin Towers East, 19th Floor, Atlanta, Georgia 30334. Package Title: Georgia Department of Education Regulations and Procedures, IDDF Program for Exceptional Children. Date Effective: 1983.

State Definition. Hospital/Homebound refers to those students who have a medically diagnosed physical condition which restricts them to their home or a hospital for a period of time which will significantly interfere with their education. The maximum enrollment for Hospital/Homebound is eight years. Enrollment may vary according to geographic distances covered. Each student must be absent a minimum of ten school days or more. Each child will be serviced at least three hours per week.

Teacher Certification. A Georgia teacher's certificate is required.

HAWAII

Department of Education, Honolulu, Hawaii 96813. (808) 548-2211. Educational package currently under revision.

IDAHO

State Department of Education, Special Education, Len B. Jordan Office Building, Boise, Idaho 83720; Jerry L. Evans, State Superintendent of Public Instruction. Package Title: Idaho State Board of Education Rules and Regulations Pertaining to Special Education and Federal Regulations Under P.L. 94-142, the Education of All Handicapped Children Act. Date Effective: July 1985.

State Definition. Homebound program model: a model which is for students who are unable to attend school due to temporary illness, accident, or an unusual handicapping condition. A student must be absent from school ten consecutive days or a physician's statement must certify in advance that absence will exceed this period of time.

Teacher Certification. The homebound teacher must hold a valid Idaho teacher's certificate in elementary or secondary education.

ILLINOIS

Illinois State Board of Education, 100 North First Street, Springfield, Illinois 62777-0001. Package Title: Title 23: Education and Cultural Resources, Subtitle A: Education, Chapter 1 State Board of Education, Subchapter F: Instruction for Specific Student Populations, Part 226, special education; and booklet: Home or Hospital Services. Date Effective: 1986.

State Definition. The home and hospital program shall be provided to any child with a health or physical impairment which in the opinion of a licensed medical examiner will cause an absence from school for more than two consecutive weeks, and for whom school personnel determine that such a program can be of educational benefit. A child who requires a home or hospital program, on a temporary basis, shall be provided with instructional services sufficient to enable him or her to return to school with a minimum of difficulty. Instructional time shall not be less than five hours per week in order to qualify for full reimbursement. A child whose home or hospital instruction is provided through a home-school, telephone or other similar device, shall be provided at least two hours per week of direct instruction.

Teacher Certification. An Illinois teacher's certificate is required as well as documented background in the appropriate subject matter in order to be able to carry the curriculum from the school to the home or hospital.

Interesting Features in State Legislation. When a student, for health reasons, requires additional work to complete the preceding year's educational program, he may be provided with home instructional services during the summer.

INDIANA

Indiana Department of Education, Division of Special Education, Room 229 State House, Indianapolis, Indiana 46204. (317) 269-9442; Beverly Fay, Section Manager, Division of Special Education. Package Title: Rules, Regulations and Policies Adopted and Promulgated by the Commission on General Education of the Indiana State Board of Education, State of Indiana, Rule S-1. Date Effective: July 1984.

State Definition. Homebound and/or school-home telephone programs provide instruction to children unable to attend school because of physical handicaps or special health problems. Homebound teaching shall be initiated only after all other possibilities have been exhausted, with the goal of providing free appropriate public education for all children, regardless of physical limitation. The statement of the physician must indicate the child will be homebound for at least four weeks or less than four weeks at the close of the school year, enabling the child to complete the regular school work. The number of homebound children per teacher shall not exceed five at any one time. Instruction is limited to one hour per day, five days a week (elementary) and one hour per day, five days a week, per each subject (secondary) in which student is enrolled.

Teacher Certification. Teacher of special education children or homebound must be certified in the areas of the children's handicaps.

IOWA
Department of Education, Grimis State Office Building, Des Moines, Iowa 50319-0146. Package Title: Rules of Special Education, State of Iowa Department of Public Instruction. Date Effective: 1985.

State Definition. Itinerant home services or hospital services: Pupils requiring special education shall not be denied special education when their condition precludes school attendance. Appropriate special education shall be provided through home or hospital instruction.

Teacher Certification. Itinerant hospital services and homebound services require special education certification.

Interesting Features in State Legislation. When it is necessary, as determined by the director, to provide a home instruction program for a pupil requiring special education who has been removed from school because of unacceptable school behaviors, the program shall be reviewed by the diagnostic educational team, including the parents, at least every thirty calendar days to review other alternatives or to determine that home instruction continues to be appropriate.

KANSAS
Kansas State Department of Education, Kansas State Education Building, 120 East 10th Street, Topeka, Kansas 66612-1103; James E. Marshall, Director, Special Education Administration. Package Title: State Plan for Special Education, State Regulations for Special Education. Date Effective: July 1987.

State Definition. Homebound instruction means a plan for the delivery of educational services under which educational services are provided in the home of a child whose health problems are so serious that school attendance is impossible, or who is temporarily disabled by physical or mental illness. In some cases, students with severe and/or unusual handicapping conditions may receive short-term homebound instruction as temporary measures until more appropriate arrangements can be made.

Teacher Certification. All homebound and hospital instructional services shall be provided by individuals with a Kansas teaching certificate that is valid at the level of instruction to be provided. Each individual who is a full-time teacher in homebound or hospital shall have completed a program which qualifies the individual to be fully certified in at least one of the special education subject areas.

Interesting Features in State Legislation. Homebound services to a student with behavior disorders are limited by K.A.R. 91-12-55 (C) (Y) to no more than two months.

KENTUCKY
Kentucky Department of Education, Office of Education for Exceptional Children, Capital Plaza Tower, Frankfort, Kentucky 40601; Alice McDonald, Superintendent of Public Instruction. Package Title: Kentucky Administrative Regulations (Related to Exceptional Children). Date Effective: May 1986.

State Definition. K.R.S. 159.030 provides for home and hospital instruction for all pupils whose physical or mental condition renders school attendance inadvisable. This regulation is necessary to assure uniformity in providing special education and related services in the home and/or hospital setting and to conform with Public Law 94-142, and in order to assure uniform educational services for nonexceptional children in the home or hospital setting. The average caseload is ten students, servicing K–12 grades with a minimum of two one-hour visits per week.

Teacher Certification. A Kentucky teacher certification is required to teach hospital/homebound programs.

LOUISIANA

Department of Education, P.O. Box 94064, Baton Rouge, Louisiana 70804-9064; Thomas G. Clausen, State Superintendent. Educational package currently under revision.

MAINE

State of Maine, Department of Educational and Cultural Services, State House Station 23, Augusta, Maine 04333. Package Title: Maine's Special Education Regulations. Date Effective: 1984.

State Definition. Any instruction offered to an exceptional student in a hospital or home situation shall be provided by an appropriately certified special education teacher, or by a certified regular teacher, or by a substitute teacher for that administrative unit who has been previously registered as a substitute with the division of teacher certification and placement. The hospital/homebound instruction shall consist of at least two hours of direct instruction per subject per week or a minimum of ten hours of direct instruction per week, whichever is greater. If the duration of the hospital/homebound instruction is anticipated to exceed ten school days, a PET (Pupil Evaluation Team) shall convene to devleop a new IEP.

Teacher Certification. Stated above in state definition.

Interesting Features in State Legislation. Hospital/homebound instruction shall not be conducted for more than 60 calendar days without prior approval by the commissioner. Hospital/homebound instruction in excess of 60 days shall be provided by a certified special education teacher.

MARYLAND

Maryland State Department of Education, 200 West Baltimore Street, Baltimore, Maryland 21201-2595; Ms. Marjorie Shulbank, Division of Special Education. (301) 333-2478. Package Title: COMAR 13A-05.01, Programs for Handicapped Children. Date Effective: May 1978.

State Definition. Home and hospital instruction is designed to provide short-term itinerant instructional services to students with physical disabilities or in emotional crisis. Services provided include instructional service to the student who is being maintained at home or in a hospital for purposes of convalescence or treatment, and is restricted by a physician for reasons of physical health from attending a school-based program.

Teacher Certification. A Maryland teacher's certificate is required.

Interesting Features in State Legislation. Instructional service to a student in emotional crisis who is being maintained at home or in a hospital shall be available only on an emergency basis. This service may not exceed 60 consecutive school calendar days (minimum of 6 hours per week) pending placement in an established educational program.

MASSACHUSETTS

The Commonwealth of Massachusetts, Department of Education, Quincy Center Plaza, 1385 Hancock Street, Quincy, Massachusetts 02169. Package Title: 766 Regulations, Massachusetts Department of Education. Date Effective: September 1986.

State Definition. There are two types of programs within this prototype, Type A and Type B. In Type A program, the entire program is provided without team involvement. In Type B program, the team and the administrator of special education develop an IEP for the child. TYPE A PROGRAMS: Each school committee shall provide a Type A home or hospital program to each child who, in the judgment of the child's physician, will have to remain at home or in a hospital on a day or overnight basis, or any combination of both, for a period of not less than 14 or more than 60 days during any school year. TYPE B PROGRAMS: A child who, in the judgment of the child's physician, will have to remain at home or in a hospital for more than 60 days during any school year in order not to endanger the health or safety of such child or that of others.

Teacher Certification. A Massachusetts teacher's certificate is required as well as an endorsement in at least one area of special education.

MICHIGAN

Michigan Department of Education, Special Education Services, Box 30008, Lansing, Michigan 48909. Package Title: Revised Administrative Rules for Special Education. Date Effective: July 1987.

State Definitions. RULE 46: Specific requirements for homebound and hospitalized services are as follows:

1. Homebound services shall be initiated within 15 school days after verification, by a licensed physician, of a medical handicap which requires the eligible special education student to be confined to the home. Such verification shall indicate the anticipated duration of the required confinement.

2. Homebound teachers shall be assigned not more than 12 students at any one time.

3. Students receiving homebound or hospital services shall receive a minimum of two nonconsecutive hours of instruction per week. Related services personnel may supplement, but not substitute for the teacher's instruction.

4. Homebound and hospitalized services shall not be substituted for special education programs. Rather, the service shall endeavor, to the extent appropriate, to present curricular experiences which are being provided in the program where the student is currently enrolled.

Teacher Certification. The homebound teacher must hold a Michigan teacher's certificate, an elementary or secondary certificate, and at least one certification in an area of special education.

Interesting Features in State Legislation. Michigan has additional requirements, as of September 1, 1990, for any person wishing to teach special education in Michigan. They must also possess an endorsement in elementary or secondary special education, and not less than a 180-hour practicum in the specific area of impairment for each additional endorsement.

The Michigan special education package had rules and regulations far above the minimal standards of P.L. 94-142. The package not only stated rules but also detailed the qualifications, through colleges and universities. It was a very impressive package.

MINNESOTA

Department of Education, Capitol Square Building—550 Cedar Street, St. Paul, Minnesota 55101. Package Title: Minnesota: Rules of the State Board of Education. Date Effective: February 1984.

State Definition. Homebound/handicapped pupil placement: when district services are required, a district must provide regular education, instruction, and related services in a facility or home to a pupil placed there for care and treatment. The services must be provided to a pupil who is (1) prevented from attending the usual school site for 15 consecutive days, or (2) other health-impaired and predicted by the team to be absent for 15 intermittent days.

Teacher Certification. A homebound teacher must hold a Minnesota teacher's certificate.

MISSISSIPPI

State Department of Education, Bureau of Special Services, P.O. Box 771, Jackson, Mississippi 39205-0771. Educational package currently under revision.

MISSOURI

Missouri Department of Elementary and Secondary Education, Section of Special Education, Post Office Box 480, Jefferson City, Missouri 65102. Package Title: Missouri State Plan, Fiscal Year 1987–1988: State Plan for Part B of the Education of the Handicapped Act as Amended by Public Law 94-142. Date Effective: 1987.

State Definition. Any handicapped student meeting the definitions of 35 CFR 300.5(1-8) between the ages of 5 through 21 years, who because of the nature or extent of his/her handicapping condition, requires homebound instruction or instruction during hospitalization care, shall upon approval by the state Department of Elementary and Secondary Education, receive educational services during the school year within his facility of confinement for as long as the handicapping condition prevents the student from safely or adequately attending school. There will be at least five hours of instruction each week.

Teacher Certification. A Missouri teacher's certificate is required.

MONTANA

Office of Public Instruction, Helena, Montana 59620. Ed Argenbright, Superintendent. Sue Paulson, Department of Educational Services. Package Title: Special Education: Reference Manual, Montana Laws and Rules. Date Effective: September 1987.

State Definition. Services to any homebound and/or hospitalized students may be provided when a medical doctor verifies that a student is hospitalized or provides medical documentation and reasons for the student's need to remain out of school.

Teacher Certification. A teacher of homebound and/or hospitalized students need only hold a valid teaching certificate.

NEBRASKA

Nebraska Department of Education, 301 Centennial Mall South, P.O. Box 94987, Lincoln, Nebraska 68509. Package Title: Nebraska Department of Education Rule 51, Regulations and Standards for Special Education Programs, Title 92, Nebraska Administrative Code Chapter 51. Date Effective: September 1987.

State Definition. Homebound or hospital educational services shall be provided for verified handicapped children with health or physical limitations. The child's IEP shall reflect the amount of instructional or supportive service time to be provided. Direct instructional time shall not be less than five hours per week unless otherwise stipulated by a physician.

Teacher Certification. Any teaching endorsement is acceptable with the Nebraska Department of Education.

NEVADA

Special Education Branch, Nevada Department of Education, Capitol Complex, 400 West King Street, Carson City, Nevada 89710. (702) 885-3140. Package Title: Standards for Administration of Special Education Programs. Date Effective: June 1979.

State Definition. Homebound means a mental or physical disability requiring temporary instruction in a home or hospital. Regular students, who for reasons of mental or physical disability require temporary instruction in a home or hospital setting, need only to be certified by a licensed physician or a certified psychologist. The caseload for teachers providing instructional services to physically handicapped students confined to home or hospital shall not exceed ten students per week. Homebound tele-teaching class size per instructional period shall not exceed 15 students to receive instruction at any one time.

Teacher Certification. A teacher shall hold a certificate in the area of exceptional pupil education with endorsements in the areas of exceptionality represented in the special education unit. Exceptions to the certification requirements may be permitted with the approval of the Nevada Department of Education.

NEW HAMPSHIRE

Department of Education, Special Education Bureau, 101 Pleasant Street, Concord, New Hampshire 03301. Package Title: New Hampshire State Board of Education, New Hampshire Standards for the Education of Handicapped Students. Date Effective: May 1984.

State Definition. Educationally handicapped students ages 3 to 21 may receive a homebased program on a temporary basis. Such programs shall not exceed 45 days unless exception is granted by the State Director of Special Education upon written request from the superintendent of schools. Homebased program shall minimally include five hours per week of specifically designed instruction. The homebased program may also include educationally related services as specified in the IEP. Any educationally related services so provided will be in addition to the five hours of specially designed instruction.

Teacher Certification. All teachers of the handicapped shall have valid New Hampshire certification with an endorsement appropriate for the educationally handicapping condition of the students to be served. All regular education professional staff who instruct educationally handicapped students shall have access to certified special education personnel for consultation and advice.

NEW JERSEY

New Jersey Education Association, 180 West State Street, P.O. Box 1211, Trenton, New Jersey 08607-1211. Package Title: New Jersey Regulations on Special Education, Chapter 28: Special Education, New Jersey Administrative Code Title 6 Education. Date Effective: June 1987.

State Definition. Instruction provided in lieu of classroom instruction for pupils classified by the school physician as eligible for home instruction shall meet the following criteria: Instruction shall be provided at the pupil's place of confinement; the pupil shall be carried on an individual instruction register; instructional services shall begin within seven calendar days after eligibility has been established; instruction shall be provided for no fewer than five hours per week. The five hours of instruction per week shall be accomplished in no fewer than three visits by a teacher on three separate days. Also, instruction may be provided up to 60 calendar days in a school year (referrals can be made from a competent physician for a longer period of time).

Teacher Certification. The teachers providing instruction shall be appropriately certified for the subject or level in which the instruction is given.

Interesting Features in State Legislation. When instruction is provided by direct communication to a classroom program by telephone or television, this instruction shall be in addition to the basic five hours of instruction by a teacher.

NEW MEXICO

Department of Education, Sante Fe, New Mexico 87503. (505) 827-4011. Educational package currently under revision.

NEW YORK

New York State Education Department, Division of Program Development, Room 1071, Education Building Annex, Albany, New York 12234. Package Title: Regulations of the Commissioner of Education, Subchapter P, Part 200: Children with Handicapping Conditions. Date Effective: February 1987.

State Definition. Pupils with handicapping conditions who are recommended for home/hospital instruction by the committee on special education shall receive individualized instruction as follows: a minimum of five hours per week at the elementary level, preferably one hour daily; or minimum of ten hours per week at the secondary level, preferably two hours daily.

Teacher Certification. Special education instruction shall be provided by individuals appropriately certified or licensed.

Interesting Features in State Legislation. Twelve-month programming is available for those pupils whose needs are to maintain developmental levels.

NORTH CAROLINA

North Carolina Department of Public Instruction, 116 West Edenton Street, Education Building, Raleigh, North Carolina 27603-1712. Package Title: Rules Governing Programs and Services for Children With Special Needs. Date Effective: July 1987.

State Definition. Any child with special needs who is confined for four weeks or longer to a hospital or home for treatment or for a period of convalescence is eligible for this program. The child should be expected by a competent medical authority to be away from the classroom for a minimum of four weeks.

Teacher Certification. A North Carolina teacher's certificate is required as well as a certification in at least one area of special education.

Interesting Features in State Legislation. The caseload for homebound can be up to 12 pupils and instruction is based upon individual needs for an average of 5 hours per week unless prohibited for medical reasons.

NORTH DAKOTA

North Dakota Department of Public Instruction, Bismarck, North Dakota 58505; Dr. Wayne G. Sanstead, Superintendent. Package Title: Special Education in North Dakota, Guide 1 — Laws, Policies, and Regulations for Special Education for Exceptional Students; Also, Supplement to Guide 1. Date Effective: August 1986.

State Definition. If the student is temporarily or periodically confined to home or hospital, instruction appropriate to the student's health condition is to be provided at that setting. The purpose of the home and hospital program is to maintain the student's school progress and to keep the student in touch with peers. The student must be well enough to pursue at least a minimal program but may not always carry a full course load. The school progress records are to be kept in the school file. A full time teacher shall serve five individual homebound students or up to ten in a hospital group.

Teacher Certification. A valid North Dakota educator's professional certificate in elementary or secondary education is required.

Interesting Features in State Legislation. Home to school telephone for instructional purposes should be explored for long-term home instruction.

OHIO

State of Ohio, Department of Education, Division of Special Education, 933 High Street, Worthington, Ohio 43085-4087. Package Title: Rules for the Education of Handicapped Children. Date Effective: July 1982.

State Definition. Home instruction is an individualized special education program provided to a child with a handicap which prevents the child from attending a regular or special education program even with the aid of special transportation.

Teacher Certification. An Ohio teacher's certificate is required.

Interesting Features in Legislation. The teacher responsibilities specifically included assisting in the development of the IEP, providing an instructional program, periodic reports, and coordinating with school personnel in the successful return of the child to the regular school program.

OKLAHOMA

Oklahoma State Department of Education, Oliver Hodge Building, 2500 North Lincoln Boulevard, Oklahoma City, Oklahoma 73105-4599; John M. Folks, State Superintendent. Package Title: Policies and Procedures Manual for Special Education in Oklahoma. Date Effective: 1988.

State Definition. The program provides the opportunity for children to enjoy achievement in the academic subjects of our public schools and advance in their efforts to obtain an education at their rate of development, when they are unable to attend public school because of illness. To be eligible, a student must be absent from school a minimum of two weeks. Each homebound student must be provided instruction one hour per day, three days per week; this is considered a unit or class of homebound teaching.

Teacher Certification. Teachers of homebound children shall hold a valid Oklahoma teacher's certificate. A special education certificate is not required.

Interesting Features in State Legislation. If the child's education has been interrupted because of illness, the State Board of Education may grant permission for him to remain on the program an additional year for each year that his education was interrupted, or until the student reaches his twenty-sixth birthday, providing that his progress in schoolwork is satisfactory and the extension of time is necessary for the completion of the 12 grades.

OREGON

Oregon Department of Education, 700 Pringle Parkway S.E., Salem, Oregon 97310-0290. Packet Title: Oregon Administrative Rules, Department of Education, Chapter 581. Date Effective: April 1987.

State Definition. Standards for home, hospital, institutional or other regularly scheduled instruction: School districts may provide home, hospital, institutional, or other regularly scheduled instruction to any eligible student with a mental, physical, emotional, or learning problem or to individuals who are pregnant. The home, hospital, institutional, or other regularly scheduled program shall be appropriate to the unique educational needs of the student.

Teacher Certification. An Oregon teacher's certificate is required.

Interesting Features in State Legislation. Throughout most of the defined segments in Oregon's administrative rules, the information was vague and displayed minimal alterations to the federal legislation for handicapped children (P.L. 94-142).

PENNSYLVANIA

Department of Education, Harrisburg, Pennsylvania 17120. (717) 787-2121. Educational package currently under review.

RHODE ISLAND

Special Education Program Services Unit, Rhode Island Department of Education, 22 Hayes Street, Providence, Rhode Island 02908. Package Title: Regulations of the Board of Regents for Elementary and Secondary Education Governing the Special Education of Handicapped Children. Date Effective: June 1984.

State Definition. Homebound and hospital instruction shall take place on the specific recommendation of the school district administrator of special education. Such recommendation shall be based on a physician's diagnosis and statement that the child will be absent from school for more than 30 consecutive days. (Contagious diseases are excluded under the provisions of these regulations.) The minimum number of hours of instruction shall be three per school week at the elementary level of education and four at the secondary level unless fewer hours are recommended by the physician. The use of the home to school telephone system should be employed whenever possible. In such cases, however, a teacher should provide instruction in the child's home for at least one hour each school week.

Teacher Certification. Teachers of the homebound shall hold Rhode Island teaching certificates in the area appropriate to the health impaired and physically disabled child and/or to such child's primary handicapping condition.

Interesting Features in State Legislation. The Rhode Island state definition of "other health impaired" includes traumatic brain injured.

SOUTH CAROLINA

Department of Education, Columbia, South Carolina 29211. (803) 758-0221. Educational package currently under revision.

SOUTH DAKOTA

Division of Education, Section for Special Education, Richard F. Kneip Building, 700 Governors Drive, Pierre, South Dakota 57501-2293. Package Title: Administrative Handbook for Special Education, State of South Dakota. Date Effective: 1983.

State Definition. An educational program shall be designed to serve a child who is hospitalized or homebound. When further assessment of a child is needed, the child may be assigned to a program on a temporary basis for a period not to exceed six weeks.

Teacher Certification. Each school district having special education programs shall employ special education personnel who have the special education endorsement as provided in Article 24:02.

TENNESSEE

State of Tennessee, Department of Education, Office of Commissioner, Cordell Hull Building, Nashville, Tennessee 37219-5335. Package Title: Special Education Programs and Services (0520-1-3-09). Date Effective: March 1987.

State Definition. Other related services (to special education): A description of the frequency (range of time per session and number of sessions per week) and anticipated duration (number of days, weeks, and months) of specific special education and related services to be provided.

Teacher Certification. Not stated.

Interesting Features in State Legislation. This state legislation lacked any specific information on a homebound or hospital program, teacher certification or responsibilities. The copy itself was poorly printed and barely legible.

TEXAS

Texas Education Agency, W.B. Travis Building, 1701 N. Congress Avenue, Austin, Texas 78701. Package Title: State Board of Education Rules for Handicapped Students (Including Federal Regulations and State Law). Date Effective: September 1986.

State Definition. Homebound: This instructional arrangement is for providing special education instruction in the student's home or hospital room. The instructional arrangement will be used for eligible handicapped students who are served at home or hospital bedside or who are considered to be homebased. Students served on a homebound or hospital basis are expected to be confined for a minimum of four consecutive weeks as documented by a physician. Homebased instruction may be provided as an option for eligible handicapped students removed to an alternative education program as a result of disciplinary action. Home instruction may be used for prekindergarten students whose developmental levels are such that they are not capable of participating in special education classes for early childhood.

Teacher Certification. Teachers assigned full time to teaching students who are orthopedically handicapped or other health impaired with the teaching station in the home or a hospital shall not be required to hold a special education certificate or endorsement as long as the personnel file contains an official transcript indicating that the teacher has completed a three-semester-hour survey course in the education of the handicapped and three semester hours directly related to teaching physically handicapped children.

UTAH

Utah State Office of Education, 250 East Fifth South, Salt Lake City, Utah 84111; Walter D. Talbot, State Superintendent. Package Title: Rules and Regulations for Education Programs for the Handicapped. Date Effective: November 1981.

State Definition. This program is an instructional program designed for identified handicapped students who are permanently or temporarily homebound or hospitalized. The student must have an expected absence of at least two weeks. Homebound instruction time per student should average two hours per week.

Teacher Certification. Teachers serving in a classroom for physically handicapped or in service to the homebound or hospitalized (handicapped) must have one of the special education endorsements.

VERMONT

Special Education Unit, Vermont Department of Education, 120 State Street, Montpelier, Vermont 05602. Package Title: Special Education Rules from the Vermont State Board of Education Manual of Rules and Practices. Date Effective: May 1982.

State Definition. Homebound and hospital instruction: Pupils are eligible for homebound and hospital instruction whenever they are unable to attend school for a period of ten consecutive school days or more because of pregnancy or a medical disability. Elementary pupils who receive homebound instruction shall receive an average of two hours per week. Secondary students shall receive an average of two hours per subject.

Teacher Certification. Vermont teacher's certificate is required.

VIRGINIA

Commonwealth of Virginia, Department of Education, P.O. Box 6 Q, Richmond, Virginia. Package Title: Regulations Governing Special Education Programs for Handicapped Children and Youth in Virginia. Date Effective: January 1985.

State Definition. Homebound instruction shall be deemed appropriate for a handicapped child only when such placement is stipulated in the child's IEP and is in accordance with the requirements of the least restricted environment. Homebound instruction shall be deemed appropriate for non-handicapped children when they become temporarily disabled to the extent that they cannot attend regular classes.

Teacher Certification. A Virginia teacher's certificate is required.

Interesting Features in State Legislation. Reimbursement is available for 60 percent of an established hourly rate for teachers employed to provide such instruction. Such rates shall be determined annually.

WASHINGTON

Department of Education, Olympia, Washington 98504. (206) 753-5000. Educational package currently under review.

WEST VIRGINIA

State Department of Education, Charleston, West Virginia 25305-2960-26. Package Title: Regulations for the Education of Exceptional Students. Date Effective: July 1987.

State Definition. The public agency shall include home-teaching or visiting teacher services for children who are homebound due to injury or who, for any other reason as certified by a licensed physician, are homebound for a period that has lasted or will last more than three weeks. There are two groups of students eligible to receive home/hospital instruction: (1) Students who meet the eligibility criteria for one or more of the program areas defined in the regulations for the education of exceptional students and who evidence a severe handicapping condition or conditions which prevent them from attending school, even with the aid of special transportation; (2) Students with injuries, non-communicable illnesses, or health conditions which prevent the student from attending school for more than three weeks. Students placed on extended home instruction shall submit a physician's statement of need for continued home instruction when the term of home instruction reaches six months in length.

Teacher Certification.

1. Teachers providing temporary home-teaching or visiting-teacher services, including regular and special education, must hold a valid teaching license, with an endorsement appropriate to the programmatic level of instruction (early, middle, adolescent).

2. Teachers providing home-teaching or visiting-teaching to eligible handicapped students must hold a valid license with an endorsement for each area of exceptionality being served.

WISCONSIN

Wisconsin Department of Public Instruction, Division for Handicapped Children and Pupil Services, 125 South Webster Street, P.O. Box 7841, Madison, Wisconsin 53707. Package Title: Chapter PI11: Rules Implementing Subchapter V of Chapter 115, Wis. Stats. Date Effective: February 1983.

State Definition. A homebound instruction program is a special education program in which a teacher serves children with exceptional educational needs in the home, hospital, a sanitarium, or a convalescent home. The program may include not only direct teaching services but also correspondence courses and telephone instruction.

Teacher Certification. This program shall require a teacher to hold a valid Wisconsin teacher's license.

WYOMING

Wyoming State Department of Education, Curriculum and Instruction Division, Hathaway Building, Cheyenne, Wyoming 82002. Package Title: Wyoming State Board of Education Rules and Regulations Governing Services for Handicapped Children in Wyoming School Districts. Date Effective: June 1986.

State Definition. No homebound definition was stated. "Other health impairment" was defined using the federal (P.L. 94-142) definition.

Teacher Certification. Individuals who provide special education and related services to a handicapped child placed in a homebound or hospital setting must meet the certification standards prescribed by the State Department of Education.

Interesting Features in State Legislation. There was no mention, throughout the Wyoming legislation, of a homebound program. There was a brief section on homebound contracting, for funding purposes.

Appendix B:
Support Agencies

Following are agencies that offer support to families of chronically or terminally ill children. Agencies vary in terms of services and functions. Most, however, provide literature, a "listening ear" or hotline, and possibly referral to local support groups for parents and children.

AIDS Hotline, National
P.O. Box 3481
Houston TX 77253-3481

**Alexander Graham Bell
Association for the Deaf**
3417 Volta Place, N.W.
Washington DC 20007

Allergy Foundation of America
801 Second Avenue
New York NY 10017

American Brittle Bone Society
1256 Merrill Drive
Marshalton
West Chester PA 19380

American Cancer Association
777 Third Avenue
New York NY 10017

**American Coalition of Citizens
with Disabilities**
1200 15th Street, N.W.
Suite 201
Washington DC 20005

American Council for the Blind
Suite 506
1211 Connecticut Avenue, N.W.
Washington DC 20036

American Diabetes Association
2 Park Avenue
New York NY 10016

American Foundation for the Blind
15 West 16th Street
New York NY 10011

American Heart Association
7320 Greenville Avenue
Dallas TX 75231

American Lung Association
1740 Broadway
New York NY 10019

**American Parkinson Disease
Association**
116 John Street
New York NY 10038

American Trauma Society
Arlington and Detroit Avenue
Toledo OH 46615

**Architectural and Transportation
Barriers Compliance Board**
Switzer Building
Washington DC 20201

Arthritis Foundation
1314 Spring Street
Atlanta GA 30309

Association for the Care of Children's Health
3615 Wisconsin Avenue
Washington DC 20016

Association for Children and Adults with Learning Disabilities
4156 Library Road
Pittsburgh PA 15234

Association for Children with Retarded Mental Development
162 Fifth Avenue, 11th Floor
New York NY 10010

Association for Education and Re-habilitation of the Blind and Visually Impaired
206 N. Washington Street, Suite 320
Alexandria VA 22314

Association for the Severely Handicapped
7010 Roosevelt Way, N.E.
Seattle WA 98115

Association of Birth Defect Children
3201 East Crystal Lake Avenue
Orlando FL 32806

Beginnings for Parents of Hearing Impaired
P.O. Box 10565
Raleigh NC 27605

Braille Authority of North America
American Foundation for the Blind
15 W. 16th Street
New York NY 10011

Cancer Hotline
4019 N. Roxboro Road
Teer House
Durham NC 27704
An example of a local cancer information service. Your city, state, or region may have a similar service. Contact the Cancer Hotline, National.

Cancer Hotline, National
1-800-4-CANCER (Continental U.S.);
1-800-638-6070 (Alaska);
1-800-524-1234 (Hawaii)

Cancer Information Center, American
1600 Pierce Street
Denver CO 80214

Cancer/Colon Rectal
Warren Lambeth Company
Morris Plains NJ 07950

Catholic Association of Persons with Visual Impairment
P.O. Box 7196
New York NY 10116

Center for Medical Consumers and Health Care Information
237 Thompson Street
New York NY 10012

Center for Sickle Cell Anemia
College of Medicine
Howard University
520 West Street N.W.
Washington DC 20001

Child Abuse Listening Mediation
P.O. Box 718
Santa Barbara CA 93102

CHIDHELP USA, Inc.
6463 Independence Avenue
Woodland Hills CA 91370

Children's Hospice International
1101 King Street, Suite 131
Alexandria VA 22314

Children's Liver Foundation
Seven Highland Place
Maplewood NJ 07040

Children's Transplant Association
P.O. Box 2106
Laurinburg NC 28352

Children's Wish Foundation
32 Perimeter Center East, N.E.
Suite 100
Atlanta GA 30346

Child's Wish Come True
P.O. Box 1067
Webster MA 01570

Compassionate Friends
P.O. Box 1347
Oakbrook IL 60521

Consumers Organization for the Hearing Impaired
P.O. Box 8188
Silver Spring MD 20907

Council for Exceptional Children
1920 Association Drive
Reston VA 22091

Cerebral Palsy, United/Association, Inc.
66 East 34th Street, Third Floor
New York NY 10016

Cystic Fibrosis Foundation
6000 Executive Boulevard, Suite 309
Rockville MD 20852

Diabetes Foundation, Juvenile
432 Park Avenue South
New York NY 10016

Disability Rights Education and Defense Fund
2212 Sixth Street
Berkeley CA 94710

Do It Now Foundation
P.O. Box 21126
Phoenix AZ 85036

Down's Syndrome International
11 N. 73rd Terrace, Rm K
Kansas City KS 66111

Dysautonomia Foundation
370 Lexington Avenue, Suite 1504
New York NY 10017

Epilepsy Foundation of America
4351 Garden City Dr.
Landover MD 20785
(301) 459-3700

Epilepsy Information Service
300 South Hawthorne Road
Winston-Salem NC 27103

Families Anonymous
P.O. Box 528
Van Nuys CA 91408

Foundation for Children with Learning Disabilities
99 Park Avenue, 6th Floor
New York NY 10016

Foundation for Exceptional Children
1920 Association Drive
Reston VA 22091

Friedreich's Ataxia Group in America, Inc.
Box 11116
Oakland CA 94611

Governors Advocacy Council for Persons with Disabilities
1318 Dale Street, Suite 100
Raleigh NC 27605
(An example of a state advocacy organization. Your state may have a similar group. Contact your state's division of handicapped or rehabilitation services.)

Handicap Introductions
P.O. Box 232
124 S. Main Street
Coopersburg PA 18036

Heal the Children
North 1603 Belt
Spokane WA 99205

Health Information Center, National ODPHP (Office of Disease and Health Promotion)
P.O. Box 1133
Washington DC 20013-1133

Hearing and Speech Action, National
10801 Rockville Pike
Rockville MD 20852

Heart Disease Hotline
P.O. Box 54305
Atlanta GA 30308

Hospice of North Carolina
800 St. Mary Street, Suite 303
Raleigh NC 27605
(Your state may have a similar
organization; or contact the National
Hospice Organization.)

**Jewish Association for Retarded
Citizens**
17288 W. 12 Mile Road
Southfield MI 48076

Jewish Braille Institute of America
110 E. 30th Street
New York NY 10016

Joseph Kennedy Jr. Foundation
1701 K Street N.W., Suite 205
Washington DC 20006

Juvenile Diabetes Foundation
432 Park Avenue, S.
New York NY 10016

Kidney Fund, America
7315 Wisconsin Avenue
Suite 203
Bethesda MD 20814-3266

Leukemia Society of America
733 Third Avenue
New York NY 10017

Lung Disease/Asthma
National Jewish Center for
Respiratory Disease
1400 Jackson Street
Denver CO 80206

Lupus Foundation of America, Inc.
11675 Holly Springs Drive
St. Louis MO 63141

Mainstream Inc.
1200 15th Street, N.W.
Washington DC 20005

Make Today Count
P.O. Box 222
Osage Beach MO 65065

Make a Wish Foundation of America
4501 N. 16th Street, Suite 205
Phoenix AZ 85016

**March of Dimes Birth Defects
Foundation**
1275 Mamaroneck Avenue
White Plains NY 10605

Multiple Sclerosis, National Society
205 East 42nd Street
New York NY 10017

**Muscular Dystrophy Association of
America**
810 Seventh Street
New York NY 10019

National Amputation Foundation
12-45 150th Street
Whitestone NY 11357

**National Association for Down's
Syndrome**
P.O. Box 4542
Oak Brook IL 60521

**National Association for Sickle Cell
Disease**
4221 Wilshire Blvd., Suite 360
Los Angeles CA 90010

**National Association for Visually
Handicapped**
22 W. 21st Street
New York NY 10010

National Ataxia Foundation
600 Twelve Oaks Center
15500 Wayzata Blvd.
Wayzata MN 55391

National Burn Victim Foundation
308 Main Street
Orange NJ 07050

National Cancer Care Foundation
1180 Avenue of the Americas
New York NY 10036

National Down's Syndrome Society
141 Fifth Avenue
New York NY 10010

National Easter Seal Society
2023 West Ogden Avenue
Chicago IL 60612

National Federation for the Blind
1800 Johnson Street
Baltimore MD 21230

National Head Injury Foundation
P.O. Box 567
Framingham MA 01701

National Headache Foundation
5252 N. Western Avenue
Chicago IL 60625

National Hemophilia Foundation
25 West 39th Street
New York NY 10018

National Hospice Organization
Suite 307
1901 North Fort Myer Drive
Arlington VA 22209
(703) 243-5900

National Information Center for Handicapped Children and Youth
P.O. Box 1492
Washington DC 20013

National Kidney Foundation
Two Park Avenue
New York NY 10016

National Legislative Council for the Handicapped
P.O. Box 262
Taylor MI 48180

National Leukemia Association
Roosevelt Field Lower Concourse
Garden City NY 11530

National Multiple Sclerosis Society
205 E. 42nd Street
New York NY 10017

National Spinal Cord Injury Association
149 California Street
Newton MA 02158

National Tay-Sachs and Allied Disease Association, Inc.
200 Park Avenue South
New York NY 10003

Osteogenesis Imperfecta, Inc.
P.O. Box 245
Eastport NY 11941

Parents of Down's Syndrome Children
c/o Montgomery County Association for Retarded Citizens
11600 Nebel Street
Rockville MD 20852

People with Aids Coalition
263A W. 19th Street, #125
New York NY 10011

Recording for the Blind
20 Roszel Road
Princeton NJ 08540

Self-Help for Hard of Hearing People
7800 Wisconsin Avenue
Bethesda MD 20814

Sick Kids Need Involved People
216 Newport Drive
Severna Park MD 21146

Sickle Cell Disease
4221 Wilshire Blvd.
Suite 360
Los Angeles CA 90010

Special Olympics
1350 New York Avenue, N.W.,
Suite 500
Washington DC 20005

Spina Bifida
1700 Rockville Pike
Suite 540
Rockville MD 20852

Spinal Cord Injuries
2201 Argonne Drive
Baltimore MD 21218

Starlight Foundation
10100 Santa Monica Blvd., Suite 785
Los Angeles CA 90067

Tourette's Syndrome Association
42-40 Bell Blvd.
Bayside NY 11361

We Can Do!
P.O. Box 723
Arcadia CA 91006

Wernicke-Korsakoff Syndrome
P.O. Box 3337
La Jolla CA 92038

A Wish With Wings
P.O. Box 110418
Arlington TX 76007

Glossary

abscissa. The horizontal line of a graph on which the independent variable is indicated.

acalculia. Loss of ability to perform mathematical functions.

acceleration. When inappropriate behavior is increased in self-control programs.

accountability. Objective demonstration of the effectiveness of a given program.

acquisition. During conditioning, process by which an organism learns a new response.

acrophobia. Fear of high places.

acute. Severe, rapid onset of disorder, lasting a short time.

adaptation. The process of changing behavior to fit changing circumstances.

adaptive daily living skills. Often called ADL skills or social adaptive skills, these include hygiene, dressing, budgeting, cooking, housework, leisure skills, and peer socialization.

adjunctive behavior. Behavior which occurs after reinforcement, or during the post-reinforcement pause.

affect. To cause a change in something (behavior or stimulus).

aggression. Behavior that one person enacts with the intention of harming or destroying another person or object.

agnosia. Loss of ability to identify familiar objects through a particular sense organ.

agoraphobia. Fear of open spaces. Inability to recall the kinesthetic patterns that go into writing, i.e., unable to relate mental images of words to the motor movements for writing.

agrammalogia. Inability to recall the structure of sentences.

agraphia. The pathologic loss of the ability to write.

AIDS. Acquired Immune Deficiency Syndrome, a severe manifestation of infection with human immunodeficiency virus.

alexia. Loss of ability to deal with visual language symbols while vision and intelligence remain intact.

allergen. A substance which may produce an allergic reaction.

allergy. Hypersensitivity to certain chemicals, e.g. air pollutants, and other substances, marked by such symptoms as asthma attacks, itching, skin rashes.

alopecia. Baldness, often a side-effect of radiation therapy.

alveoli. Structures of the lungs which are each subdivided into tiny thin-walled air sacs. There are more than 750 million alveoli in the lungs, allowing the exchange of oxygen and carbon dioxide.

ambulation. The act of walking or moving from place to place.

ametropia. An abnormality of the eye. When it is at rest, light rays are not focused on the retina, but rather in front of or behind it.

aminophylline.   A drug that dilates the bronchial tubes.

amnesia.   Lack or loss of memory. With some individuals the deficiency is intermittent and the person will remember things at one time but not another.

amniocentesis.   A clinical procedure that can identify abnormal chromosomes in a developing fetus.

amusia.   Loss of ability to produce or to comprehend musical sounds.

analgesic.   Any substance producing insensitivity to pain without loss of consciousness.

analysis.   Task of finding out and describing the precise set of conditions that give rise to specific events.

anaphylactic shock.   A very serious, rare condition in which an allergic reaction to medication causes sudden shock to the body. Symptoms are counteracted by prompt administration of adrenalin.

anarthria.   Loss of ability to form words accurately due to brain lesion or damage to peripheral nerves which carry impulses to the articulatory muscles (dysarthria is a partial impairment).

anecdotal evidence.   Casual, unsystematic observations which are rarely sufficient evidence for generalizations but provide the basis for hypotheses.

anecdotal method.   Method of presenting data using popular accounts based on observation.

anemia.   Decrease in the number of red blood cells or in their hemoglobin content. This decreases oxygen-carrying capacity of blood.

anorexia nervosa.   Chronic failure to eat for fear of gaining weight.

anoxia.   Failure to properly use the necessary amount of oxygen in the blood.

antecedents.   Objects and events that precede the behavior in question.

antibiotics.   Medications used to combat bacterial infections.

antibody.   A protein made by lymphocytes which is capable of interacting with a foreign substance to neutralize it.

antidepressant.   A drug used to elevate mood in depressed patients.

antigen.   A foreign substance (e.g. virus) which stimulates production of neutralizing proteins (antibodies) by lymphocytes.

antihistamine.   A drug that blocks the effects of histamine, a chemical responsible for many symptoms of allergy when released by mast cells during an allergic reaction.

antisocial behavior.   Behavior that violates rights of others, usually associated with antisocial personality.

anxiety.   A state of increased physiological arousal and generalized feeling of fear and apprehension.

anxiety disorders.   Group of psychological disorders including generalized anxiety, phobia, and obsessive-compulsive disorders.

aphasia.   A generic term for various types of communication disorders.

applied behavior analysis.   Interventions derived from the principles of behavior analysis, designed to change behavior in measurable and accountable ways.

applied behavior analyst.   Individual who has demonstrated professional competencies in designing, implementing, evaluating and communicating the results of an applied behavior analysis program.

applied research.   Research that concerns the analysis of variables and behaviors that are socially important.

apraxia.   Loss of ability to perform purposeful movements.

artificial prompt.　Discriminative stimulus that is not usually present in the environment.

aspiration.　Procedure by which a liquid is sucked by vacuum pressure into a syringe.

associative learning disability.　Condition arising from various causes in which individual cannot make or retain associations between meanings and symbolic representations. Occurs frequently in oral language.

asthma.　A disease characterized by narrowing of the bronchial tubes that is brought on by some irritant. There is increased production of mucus by the bronchial cells, and secretions further clog up bronchial tubes.

asymbolia.　Loss of ability to use or understand symbols, such as those used in mathematics, chemistry, music, etc.

ataxia.　A type of cerebral palsy exhibiting lack of muscle control, poor coordination and lack of spatial position.

atherosclerosis.　A narrowing and sometimes obstruction of the opening of the blood vessels.

athetosis.　Type of cerebral palsy exhibiting involuntary, purposeless movements.

atrophy.　Decrease in size or deterioriation of tissue.

attending.　A person attends to a stimulus when that stimulus exerts some form of stimulus control over the person's actions.

attention deficits (hyperactivity).　Childhood disorder characterized by an inability to focus attention or follow instructions consistently.

attribution.　Process of understanding behavior by making inferences about its underlying causes.

auditory aphasia (receptive aphasia).　The loss of ability to comprehend spoken words.

autism.　Disorder in children characterized by the inability to relate to anything beyond the self.

auto-shaping.　Shaping of an organism where the reinforcer is freely available under conditions of deprivation and pairings with discriminative (light) stimuli.

auto-suggestion.　When suggestion comes from the subject himself, as opposed to emanating from another.

aversive stimulus.　A stimulus whose removal is reinforcing.

avoidance behavior.　A behavior that increases in frequency when it delays or avoids completely an aversive stimulus.

baseline.　The strength or level of behavior before an experimental variable or procedure is introduced.

basic instructional level.　Highest difficulty level of reading material at which the student can function to meet criteria of 95 percent word recognition and 75 percent comprehension.

behavior.　Any activity that can be observed, recorded, and measured.

behavior, verbal.　Behavior which employs words in any form — printed, written, oral, signed, etc. — shaped by mediated reinforcement and interactions within the field.

behavior deficits.　When a certain behavior occurs at a lower frequency than is appropriate to the situation, with resulting impairment of an individual's social, intellectual and practical skills.

behavior excesses.　When certain behavior occurs at a higher frequency than is adaptive according to what is appropriate to the situation.

behavior modification.   A method of psychotherapy which uses learning principles to improve behavior.

behavior ratings.   Observation and recording of the occurrence of specific behaviors or classes of behaviors.

behavior segment.   The smallest descriptive unit of a response to a stimulus.

behavior therapy.   Term to describe therapies originally taken from learning principles but now including methods from other psychological research areas.

behavior-analysis procedures.   Interventions that are used to bring about behavioral change through application of behavioral principles.

behavioral contract.   The goals and procedures of treatment, mutually agreed upon by the client and other involved persons.

behavioral dimensions.   Measurable descriptive characteristics of a behavior such as number of occurrences, intensity, duration, topography, and accuracy.

behavioral field.   The sum at any given time of all events, conditions, and stimuli that impinge upon and influence the behavior of the organism.

behavioral medicine.   An interdisciplinary field concerned with understanding how social, psychological and biological factors interact in illness, its prevention and treatment.

behavioral method.   An approach which is derived from behaviorism in that the methods and goals, but not necessarily underlying philosophies, are accepted.

behavioral object.   Object which usually elicits or evokes a socially standardized type of behavior, such as a chair or fork.

behavioral objective.   A precise specification of the goal, including what the behavior is, where it occurs, and the criterion level.

behavioral observation.   Recording and measurement of behavior by use of a human observer, in naturalistic or controlled settings.

behavioral perspective.   A school of thought based on the assumption that conditioning is the cause of behavior.

behavioral repertoire.   All behaviors which are possible for an organism.

behavioral sampling.   Observation and recording of all the behaviors an organism engages in during prescribed segments of time, which provide a representative sample of the total behavior.

behavioral space.   The space that contains objects perceived by the organism at any one time.

behavioral technicians.   Auxiliary workers such as observers and data recorders who may be required to conduct some of the technical aspects of behavior-analysis programs.

behavioral toxicology.   The tendency of some drug users to endanger themselves as a result of impaired perception and paranoid delusions.

behaviorism.   A philosophy of psychological study holding that only observable behavior is the proper subject of investigation.

belief.   Verbal statement that functions as a discriminative stimulus, indicating which actions produce valued consequences.

benign tumor.   An abnormal growth that does not spread.

biofeedback.   Teaching voluntary control over muscular and visceral activity through the use of monitoring instruments.

biopsy.   The removal of a small part of a living tissue for examination.

-blasts.   Very young blood cells which normally develop into white blood cells. In leukemia, unusual kinds of such cells overgrow the bone marrow.

blindism.   Undesirable mannerisms and habitual movements seen in blind patients, and particularly in children or those previously institutionalized.

blood transfusion.   The administration of whole blood (cells and plasma) from a compatible donor.

bone marrow.   The inner cavity of a bone which contains the factory for developing blood cells. In leukemia, abnormal cells replace the normal cell types.

bonus time.   A group contingency package that capitalizes on the Premack principle. Time to engage in reinforcing activities is available contingent on occurrence of desirable behavior.

brain damage.   Any structural injury or insult to the brain, whether by surgery, accident or disease.

brain stem.   The point where the brain is anchored to and carries messages along the central nervous system.

bronchitis.   Inflammation of the air passages of the lungs.

bronchus.   One of the two main air passages.

bruxism.   Gnashing or grinding of the teeth, which occurs typically at night, during sleep.

bulimia.   Overeating or uncontrolled binge eating followed by self-induced vomiting.

cancer.   A harmful, uncontrolled growth of cells.

carcinogen.   Any substance known to have cancer-producing agents.

carcinoma.   A malignant tumor made up of connective tissue enclosing epithelial cells.

catheter.   A tube inserted into part of the body, often for drainage (e.g. into the bladder for drainage through the urethra).

causal explanation.   In psychology, explanation of behavior as the necessary result of antecedent factors.

causality.   An explanation of phenomena as the result of antecedent phenomena.

cell.   Smallest living unit of the body which generates energy, manufactures substances, and is capable of reproduction. A coordinated group of cells is called an organ.

central nervous system (CNS).   The brain, brain stem, and spinal cord.

cerebral palsy.   A non-progressive paralysis of the brain.

chain.   Two or more behaviors that occur in a definite order within a behavioral sequence.

chained schedules.   Two contingencies back-to-back in which the reinforcer is delivered only after behavior in both contingencies occurs.

chemotherapy.   Administration of chemical substances to kill tumor cells.

cilia.   Tiny hairlike projections, e.g. those in the lining of the airways that help move mucus upward to the throat where it can be expelled by coughing or removed by swallowing.

classical conditioning.   A form of learning where a neutral stimulus is paired with a stimulus (US) until the neutral stimulus (CS) also produces that response (CR).

closed-head injury.   A depressed skull fracture where actual pressure has been placed against the brain by a broken bone.

coded recording sheet.   An observation form with letter codes for each behavior of concern, allowing for simultaneous recording of several behaviors.

coercion.   The use of threats, aversive contingencies.

cognitive behavior therapy.   A form of behavior therapy that tries to help people control anxiety and depression by teaching them ways of interpreting and thinking about their experiences.

cognitive dissonance.   Motivation state which exists when an individual's cognitions are inconsistent with each other.

cognitive perspective.   An approach which regards the individual's patterns of thinking as the major determinants of his or her behavior.

cognitive therapy.   Cognitive restructuring techniques which hold that emotional disorders are caused by irrational thoughts.

collateral behavior.   Behavior which is parallel to the behavior producing reinforcement.

communication handicap.   Problems involving hearing or speech that result in impairment of communication.

complex behavior.   Behavior consisting of two or more subsets of responses.

compliance.   Agreeing to behave according to the requests or demands of another person.

compulsions.   Recurrent, ritualistic behavior sequences experienced as irresistible.

concept.   A categorization of the salient people, objects and events in the environment.

concretism.   Approach to thinking and behavior in which students handle each situation as a unique one. Such students do not see essential similarities between situations which normal students accept as similar or even identical.

conditioned aversive stimulus.   A stimulus which has the properties of an aversive stimulus after being paired with an aversive stimulus.

conditioned reflex.   Basic mechanisms of learning whereby if a neutral stimulus is paired with a nonneutral stimulus, the organism will eventually respond to the neutral stimulus.

conditioned response.   In classical conditioning, the response that results from pairing the conditioned stimulus with the unconditioned stimulus.

conditioned stimulus.   In classical conditioning, the stimulus that is paired with the unconditioned stimulus and eventually comes to elicit the conditioned response.

conditioning, operant. *See* **operant conditioning.**

confounding variables.   Variables that introduce ambiguity into an experimental study (e.g. history, maturation, instrumentation, etc.).

congenital.   Taking place some time between conception and birth.

consequences.   Changes produced in the world that follow and influence behavior.

construct, empirical.   A construct determined as a result of experimentation.

construct, hypothetical.   Concepts introduced in theory with the aim of explaining behavioral data.

contingencies.   Operant relationship between antecedents, behavior and consequences which generally is predictive of future probabilities of responding.

contingency control.   The ability to manipulate the environmental antecedents and consequences of a given behavior to achieve a specific behavioral goal.

contingency managers.   Individuals — parents, nurses, teachers, counselors, therapists, clients themselves — who conduct the day-to-day operation of a behavior program.

contingent observation.   A reductive procedure that contains elements of time-out.

continuous response.   A response with no clear beginning or end.

continuum.   A curve, graph of variable which has no abrupt changes between any two points.

contrast.   The intensification of differences between two given stimuli produced by the contiguous presentation of them.

cortisone.   A hormone that helps regulate the inflammatory or allergic responses in the body.

cranial radiation.   X-ray treatment directed toward the brain, to prevent leukemic cells from growing there.

creatine phosphokinase (CPK Test).   Blood test that shows the elevated level of muscle enzyme for muscular dystrophy.

creative behavior.   A new response or set of responses that is in some sense new and appropriate to the setting.

criterion analysis.   A method of factor analysis using the criterion variable in the test matrix.

criterion level.   Standard used to indicate when the behavioral goal has been reached.

cromolyn sodium.   Generic name for a drug used to treat asthma.

cue (discriminative stimulus).   A stimulus in whose presence a response is likely to yield reinforcement.

culturally handicapped.   Children whose cultural environment of school is radically different from their rearing environment. Differences usually are religious, socio-economic, racial, or educational.

cumulative graph.   The dependent variable value for an independent variable is added to the preceding dependent variable.

cystitis.   An inflammation of the bladder with pain, burning and blood in the urine.

data.   Records of the observations or measurements in an empirical study.

deceleration.   When inappropriate behavior is decreased in a self-control program.

demand characteristics.   A methodological problem where subjects' responses are strongly determined by the research setting.

demography.   The statistical study of human populations including birth and death rates, income, geographic distribution, and so forth.

deoxyribonucleic acid (DNA).   A substance which contains information to direct activities of a cell; DNA is organized in long threads called chromosomes.

denial.   Refusal to acknowledge the source of distress.

dependent variables.   A variable measured in an experiment but not manipulated.

depression.   An emotional state characterized by intense and unrealistic sadness.

deprivation.   Period of time during which there is no contact with a reinforcer.

deprivation, sensory.   A level of stimulation that has been reduced or altered so that it no longer allows the individual's normal range of stimulation.

deprivation, sleep.   Chronic prevention of sleep causing psychotic behavior and a decrease in performance and EEG alpha activity.

description.   Procedures by which events and their relationships are defined, classified, or categorized.

developmental sequence.   The normal order in which behavior develops for a given species.

deviation IQ.   Measure of intelligence with a test in which scores are standardized with an average score of 100 and a standard deviation specific to the test used.

diagnosis.   Identification of disorders on the basis of observed symptoms, usually given a classification.

direct observational recording.   A method in which a human observer records behavioral data as it occurs.

discontinuous variable.   A variable having values which are not on a continuum, but have discrete and abrupt changes from one magnitude to the next magnitude.

discrete response.   A behavior that has a clear beginning and end.

discrimination.   In operant conditioning, process of learning to respond differently to stimuli that are differently reinforced.

discriminative stimulus.   In operant conditioning, the stimulus that signals a response will be reinforced.

dissemination.   The spread of a disease throughout the body, usually through the blood.

diuretic.   Any substance that increases the passing of urine.

Down's syndrome.   A congenital condition, caused by a chromosomal deformity, resulting in moderate to severe retardation.

Duchenne muscular dystrophy.   The most common type of muscular dystrophy, causing progressive weakness of limbs and trunk.

duration.   The time between the onset and termination of a response.

dysgraphia.   Partial inability to express ideas by writing; usually associated with brain injury or dysfunction.

dyskinesia.   Partial impairment of voluntary movement abilities resulting in incomplete movements, poor coordination, and clumsy behavior.

dyslexia.   Partial inability to read, or to understand what one reads silently or aloud.

dyspnea.   Difficult or labored breathing.

echoic behavior.   Relationship where the stimulus is auditory and the imitative response is speaking.

echolalia.   Infantile speech pattern based on repeating sounds or words, also characteristic of catatonic schizophrenia.

ecological validity.   Relationship within a set of environmental circumstances between a proximal and distal stimulus, where the occurrence of one stimulus increases the occurrence of the other.

ecology, human.   The study of human organisms in relation to the physical and social environment which constitutes their life space.

ecology, psychological.   The interaction of environmental variables and personal susceptibility in the development of a disorder.

effect.   The result or outcome of change upon behavior.

electroencephalogram (EEG).   A method of recording the electrical activity of the brain, especially of the cerebral cortex.

electromyography (EMG).   Measures electrical impulses in muscular contractions.

elicit.   In respondent or classical conditioning, a verb that denotes the effect of a conditioned or unconditioned stimulus upon a conditioned or unconditioned response.

emit.   In operant conditioning, a verb that describes the occurrence of behavior in the absence of any known eliciting stimulus.

empathy.   The process of taking another person's perspective.

emphysema. Chronic obstructive pulmonary disease that is characterized by decreased elasticity of the lungs. The air sacs in the lungs become overly stretched, and the capacity of lungs to exchange oxygen and carbon dioxide is reduced.

empirical. Based on facts and experience, systematic observation and experiment rather than on theory or general philosophical principles.

empirical construct. Hypothetical construct based on observed facts.

empirical law. Principle based on empirical data or experimental findings which states the ongoing relationship between two or more sets of variables.

encopresis. A childhood disorder in which episodes of defecating alternate with longer periods of fecal retention.

enuresis. A lack of bladder control past the age when such control is normally achieved.

environment. Sum of external conditions, including social and physical factors influencing the organism.

environment, internal. Total of the internal processes occurring within the body.

environmental factors. All external conditions which may affect the individual.

epinephrine. A compound used as a bronchodilator to treat asthma.

ergonomics. The scientific study of relationships between men and machines, particularly the psychological, biological, and cultural events on the job.

errorless discrimination. Teaching the acquisition of a discrimination by carefully arranging a sequence of discriminative stimuli so that only correct responses are occasioned.

escape behavior. Behavior that is reinforced by the termination or removal of a stimulus event.

escape learning. Another name for operant conditioning with negative reinforcement.

essential hypertension. Chronically high blood pressure for which there is no organic cause.

establishing operation. Momentary strength of responding under different deprivation schedules of reinforcement.

ethical responsibility. Operating according to ethical precepts of the American Psychological Association or governing professional board.

evaluation. Determination of the relative value of a score by appraisal of comparison with a standard.

event. Occurrence or phenomenon which has a definite beginning and end.

event recording. Observational recording procedure where one records the number of occurrences of a specified discrete behavior.

evoke. In operant conditioning, response activation in the presence of a discriminative stimulus.

evoked potential. An electrical brain wave typically preceded by a sensory stimulus.

exceptional child. One who deviates significantly from the norm. Determined based on unusually high or low intelligence, physical disabilities, or emotional problems.

excitation. The process of causing physiological change in a receptor by stimulation.

experimental analysis of behavior. A scientific analysis designed to discover the functional relation between behavior and the variables that control it.

explanatory fiction. Reference to unknown or made-up causes; these explanations prevent one from the discovery of naturalistic (realisitc) conditions.

exploratory behavior. Movement or locomotion engaged in most frequently by children, animals, and lower organisms when initially orienting themselves to new situations.

expressive aphasia. The loss of ability to remember the pattern of movements required to speak words although one knows what he wants to say.

external validity. The degree to which research results can be generalized or applied to different populations, settings, and conditions.

extinction-induced aggression. The aggressive behavior that often accompanies the early phases of an extinction program in the absence of any other precipitating events. Often called "extinction burst."

extinction ratio. The ratio of unreinforced responses to reinforced responses emitted by the organism during the process of discrimination.

extrinsic asthma. Asthma caused by external agents, such as air pollutants, chemicals or cigarette smoke.

face validity. The extent to which a test seems to measure a variable because of its similarity to the criterion measure.

facioscapulohumeral muscular dystrophy. A type of muscular dystrophy where the face, scapula and arms are affected; usually onset is in the second decade of life.

false negative. An incorrect diagnosis of no illness.

false positive. An incorrect diagnosis of illness.

feedback. A process where information is returned to a system in order to regulate that system.

fetal alcohol syndrome. A group of physical deformities that appear frequently in the offspring of alcoholic women.

field theory. A systematic, mathematically described theory of psychology and social psychology which emphasizes the interrelatedness of an event and the totality of the organism's environment.

finger stick. A procedure in which a small point is opened on the fingertip and a few drops of blood gathered for routine blood examiniation (e.g. hemoglobin, white cell and plate counts).

fixed time schedule. A schedule in which a given amount of time must elapse before a response will produce reinforcement.

flaccid paralysis. Weak muscle function or no muscle functions.

frequency. Number of occurrences of some behavior.

functional analysis. Thorough analysis of the relationship of particular behavior to situations in which they occur, and their consequences.

functional relation. A lawful relation between values of two variables (usually dependent and independent variables).

gait. The process of walking or moving, related to the specific steps taken.

gene. A hereditary unit made of DNA, located on a chromosome.

generalization. When organisms conditioned to respond in certain ways to a particular stimulus also respond to similar stimuli in the same way.

generalization, generic. Similar responding in the presence of all the defining features of the training stimulus.

generalization, metaphorical. Similar responding in the presence of some, but not all, of the defining features of the training stimulus.

generalization, metonymical. Similar responding in the presence of none of the defining features of the training stimulus.

generalization, response.   The spread of effects to other classes of behavior.

generalization, stimulus.   When stimulus control is absent or incomplete.

goal.   The goal describes the target behavior and how it is to be changed. Goals should be translated into behavioral objectives.

Gower's sign.   A classic sign of muscular dystrophy indicating weakness of thigh muscles. A three-year-old, for example, will try to get up from the floor and literally have to "walk-up" his body to an erect position.

head-banging.   Uncontrolled physical movements characteristic of a young child in a temper tantrum.

head-knocking.   Hitting the head against the wall or other objects; seen in some infants, retarded adults, and children.

helplessness-hopelessness syndrome.   The depressed person's conviction that he is both unable to help himself and unlikely to be helped by external forces.

hemiplegia.   Paralysis of half of one side of the body.

hemispherical dominance.   Refers to the fact that one cerebral hemisphere generally leads the other in control of body movement, resulting in preferred use of left or right side.

hemophilia.   A rare, hereditary bleeding disorder of males, inherited through the mother and caused by a deficiency in making one or more blood-clotting proteins.

herpes simplex virus I (HSVI).   A virus that results in cold sores or fever blisters, most often on the mouth or around the eyes. Virus may lie dormant for months or years in nerve tissue or flare up under stress, trauma, infection or immunosuppression. There are no cures for herpes viruses.

herpes simplex virus II (HSVII).   The virus causing genital herpes infections. Infection results in painful sores on the genitals or anus. It accounts for one of the most common sexually transmitted diseases in the United States.

histamine.   A chemical released by mast cells and responsible for swelling and itching with a hay fever or related allergies.

home reports.   Contingency package that coordinates interventions between home and training facility.

homebound program.   Specialized educational program that services the community and children who are out of school for medical and emotional reasons.

homeostasis.   An ideal or optimal level of physiological functioning that maintains an organism on an even keel.

homosexuality.   Sexual activity directed toward one's own sex.

hydrocephalus.   A term that means water on the brain. An associated deformity in 90 to 95 percent of children with myelomeningoceles/spina bifida.

hyperactivity. *See* **attention deficits.**

hysteria.   A physical disability for which no organic cause can be found.

iatrogenic.   Problems uninentionally produced by a medical practitioner or practice.

idiosyncrasy.   A characteristic peculiar to an individual that can be attributed to any general psychological factor.

imagery.   A reproduction arising from the memory of a sense experience in the absence of sensory stimulation.

imitation.   Matching the behavior of a model, or engaging in behavior similar to that observed.

imitative proof.   A discriminative stimulus designed to occasion an imitative response.

immediate instructional level.   The lowest difficulty level of material at which there is evidence of need for instructional aid.

immobility.   A state of temporary inability to move, as seen in the tonic immobility cases or that of states of hypnosis.

immune system.   The natural system of defense mechanisms in which specialized cells and proteins in the blood and other body fluids work together to eliminate disease-producing microorganisms and foreign substances.

immunostimulant.   Any agent that will trigger a body's defenses.

immunotherapy.   An experimental technique which attempts to stimulate the patient's own immune system to fight leukemia cells.

imprinting.   Changing a neutral stimulus into a reinforcer by exposing the newborn to that stimulus.

inappropriate effect.   A subjective feeling in which emotional responses are totally unsuited to the immediate context.

incentives.   Environmental events that motivate the organism in certain directions.

incompatible behavior.   A specific alternative response that competes with a simultaneous behavior.

incubation.   A period of time when a phobic reaction intensifies as the person avoids the original stimulus.

independent variable.   A variable that is measured and manipulated in an experiment.

indirect observation.   A method of obtaining behavioral data that relies on self-reports or on "memory" of what occurred.

induction, negative.   Conditioning of inhibition due to preceding excitation of proximal stimuli.

induction, positive.   Conditioning of excitation in a stimulated area due to preceding or proximal stimuli.

inference.   A form of constructive memory in which people fill in information missing from memory using general knowledge about a situation.

inference, impure.   False or distorted guesses about why things happen. Explanations are invented rather than based on known contingencies.

inference, pure.   When a description draws from natural events even though there are none around.

informed consent.   In human services, clients, patients and parents have the right to be informed about proposed outcomes and procedures and their risks and benefits before giving consent.

infusion.   A procedure in which a medication is administered directly into a vein, usually over a period of time (IV drip).

inhibiting stimuli.   Antecedent stimuli that signal nonreinforcement or an aversive consequence for a particular behavior.

intensity.   The strength or "force" with which a response occurs for reinforcement.

interaction effect.   In a research study, when the effect of one independent variable differs depending on the level of a second independent variable.

interbehaviorism.   Type of psychology, founded by J.R. Kantor, that studies how organisms and objects interact within a naturalistic field (the environment).

intermittent schedules.   Occasional, rather than consistent, consequences for a response.

internal consistency.   When different parts of a test should yield the same results.

interpretation of the stimulus.   Responding to a stimulus in light of one's own memories, beliefs, and expectations before reacting.

inter-response time. The time it takes between two consecutive responses.

inter-trial interval. The time it takes between the end of one trial (when the reinforcer ends) and the beginning of the next trial.

interval schedules. Schedule of reinforcement where a reinforcer (or some consequence) is delivered only after a certain amount of time has passed.

intraverbal behavior. A response controlled by a verbal stimulus where there is no point-to-point correspondence between stimulus and response.

intrinsic asthma. Hypersensitivity that is caused by internal factors not from stimulation by allergens (e.g. sinus infection).

Kaposi's sarcoma. A cancer or tumor of the blood and lymphatic vessel walls. It appears as blue-violet to brownish skin blotches or bumps. Before rise of AIDS, it was rare in the U.S. and Europe, where it occurred primarily in men over age 50.

kinesthesis. The sense of body movement and movements of particular body parts, such as muscles, tendons and joints.

laceration. In reference to brain damage, indicates a severe injury in which a bullet or piece of metal enters the skull and directly ruptures and destroys brain tissue.

larynx. The organ of voice production (voice box).

latency. The time between the termination of a stimulus and onset of response.

laterality. General term used to cover patterns of dominance relative to brain hemispheres.

learned helplessness. The depressive's inability to initiate adaptive responses, possibly due to a helplessness conditioned by earlier, inescapable trauma.

learning. An enduring change in behavior caused by experience or practice.

learning disability. A specific deficit in perceptual, integrative or expressive processes which severely impairs learning efficiency.

learning history. The sum of an individual's behaviors that have been conditioned or modified as a function of environmental events.

leukemia. Cancer of the white blood cells.

leukocyte. A white blood cell.

life space. The entire set of phenomena in the environment and in the organism itself which influences present behavior.

limited hold. A restriction placed on a schedule requiring that the response for reinforcement be emitted within a particular time limit or reinforcement will not be made available.

lordosis. Curvature of the spine resulting in a sway back.

lymph nodes. Collections of lymphocytes gathered in different locations in the body (neck, armpit, groin), which become enlarged when inflammation is present.

lymphadenopathy. Enlargement of the lymph nodes.

lymphocyte. A type of white blood cell which is active in immune reactions, producing antibodies or other defense substances.

lymphomas. Cancers that attack lymph nodes and bone marrow.

maintenance. Applying schedules of reinforcement, altering reinforcers, and fading artificial prompts to allow continuation of behavior under natural conditions.

maladaptation. The failure of an individual to develop behavioral patterns necessary for personal and social success.

malignant tumor. A fatal, uncontrolled growth of cells.

mand.   Speech (verbal behavior) whose function is to make a request of (enjoin) another person's behavior during different schedules of deprivation and reinforcement.

mediation.   Sequences of more or less standard responses and events that fill the time between a response producing reinforcer and the occurrence of that reinforcer.

medium of contact.   Stimulus that allows person and object to interact (light waves, air waves, etc.).

memory span.   A measure of the amount of material that can be acquired and retained in one presentation.

meningocele.   Out-pouching consists of coverings of spinal cord. The spina bifida indiviudal's spinal cord is usually covered with skin.

mental age.   A measure of an individual's performance on an intelligence test expressed in terms of years and months.

mental retardation.   A condition characterized by intellectual ability that is significantly below average and by a serious deficiency in adaptive behavior.

metastasis.   The spread of disease from one part of the body to another.

mixed asthma.   Asthma in which the causes are both extrinsic (allergies) and intrinsic (infection).

model.   The person whose behavior is imitated.

mongolism. *See* Down's syndrome.

monocyte.   A phagocytic white blood cell that engulfs and destroys bacteria and other disease-producing microorganisms.

mood.   A sustained emotional state that colors perception, thought, and behavior.

motivation.   The desire, need, and interest that arouse an organism and direct it toward a specific goal.

motor habits.   Related to tics, these are repetitive, nonfunctional patterns of motor behavior that seem to occur in response to stress.

motor skills.   Skills of muscular movement.

muscular dystrophy.   A progressive weakness of all muscle groups characterized by a degeneration of muscle cells and their replacement by fat and fibrous tissue.

mutation.   Change in the composition of a gene that results in altered structure of offspring as compared to the parent.

mutism.   Cessation of speech, often characteristic of catatonic schizophrenia.

myelodisplasia.   A defective development of the spinal cord. A medical term for spina bifida.

myelomeningocele.   An outpouching of the spinal cord through the back where the bony vertebral column has failed to form.

narrative recording.   A written, running account of behavior in progress.

natural concepts.   A categorization of everyday objects into a class that has vague boundaries, with a clear prototype representing a good example of the concept.

natural events.   Observations made of confrontable objects and events within the field of psychological interactions.

natural sciences.   Sciences which study nature, i.e., physics, chemistry, biology, geology, etc.

naturalistic observations.   The study of behavior in its natural environment where the observer attempts not to interfere with the natural behavior of the subject.

negative feedback. Feedback in which the turning on of one component of a system leads to the turning off of another component, thereby regulating the system. It also denotes corrective (remedial) feedback.

neoplastic. Cancerous, leukemic or malignant. All of these terms refer to cells which grow without responding to normal control mechanisms.

neuroblastoma. Tumor of the nerve cells.

neurological. Related to the nervous system. Neurological problems are those arising from disease or damage to the nervous system.

neurons. Cells of the nervous system that connect motor and receptor cells and transmit information throughout the body.

neutral stimulus. Object or event that is neutral with respect to some property that it may later acquire. It does not reliably affect behavior in any known way.

novel stimulus. Any change in the background level of stimulation that attracts attention.

objective measurement. Recording behavioral data unbiased by the observer's feelings or interpretations.

observation. An intentional or explicit examination of the situation or thing in order to ascertain facts or particulars about it.

observational learning. Learning as a result of watching models be reinforced for certain behaviors.

observer. An individual who examines a situation or an object closely to report on it or understand it clearly.

obsessions. Recurrent thoughts or images experienced as involuntary intrusions into consciousness.

obsessive-compulsive disorder. Form of anxiety characterized by highly frequent actions that the person poorly controls.

occasion. To increase the likelihood of the emission of a response by arranging prior stimulus conditions.

one-trial learning. Mastery of a skill or an association on the first trial.

operant. A unit of behavior defined by its effect on the environment.

operant, concurrent. Two or more topographically different responses capable of being performed at the same time or in rapid succession with little mutual interference.

operant behavior. Behavior whose rate or probability of occurrence is controlled primarily by its consequences.

operant class. A class of behaviors that is susceptible to change by consequences.

operant conditioning. Form of learning where the response probability is increased or decreased depending on the consequences of that response.

operant level. The frequency of the response prior to any special consequences (interventions).

operational definition. A definition of a variable in terms of observable events or behavior that can be measured.

ordinate. The vertical line of a graph where the dependent variable is placed.

orienting response. A pattern of physiological reactions to a novel stimulus that enhances the body's ability to respond efficiently.

orthopsychiatry. A cross-disciplinary science combining child psychiatry, developmental psychology, pediatrics, and family care.

orthoses. Self-standing braces.

osteogenesis imperfecta.   A defect of bone formation characterized by bone fragility and sometimes deafness, resulting in multiple fractures even before birth and in infancy.

osteosarcoma.   A malignant tumor arising from fibrous tissues in the bone.

overlearning.   When responses to be made in anxiety settings are rehearsed repeatedly.

pain.   Self-aware response made when a punisher makes contact.

pancytopenia.   A decreased number of red cells, white cells, and platelets.

paraplegia.   Paralysis of the legs and lower part of the body.

parapodium.   Braces to support the trunk and lower limbs.

pedophilia.   Child molesting. Adult gratification through sexual contacts with children.

peer self-help groups.   Groups of people who share a special problem and meet to discuss that problem without the help of mental health professionals.

petechiae.   Small red pin-point hemorrhages in the skin which usually occur when blood platelets are low.

pharynx.   The throat. The section of the digestive tract that extends from the nasal cavities to the larynx, and there becomes continuous with the esophagus.

physical guidance.   A form of response priming where the appropriate body part or parts are assisted through the proper motion.

pneumonia.   A disease of the lungs that is characterized by inflammation and caused by viruses, bacteria and physical or chemical agents.

post-reinforcement rate.   A pause in responding that occurs immediately after reinforcement has been delivered, characteristic of fixed-ratio and fixed-interval schedules.

prediction.   One of the objectives of the scientific method: the ability to predict the relationship between events.

prelanguage control.   Simple stimulus control when specific stimuli are discriminative stimuli for specific acts.

Premack principle.   Principle stating that if one activity occurs more frequently than another, that activity will be an effective reinforcer for the less frequent activity.

prevalence.   Frequency of a disorder in a particular population.

principles of behavior.   Lawful relations between behavior and the variables that control it.

principles of reinforcement.   The basic mechanism for predicting and controlling human behavior.

probability.   Term describing the frequencies with which events occur.

probe.   A phase in a behavior analysis experiment to test the effect of a given intervention.

prognosis.   A forecast as to the recovery or outcome of an attack of disease, based on the symptoms and current knowledge of the disease.

prompt.   A discriminative stimulus presented to "assist" a given response.

proprioceptive stimuli.   Inner stimuli produced by the position of muscles.

pseudohypertrophism.   The enlargement of the muscles due to replacement of muscle with fat.

psychiatric diagnosis.   Classification of a patient's problem within the taxonomy of psychiatric disorders developed by the psychiatric profession.

psychoactive drug.   A drug that alters one's psychological state.

psychological assessment.   Systematic analysis of a person and his or her life condition.

psychological test.   Assessment technique where subject is presented with a series of stimuli to which he or she is asked to respond.

psychopathology.   Abnormal psychology.

psychophysiological disorders.   Harmful changes in tissue structure caused by maladaptive responses the body systems make in the presence of learned stress.

punisher, negative.   A stimulus which if terminated or removed following a response results in a decreased frequency of that response.

punisher, positive.   A stimulus which if presented following a response results in a decreased frequency of that response.

punishment, negative.   Termination or removal of a stimulus following a response, which results in a decreased frequency of that response.

punishment, positive.   Presentation of a stimulus following a response, which results in a decreased frequency of that response.

quadraplegia.   Paralysis of both arms and both legs; also called tetraplegia.

rapport.   A comfortable and warm atmosphere between two individuals, especially that established between subject and experimenter or between patient and therapist.

ratio strain.   Decrease in rate of responding due to making the ratio of consequences to behavior (the schedule) too high or too low.

reactional biography.   Total life history of organism's biological and psychological development.

reactivity.   The effect produced by experimental activities other than the independent variable.

receptive aphasia.   *See* **auditory aphasia.**

receptors.   Specialized cells suited to absorb certain forms of stimulus energy.

reciprocal inhibition.   The elicitation of a particular spinal reflex when accompanied by the inhibition of another.

reconditioning.   The strengthening or reestablishment after extinction of a conditioned response.

referral.   The process by which the educational system seeks to secure special education services for the exceptional child.

reflex.   A specific, involuntary response to a stimulus that does not involve learning.

reify.   To invent things that help explain how natural things relate. To turn a relationship between natural things into a thing itself.

reinforcement, accidental.   The unplanned coincidence of a response and a reinforcing event.

reinforcement, alternative.   Reinforcement that occurs according to either a fixed-ratio or fixed-interval schedule, depending on which condition is satisfied first.

reinforcement, aperiodic.   Reinforcement schedules in which reinforcement occurs irregularly and intermittently.

reinforcement, conditioned.   A reinforcing event which acquires its effectiveness from pairings with other reinforcers.

reinforcement, contingent.   A reinforcing event that occurs only as a consequence of the specified behavior.

reinforcement, continuous.   A schedule of reinforcement in which each occurrence of a response is reinforced.

reinforcement, homogeneous.   The simultaneous presentation of two stimuli, each of which elicits the same response.

reinforcement, interlocking. Intermittent reinforcement schedule consisting of decreasing ratio of required response per reinforcement.

reinforcement, negative. Termination or removal of a stimulus following a response, which results in an increased frequency of that response.

reinforcement, noncontingent. Arbitrary reinforcement unrelated to behavior.

reinforcement, partial. Schedule of reinforcement where reinforcer is delivered only part of the time of organism emits the response.

reinforcement, positive. Presentation of a stimulus following a response, which results in an increased frequency of that response.

reinforcement, predelay. A modification of the delayed response technique, where responding after a delay is reinforced.

reinforcement density. Frequency of rate with which responses are reinforced.

reinforcer, artificial. A reinforcer that is not usually present in the natural setting or is not a natural consequence for that behavior.

reinforcer, back-up. Object or event that has already demonstrated its reinforcing effect on a person, used in exchange for tokens, points, or other such conditioned reinforcers.

reinforcer, conditioned. A stimulus that becomes reinforcing after being associated with a primary reinforcer.

reinforcer, generalized conditioned. A conditioned reinforcer that is not dependent on any state of deprivation and which becomes reinforcing through pairings with other conditioned and unconditioned reinforcers.

reinforcer, negative. A stimulus which if terminated or removed following a response results in an increased frequency of that response.

reinforcer, positive. A stimulus the presentation of which increases responding.

reinforcer, primary. Same as unconditioned reinforcer.

reinforcer, secondary. Same as conditioned reinforcer.

reinforcer, unconditioned. A stimulus that is usually reinforcing in the absence of any prior learning history.

reliability. Extent to which a measurement device yields consistent results under varying conditions.

repertoire, behavioral. The behavior that a particular organism is able to emit over a succession of learning conditions.

replicate. To repeat a study and its methodology.

respondent behavior. Behavior which is elicited by specific stimuli, both learned and unlearned.

response, consummatory. A concluding response in a series of responses which brings the organism to a state of adjustment.

response, differential. Response to only one of several stimuli.

response, implicit. Muscular and glandular responses not directly observable without the appropriate instruments.

response, stereotyped. A behavior that is consistently occasioned by some problem situation, varies little in its topography, and is altered little by its consequences.

response bias. Responses occurring in a wide range of settings and stimuli because of a lengthy history of reinforcement.

response class. A category of behaviors of an organism, all of which tend to produce the same or similar consequences.

reponse hierarchy. A class of behaviors, parts of behaviors or behavior patterns which are arranged in the order of their probability of occurrence.

response patterns. A qualitative and quantitative grouping of responses into a distinct unit of activity.

response probability. Relative frequency of responding over a number of opportunities.

response sequence. Responses that form serial dependencies; interpreted as concurrent or sequential responses.

response set. A test-taking attitude that leads subjects to distort their responses.

response specificity. An individual's patterns of autonomic responses, which carry over from one type of stress to another.

response strength. A measure of the magnitude or intensity of a response.

retardation. General failure to benefit from normal training and experience, such that minimal mastery of skills and knowledge the culture requires is not attained.

reward. Everyday term meaning the same thing as reinforcer.

ribonucleic acid (RNA). A nucleic acid associated with the control of chemical activities inside a cell. One type of RNA transfers information from the cell's DNA to the protein-ormi system of a cell outside the nucleus. Some viruses carry RNA instead of the more familiar genetic material DNA.

rigidity. Inflexibility or stiffness; usually associated with tension in a muscle which gives way in little jerks when the muscle is passively stretched.

rule. A self- or independently made statement that describes (1) the nature of the response, (2) the relevant settings or stimulus conditions, and (3) the results (consequences) of the response in that setting.

rule control. Stimulus control in which rules function as discriminative stimuli.

scale. Any series of items progressively arranged according to value or magnitude.

scheme. General knowledge about a particular situation that influences the organization and storage of new memories.

scoliosis. A lateral or side-to-side curvature of the spine in the shape of an elongated letter "S".

self-awareness. Ability to offer verbal responses that correctly describe one's actions and why they occur.

self-control. A self-management program where one attempts to change some aspect of his or her own behavior.

self-disclosure. Telling another person about one's own needs, thoughts, feelings, behavior, and background.

self-report inventory. Assessment technique asking subjects direct questions about their personality or about events in their lives.

sequence analysis. A description of an individual's behavior, and the events that appear to precede and follow those behaviors.

setting events. These are not the stimuli with which an organism interacts directly but are the contexts of those interactions (e.g. room temperature, noise, social-cultural aspects, etc.).

sheltered workshop. Special work center, designed to meet the needs of retarded or injured people who are employed there.

sickle cell anemia. A hereditary form of anemia occurring mainly among blacks, characterized by sickle-shaped cells and an abnormal type of hemoglobin.

It is accompanied by acute abdominal pains, ulceration of legs, and bone pain.

simultaneous conditioning.   When the conditioned and unconditioned stimuli begin and end at the same time.

specific reading disability.   Inability to acquire reading ability where there is no mental retardation or serious deficiencies. (Labeled as word-blindness in 1896.)

spina bifida.   A congenital cleft in the bony encasement of the spinal cord, with meningila protrusion.

spirometer.   A device that measures the amount of air inhaled and exhaled. Used to measure the amount of airway obstruction in patients with asthma.

spontaneous recovery (resurgence).   A process related to extinction where a learned response recurs after apparent extinction.

standard deviation.   Average distance of each value from the mean of the collection.

standardization.   Procedure in which test questions are pretested to people of varying ages, races and social backgrounds.

statistical significance.   A tool of inferential statistics to determine the probability that results have come about by chance.

steroids.   The cortisone class of drugs that dilate bronchial tubes, decrease swelling of bronchial tubes, and decrease lung inflammation.

stimulus.   Any energy configuration in the physical world.

stimulus class.   A set of stimuli which all share some common property.

stimulus control.   When the training stimulus controls the presence and future rate of the response it produces.

stimulus delta.   A stimulus in the presence of which a given response will not be reinforced.

stimulus function.   Function of stimuli peculiar to specific individuals.

stimulus generalization.   Similar responding in the presence of similar stimulus situations.

stimulus property.   An attribute of the stimulus such as topography, texture, volume, size, intensity, and so on.

stimulus-response chains.   Sequence of discriminative stimuli and responses. Each response produces some changes in the environment, which then acts as a discriminative stimulus for the following response and also acts as a conditioned reinforcer for the preceding response.

stimulus specificity.   Principle that different kinds of stress produce different patterns of physiological responses.

stress.   Conditions that cause tissue damage or physiological reactions, affecting one's ability to cope.

stuttering.   A speech nonfluency in which the even and regular flow of words is disrupted by rapid repetition of speech elements, spasms of breathing, and hesitations.

superstitious behavior.   In operant conditioning, when an organism develops repetitive behavior (although the form varies) due to noncontingent reinforcement.

supported living arrangements.   Small group homes for mildly retarded people, when supervisor is present.

symptom substitution.   The replacement of a suppressed maladaptive behavior by a new maladaptive behavior.

syndrome.   Cluster of symptoms which tends to occur in a particular disease.

synergistic effect. When combined effect of two or more drugs is greater than the sum of both drugs' effects when taken alone.

system. The placing of tasks among personnel and machines into a unit to achieve a complex and functional result.

tact. A verbal response form controlled by an immediately prior nonverbal stimulus.

tandem schedule. Two contingencies back-to-back in which the discriminative stimulus is only in the first contingency, and the reinforcer is only delivered after behavior in both contingencies occurs.

tardive dyskinesia. Muscle disorder caused by the antipsychotic drug, the phenothiazines.

target behavior. The behavior to be changed.

task analysis. Breaking down a complex behavior into its basic parts.

task selection. Presenting the various basic components of a complex task in a sequence that leads to mastery of that complex behavior.

teaching machine. A system of programmed instruction in which one works independently and at his own pace on material presented through a console on a mechanical apparatus.

terminal behavior. The behavior that is achieved at the end of a behavior analysis program.

test. A standardized set of questions administered to a group or to individuals in order to assess the presence or absence of a particular skill.

test, alternate-response. A test composed of a number of questions, each having only two possible answers.

test-retest reliability. Criterion requiring that the test yield the same results when administered to the same person at different times.

thrombocytopenia. A term used in cancer files referring to the decreased numbers of platelets in the peripheral blood.

tic. An involuntary, periodic movement of muscle groups.

topography (of response). Refers to the movement of behavior in relation to space and time and events surrounding the organism.

toxicity. A variety of unfavorable side-effects resulting from chemotherapeutic agents; these may range from mild to severe and are usually transient.

trachea. The tubelike structure through which air moves to and from the bronchi. The windpipe.

tremor. Involuntary trembling or quivering in one or more parts of the body, usually in the extremities.

tumor. A swelling or enlargement, especially one due to pathological overgrowth of tissue.

ulcer. An open sore in the walls of the stomach or in a portion of the small intestine produced by abnormally high levels of gastric activity, induced by stress.

unconditioned aversive stimulus. A stimulus object or event that functions aversively in the absence of any prior learning.

unconditioned response. A reflex (muscular, glandular) activity, elicited by an unconditioned stimulus without prior learning.

unconditioned stimulus. A stimulus which elicits a biological, unlearned response.

upper airways. The nose, mouth, and throat, through which air passes into and out of the lungs. The nasal cavities warm, filter and moisten the air as it passes through to the lungs.

validity.   The measure of how consistent a test is with other sources of information about the same subjects.

variability.   In a frequency distribution, the separation of values in the x-axis.

variable.   Any factor in a study that can vary or change.

variable interval schedules.   A schedule in which reinforcement is delivered after a variable or average amount of time passes before a response will produce reinforcement.

variable ratio schedules.   A schedule of reinforcement in which a variable or average number of responses must occur before a response can produce reinforcement.

Werdnig-Hoffman disease.   A type of muscular dystrophy. A severe and rapidly progressive neuromuscular disorder in infants.

withdrawal.   Distressing symptoms (anxiety, irritability, restlessness, etc.) that occur following cessation of regular use of alcohol or certain drugs.

word-blindness.   *See* **specific reading disability.**

Bibliography

Allison, M.G., and Allyon, T. (1980). Behavioral coaching in the development of skills in football, gymnastics, and tennis. *Journal of Applied Behavior Analysis* **13**: 297–314.

Allyon, T., and Azrin, N.H. (1965). The measurement and reinforcement of behavior of psychotics. *Journal of the Experimental Analysis of Behavior* **8**: 385–388.

_____, and _____ (1968). Reinforcer sampling: a technique for increasing the behavior of mental patients. *Journal of Applied Behavior Analysis* **1**: 13–20.

American Psychiatric Association (1980). *Diagnostic and statistical manual of mental disorders (3rd. edition).* Washington, D.C.: American Psychiatric Association.

Ascher, L.M., and Phillips, D. (1975). Guided behavior rehearsal. *Journal of Behavior Therapy and Experimental Psychiatry* **6**: 215–218.

Azrin, N.H., and Holz, W.C. (1966). Punishment. In W.K. Honig (ed.), *Operant behavior: areas of research and application.* New York: Appleton-Century-Crofts, 380–447.

_____, and Powell, J. (1969). Behavioral engineering: the use of response priming to improve prescribed self-medication. *Journal of Applied Behavior Analysis* **2**: 39–42.

Baer, D.M.; Peterson, R.M.; and Sherman, J.A. (1967). The development of imitation by reinforcing behavior similarity to a model. *Journal of the Experimental Analysis of Behavior* **10**: 405–417.

Balsam, P.D., and Bondy, A.S. (1983). The negative side-effects of reward. *Journal of Applied Behavior Analysis* **16**: 283–296.

Bandura, A. (1971). Vicarious and self-reinforcement process. In R. Glaser (ed.), *The nature of reinforcement.* New York: Academic.

_____ (1977). *Aggression: a social learning analysis.* Englewood Cliffs, N.J.: Prentice-Hall.

_____; Grusec, J.E.; and Menlove, F.L. (1966). Observational learning as a function of symbolization and incentive set. *Child Development* **37**: 499–506.

_____; _____; and _____ (1967). Vicarious extinction of avoidance behaviors. *Journal of Personality and Social Psychology* **5**: 16–23.

_____, and Parloff, B. (1967). Relative efficacy of self-monitored and externally imposed reinforcement systems. *Journal of Personality and Social Psychology* **7**: 111–116.

Barrer, A.E., and Ruben, D.H. (1984). *Readings in head injury.* Guilford, Conn.: Special Learning Corporation.

_____, and _____ (1985). Understanding the etiology of brain injury. *Forum* **12**: 19–21.

Barton, L.E.; Andrew, R.; and Repp, A.C. (1986). Maintenance of therapeutic change by momentary DRO. *Journal of Applied Behavior Analysis* **19**: 277–282.

Becker, W.C.; Engelmann, S.; and Thomas, D.R. (1975). *Teaching 2: cognitive learning and instruction.* Chicago, Ill.: Science Research Associates.

Bellack, A.S., and Hersen, M. (eds.) (1984). *Research methods in clinical psychology.* New York: Pergamon.

_____, and _____ (eds.) (1985). *Dictionary of behavior therapy techniques.* New York: Pergamon.

_____; _____; and Kazdin, A.E. (eds.) (1982). *International handbook of behavior modification and therapy.* New York: Plenum.

_____; _____; and Lamparski, D. (1979). Role-play tests for assessing social skills: are they valid? Are they useful? *Journal of Consulting and Clinical Psychology* 47: 335–342.

Benoit, R.B., and Mayer, G.R. (1975). Timeout: guidelines for its selection and use. *Personnel and Guidance Journal* 53: 501–506.

Benson, H. (1975). *The relaxation response.* New York: Avon.

Berkowitz, P., and Rothman, E. (1960). *The disturbed child.* New York: New York University Press.

Beuf, A. (1979). *Biting off the bracelet.* Philadelphia: University of Pennsylvania Press.

Bigge, J.L., and O'Donnell, P.A. (1976). *Teaching individuals with physical and multiple disabilities.* Columbus, Ohio: Merrill.

Bijou, S.W. (1958). Operant extinction after fixed-interval schedules with young children. *Journal of the Experimental Analysis of Behavior* 1: 25–29.

_____, and Orlando, R. (1961). Rapid development of multiple-schedule performance with retarded children. *Journal of the Experimental Analysis of Behavior* 4: 7–16.

Billings, D.C., and Wasik, B.H. (1985). Self-instructional training with preschoolers: An attempt to replicate. *Journal of Applied Behavior Analysis* 18: 61–67.

Bitter, J.A. (1979). *Introduction to rehabilitation.* St. Louis, Mo.: Mosby.

Blackwood, R.D. (1972). *Mediated self-control: an operant model of rational behavior.* Akron, Ohio: Exordium.

Bleck, E., and Nagel, D. (eds.) (1975). *Physically handicapped children: a medical atlas for teachers.* New York: Grune and Stratton.

Bonnstein, P.H. (1985). Self-instructional training: a commentary and state-of-the-art. *Journal of Applied Behavior Analysis* 18: 69–72.

Borkovec, T.D.; Stone, N.M.; O'Brien, G.T.; and Kaloupek, D.G. (1974). Evaluation of a clinically relevant target behavior for analogue outcome research. *Behavior Therapy* 5: 503–513.

Brolin, D.E. (1982). *Vocational preparation of persons with handicaps.* Columbus, Ohio: Merrill.

Brown, P., and Jenkins, H. (1968). Auto-shaping of the pigeon's peck. *Journal of the Experimental Analysis of Behavior* 11: 1–8.

Bryant, E.H. (1978). Teacher in crisis: a classmate is dying. *Elementary School Journal* 78: 232–241.

Burchard, J.D., and Barrera, F. (1972). An analysis of timeout and response cost in a programmed environment. *Journal of Applied Behavior Analysis* 5: 271–282.

Carey, R.G., and Buch, B.D. (1986). Positive practice overcorrection: effects of reinforcing correct performance. *Behavior Modification* 10: 73–92.

Cautela, J.R. (1967). Covert sensitization. *Psychological Reports* 20: 459–468.

Charlotte/Mecklenburg Schools (1987). *Special test arrangements for handicapped students, secondary schools handbook.* Charlotte, N.C.: Charlotte/Mecklenburg School System.

Christ, K.; Wallas, R.T.; and Haught, P.A. (1984). Degrees of specificity in task analysis. *American Journal of Mental Deficiency* **89**: 67–74.

Church, R.M. (1963). The varied effects of punishment on behavior. *Psychological Review* **70**: 369–402.

Clark, H.B.; Rowbury, T.; Baer, A.M.; and Baer, D.M. (1973). Timeout as a punishing stimulus in continuous and intermittent schedules. *Journal of Applied Behavior Analysis* **6**: 443–455.

Clark, M. (1974). *Life for the handicapped.* New York: Time-Life.

Commission on Professional and Hospital Activities (1978). *International classification of diseases (9th revision); clinical modification (vol. 2).* Michigan: Commission on Professional and Hospital Activities.

Cossairt, A.; Hall, R.V.; and Hopkins, B.L. (1973). The effects of experimenter's instructions, feedback, and praise on teacher praise and student attending behavior. *Journal of Applied Behavior Analysis* **6**: 89–100.

Crase, D. (1980). Death education resources. *Journal of School Health* **50**: 411–415.

Cruickshank, W., and Johnson, G.O. (eds.) (1967). *Education of exceptional children and youth (2nd ed.).* Englewood Cliffs, N.J.: Prentice-Hall.

Dahlgren, T., and Prager-Decker, I. (1979). A unit on death for primary grades. *Health Education* **10**: 36–37.

Deitz, S.M. (1977). An analysis of programming DRL schedules to educational settings. *Behaviour Research and Therapy* **15**: 103–111.

Delprato, D.J. (1981). The constructional approach to behavior modification. *Behaviour Research and Therapy* **11**: 49–55.

DeRisi, W.J., and Butz, G. (1975). *Writing behavioral contracts: a case simulation practice manual.* Champaign, Ill.: Research.

DeShong, B.R. (1981). *The special educator: stress and survival.* Rockville, Md.: Aspen.

Dougher, M.J. (1983). Clinical effects of response deprivation and response satiation procedures. *Behavior Therapy* **14**: 286–298.

Drabman, R.S., and Lahey, B.B. (1974). Feedback in classroom behavior modification: effects on the target and her classmates. *Journal of Applied Behavior Analysis* **7**: 591–598.

Duty, D.W.; McInnis, T.; and Paul, G.L. (1974). Remediation of negative side-effects of an ongoing response-cost system with chronic mental patients. *Journal of Applied Behavior Analysis* **7**: 191–198.

Dyer, K.; Christian, W.P., and Luce, S.C. (1982). The role of response delay in improving discrimination performance of autistic children. *Journal of Applied Behavior Analysis* **15**: 197–205.

Egeland, B. (1975). Effects of errorless training on teaching children to discriminate letters of the alphabet. *Journal of Applied Psychology* **60**: 533–536.

Ellis, A., and Grieger, R. (1977). *Handbook of rational-emotive therapy.* New York: Springer.

_____, and Harper, R.A. (1974). *A guide to rational living.* North Hollywood, Calif.: Wilshire.

Epstein, L.H.; Doke, L.A.; Sajwaj, T.E.; Sorrell, S.; and Rimmer, B. (1974). Generality and side-effects of overcorrection. *Journal of Applied Behavior Analysis* **7**: 385–390.

Fagen, S.A.; Long, N.J.; and Stevens, D.J. (1975). *Teaching children self-control.* Columbus, Ohio: Merrill.

Feindler, E.L. (1987). Clinical issues and recommendations in adolescent anger-control teaching. *Journal of Child and Adolescent Psychotherapy* **4**: 267-274.

————, and Ecton, R.B. (1986). *Adolescent anger control.* New York: Pergamon.

Florida State Department of Education, Bureau of Education for Exceptional Students (1979). *A resource manual for the development and evaluation of special programs for exceptional students (Vol. 2-H).* Gainesville, Fla.: Florida State Department of Education.

Ford, J.E. (1980). A classification system for feedback procedures. *Journal of Organizational Behavior Management* **2**: 183-192.

Foxx, R.M., and Azrin, N.H. (1972). Restitution: a method of eliminating aggressive-disruptive behaviors of retarded and brain-damaged patients. *Behaviour Research and Therapy* **10**: 15-27.

————, and Shapiro, T. (1978). The timeout ribbon: a nonexclusionary timeout procedure. *Journal of Applied Behavior Analysis* **11**: 125-136.

Freeman, J. (1978). Death and dying in three days? *Phi Delta Kappa* **60**: 118.

Fremouw, W., and Brown, J. (1980). The reactivity of addictive behaviors to self-monitoring: a functional analysis. *Addictive Behaviors* **5**: 209-217.

Girdano, D.A., and Everly, G.S. (1979). *Controlling stress and tension: a holistic approach.* Englewood Cliffs, N.J.: Prentice-Hall.

Glasgow, R.E., and Rosen, G.M. (1978). Behavioral bibliotherapy: a review of self-help oriented behavior manuals. *Psychological Bulletin* **85**: 1-23.

————, and ———— (1979). Self-help behavior therapy manuals: recent developments and clinical usage. *Clinical Behavior Therapy Review* **1**: 1-20.

Goetz, E.M.; Holmberg, M.C.; and LeBlanc, J.M. (1975). Differential reinforcement of other behavior and noncontingent reinforcement as control procedures during the modification of a preschooler's compliance. *Journal of Applied Behavior Analysis* **8**: 77-82.

Goldiamond, I.A. (1976). Self-reinforcement. *Journal of Applied Behavior Analysis* **9**: 509-514.

Gordon, A., and Klass, D. (1979). *They need to know: how to teach children about death.* Englewood Cliffs, N.J.: Prentice-Hall.

Gross, A.M., and Drabman, R.S. (1981). Behavioral contrast and behavior therapy. *Behavior Therapy* **12**: 231-246.

Guevremont, D.C.; Osnes, P.G.; and Stokes, T.F. (1986). Programming maintenance after correspondence training interactions with children. *Journal of Applied Behavior Analysis* **19**: 215-219.

Haddan, E.E. (1970). *Evolving instruction.* New York: Macmillan.

Hall, R.V.; Lund, D.; and Jackson, D. (1968). Effects of teacher attention on study behavior. *Journal of Applied Behavior Analysis* **1**: 1-12.

Hammerman, S.R. (ed.) (1973). *Communications in rehabilitation.* New York: Rehabilitation Institute.

Haney, J.I., and Jones, R.T. (1982). Programming maintenance as a major component of a community-centered prevention effort: escape from fire. *Behavior Therapy* **13**: 47-62.

Hefferline, R.F., and Keenan, B. (1961). Amplitude-induction gradient of a small human operant in an escape-avoidance situation. *Journal of the Experimental Analysis of Behavior* **4**: 41-43.

Hilgard, E.D. (1936). The nature of the conditioned response: I. The case for and against stimulus substitution. *Psychological Review* **43**: 366-385.

Homme, L.E.; Csangi, A.; Gonzales, M.; and Rechs, J. (1969). *How to use contingency contracting in the classroom.* Champaign, Ill.: Research.

Hutchinson, R.R., and Azrin, N.H. (1961). Conditioning of mental hospital patients to fixed-ratio schedules of reinforcement. *Journal of the Experimental Analysis of Behavior* **4:** 87–95.

Israel, A.C. (1978). Some thoughts on correspondence between saying and doing. *Journal of Applied Behavior Analysis* **11:** 271–276.

_____, and Brown, M.S. (1977). Correspondence training, prior verbal training, and control of nonverbal behavior via control of verbal behavior. *Journal of Applied Behavior Analysis* **10:** 333–338.

Jones, R.T., and Kazdin, A.E. (1975). Programming response maintenance after withdrawing token reinforcement. *Behavior Therapy* **6:** 153–164.

Kanfer, F. (1970). Self-monitoring: methodological limitations and clinical applications. *Journal of Consulting and Clinical Psychology* **35:** 148–152.

Kapisovsky, P.; Workman, J.; and Foster, J. (1977). *A training and resource directory for teachers serving handicapped students, K–12.* Washington, D.C: Office for Civil Rights.

Karlan, G.R., and Rusch, F.R. (1982). Correspondence between saying and doing: some thoughts on defining correspondence and future directions for application. *Journal of Applied Behavior Analysis* **15:** 151–162.

Kaufman, L.M., and Wagner, B.R. (1972). Barb: a systematic treatment technology for temper control disorders. *Behavior Therapy* **3:** 84–90.

Kazdin, A.E. (1977). *The token economy: a review and evaluation.* New York: Plenum.

_____ (1982). Symptom substitution, generalization, and response covariation: implications for psychotherapy outcome. *Psychological Bulletin* **91:** 349–365.

_____, and Bootzin, R.R. (1972). The token economy: an evaluative review. *Journal of Applied Behavior Analysis* **5:** 343–372.

_____, and Erickson, L.M. (1975). Developing responsiveness to instructions in severely and profoundly retarded residents. *Journal of Behavior Therapy and Experimental Psychiatry* **6:** 17–21.

Kelleher, R.T. (1966). Chaining and conditional reinforcement. In W.K. Honig (ed.), *Operant behavior: areas of research and application.* New York: Appleton-Century-Crofts, 160–212.

Keller, F.S. (1968). Good-bye teacher... *Journal of Applied Behavior Analysis* **1:** 79–89.

Kleinberg, S.B. (1982). *Educating the chronically ill child.* Rockville, Md.: Aspen Systems.

Knapp, T.J. (1976). The Premack principle in human experimental and applied settings. *Behaviour Research and Therapy* **14:** 133–147.

Knight, M.F., and McKenzie, H.S. (1974). Elimination of bedtime thumbsucking in homesettings through contingent reading. *Journal of Applied Behavior Analysis* **7:** 33–38.

Konarski, E.A.; Johnson, M.R.; Crowell, C.R.; and Whitman, T.L. (1980). Response deprivation and reinforcement in applied settings: a preliminary analysis. *Journal of Applied Behavior Analysis* **13:** 595–609.

Krumboltz, J.D., and Krumboltz, H.B. (1972). *Changing children's behavior.* Englewood Cliffs, N.J.: Prentice-Hall.

Lazarus, A.A. (1966). Behavior rehearsal vs. nondirective therapy vs. advice in effecting behavior change. *Behaviour Research and Therapy* **4:** 209–212.

Leach, D., and Dolan, N.K. (1985). Helping teachers increase student academic engagement rate: the evaluation of a minimal feedback procedure. *Behavior Modification* **9:** 55–71.

Leitenberg, H.; Agras, W.S.; Thompson, L.E.; and Wright, D.E. (1968). Feedback in behavior modification: an experimental analysis. *Journal of Applied Behavior Analysis* **1:** 131–138.

Lippman, L.G., and Meyer, M.E. (1967). Fixed-interval performance as related to instructions and to subject's verbalizations of the contingency. *Psychonomic Science* **8:** 135–136.

Litow, L., and Pumroy, D.K. (1975). A brief review of classroom group-oriented contingencies. *Journal of Applied Behavior Analysis* **8:** 341–347.

Lovaas, O.I.; Berberich, J.P.; Perloff, B.F.; and Schaeffer, B. (1966). Acquisition of imitative speech in schizophrenic children. *Science* **151:** 705–707.

Lovall, E.E. (1970). *Locating and correcting reading difficulties.* Columbus, Ohio: Merrill.

Maccoby, E.E., and Wilson, W.C. (1957). Identification and observational learning from fitness. *Journal of Abnormal and Social Psychology* **55:** 76–87.

MacCollulm, A. (1981). *The chronically ill child.* New York: New York University Press.

McFall, R. (1977). Analogue methods in behavioral assessment: issues and prospects. In J. Cone and R. Hawkins (eds.), *Behavioral assessment: new directions in clinical psychology.* New York: Brunner/Mazel.

———, and Twentyman, C.T. (1973). Four experiments on the relative contributions of rehearsal, modeling, and coaching to assertion training. *Journal of Abnormal Psychology* **81:** 199–218.

Mahoney, M.J. (1974). *Cognition and behavior modification.* Cambridge, Mass.: Ballinger.

Major, M. (1980). Helping the bereaved child. *Day Care and Early Education* **7:** 48–50.

Maletzky, B. (1973). Assisted covert sensitization. *Behavior Therapy* **4:** 117–119.

Mann, J. (1972). *Learning to be: the education of human potential.* New York: Free Press.

Martin, G.C.; England, G.; and England, K. (1971). The use of backward chaining to teach bed-making to severely retarded girls. *Psychological Aspects of Disability* **18:** 281–294.

———; Kehoe, B.; Bird, E.; Jensen, V.; and Darbyshire, P. (1971). Operant conditioning in dressing behavior of severely retarded girls. *Mental Retardation* **9:** 27–31.

Martin, I., and Levey, A.B. (1971). *The genesis of the classical conditioned response.* New York: Pergamon.

Matthews, B.A.; Shimoff, E.; and Catania, A.C. (1987). Saying and doing: a contingency-space analysis. *Journal of Applied Behavior Analysis* **20:** 69–74.

Mealy, J. (1968). *Pediatrics head injuries.* Springfield, Ill.: Thomas.

Menkes, J.H. (1980). *Textbook of child neurology.* Philadelphia: Lea and Febiger.

Michael, J. (1975). Positive and negative reinforcement, a distinction that is no longer necessary: or, a better way to talk about bad things. *Behaviorism* **3:** 33–44.

——— (1982). Distinguishing between discriminative and motivational functions of stimuli. *Journal of the Experimental Analysis of Behavior* **37:** 149–155.

Michaux, L.A. (1970). *The physically handicapped and the community: some challenging breakthroughs.* Springfield, Ill.: Thomas.

Mueller, J.M. (1978). I taught about death and dying. *Phi Delta Kappa* **60:** 117.

Myers, B.R. (1975). The child with a chronic illness. In R.H. Haslam and P. Valletulti (eds.), *Medical problems in the classroom.* Baltimore, Md.: University Park Press.

Nay, W.R. (1977). Analogue measures. In A.R. Ciminero, K.S. Calhoun and H.E. Adams (eds.), *Handbook of behavioral assessment*. New York: Wiley.

O'Brien, F.; Azrin, N.H.; and Henson, K. (1969). Increased communications of chronic mental patients by reinforcement and by response priming. *Journal of Applied Behavior Analysis* **2**: 23–29.

O'Connor, R.D. (1969). Modification of social withdrawal through symbolic modeling. *Journal of Applied Behavior Analysis* **2**: 15–22.

Odom, S.L.; Hoyson, B.J.; and Strain, P.S. (1985). Increasing handicapped preschoolers' peer social interactions: cross-setting and component analysis. *Journal of Applied Behavior Analysis* **18**: 3–16.

Ollendick, T.H.; Dailey, D.; and Shapiro, E.S. (1983). Vicarious reinforcement: expected and unexpected effects. *Journal of Applied Behavior Analysis* **16**: 485–491.

_____, and Matson, J.L. (1978). Overcorrection: an overview. *Behavior Therapy* **9**: 830–842.

O'Neill, D.M. (1977). *Discrimination against handicapped persons; the cost, benefits, and economic impact of implementing section 504 of the Rehabilitation Act of 1973.* Washington, D.C.: Department of Education.

Orlando, R., and Bijou, S.W. (1960). Single and multiple schedules of reinforcement in developmentally retarded children. *Journal of Experimental Analysis of Behavior* **3**: 339–348.

Panyan, M.C., and Hall, R.V. (1978). Effects of serial versus concurrent task sequencing on acquisition, maintenance, and generalization. *Journal of Applied Behavior Analysis* **11**: 67–74.

Peterson, N. (1982). On terms: feedback is not a new principle of behavior. *Behavior Analyst* **5**: 101–102.

Peterson, R.F. (1968). Some experiments on the organization of a class of imitative behaviors. *Journal of Applied Behavior Analysis* **1**: 225–235.

Pigott, H.E.; Fantuzzo, J.W.; and Gorsuch, R.L. (1987). Further generalization technology: accounting for natural covariation in generalization assessment. *Journal of Applied Behavior Analysis* **20**: 273–278.

Premack, D.T. (1965). Reinforcement theory. *Nebraska Symposium on Motivation*. Lincoln: University of Nebraska Press, 123–180.

Rescorla, R.A. (1967). Pavlovian conditioning and its proper control procedures. *Psychological Review* **74**: 71–80.

Risley, T. (1968). The effects and side-effects of punishing the autistic behaviors of a deviant child. *Journal of Applied Behavior Analysis* **1**: 21–35.

_____, and Hart, B. (1968). Developing correspondence between the nonverbal and verbal behavior of preschool children. *Journal of Applied Behavior Analysis* **1**: 267–281.

Roberts, R.N.; Nelson, R.O.; and Olson, T.W. (1987). Self-instruction: an analysis of the differential effect of instruction and reinforcement. *Journal of Applied Behavior Analysis* **20**: 235–242.

Rolider, A., and Van Houten, R. (1985). Movement suppression time-out for undesirable behavior in psychotic and severely developmentally delayed children. *Journal of Applied Behavior Analysis* **18**: 275–288.

Rosen, C.D., and Gerring, J.P. (1986). *Head trauma: educational reintegration*. San Diego, Calif.: College-Hill.

Rosen, G.M. (1976). The development and use of nonprescription behavior therapies. *American Psychologist* **31**: 139–141.

_____ (1978). Suggestions for an editorial policy on the review of self-help treatment books. *Behavior Therapy* **9**: 90.

Rosenkrans, M.A., and Hartup, W.W. (1967). Imitative influence of consistent and inconsistent consequences to a model on aggressive behavior in children. *Journal of Personality and Social Psychology* 7: 429–434.

Ruben, D.H. (1983). The effects of praise and ignoring on relevant and irrelevant verbalizations of preschool children within a classroom setting. In P.T. Mountjoy and D.H. Ruben (eds.), *Behavioral genesis: readings in the science of child psychology*. Needham, Mass.: Ginn.

_____ (1984). Analogue assessments in the behavioral treatment of drug addictions: a review. Okemos, Mich.: Best Impressions.

_____ (1985a). The validation of a behavioral programmed text for increasing self-control attitudes. *Corrective and Social Psychiatry and Journal of Behavior Technology, Methods and Therapy* 31: 7–16.

_____ (1985b). *Progress in assertiveness, 1973–1983*. Metuchen, N.J.: Scarecrow Press.

_____ (1988). Behavioral predictors of alcoholics: a "systems" perspective. *Alcoholism Treatment Quarterly* 5: 137–162.

_____ (1989). Bibliotherapy: practical considerations when writing for substance abuse readers. *Journal of Alcohol and Drug Education* 34: 70–78.

_____, and Macciomei, N.R. (1986). *Readings in muscular dystrophy*. New York: Longman.

_____, and _____ (1986). *Readings in aphasia and education*. New York: Longman.

_____, and _____ (in press). *Readings in cerebral palsy*. New York: Longman.

_____, and Ruben, M.J. (1985). Behavioral principles on the job: control or manipulation? *Personnel* 62: 61–65.

_____, and _____ (1987). Assumptions about teaching assertiveness: teaching the person or behavior? In D.H. Ruben and D.J. Delprato (eds.), *New ideas in therapy*. Westport, Conn.: Greenwood Press.

_____, and _____ (in press). *60 seconds to success*. Okemos, Mich.: Best Impressions.

Rudolph, M. (1978). *Should the children know?: encounter with death in the lives of children*. New York: Schocken.

Russell, R.K., and Sipich, J.F. (1973). Cue-controlled relaxation in the treatment of test anxiety. *Journal of Behavior Therapy and Experimental Psychiatry* 4: 47–49.

Sajwaj, T. (1977). Issues and implications of establishing guidelines for the use of behavioral techniques. *Journal of Applied Behavior Analysis* 10: 541–548.

_____; Twardosz, S., and Burke, M. (1972). Side-effects of extinction procedures in a remedial preschool. *Journal of Applied Behavior Analysis* 5: 163–175.

Salmon, D.S.; Pear, J.J.; and Kuhn, B.A. (1986). Generalization of object naming after training with picture cards and with objects. *Journal of Applied Behavior Analysis* 19: 53–55.

Scarpitti, F.R. (1977). *Social problems*. Hinsdale, Ill.: Dryden.

Schroeder, G.L., and Baer, B.M. (1972). Effects of concurrent and serial training on generalized vocal imitation in retarded children. *Developmental Psychology* 6: 293–301.

Schwarz, M.L., and Hawkins, R.P. (1970). Application of delayed reinforcement procedures to the behavior of an elementary school child. *Journal of Applied Behavior Analysis* 3: 85–96.

Shelton, J.C., and Levy, R.L. (eds.) (1981). *Behavioral assignments and treatment compliance: a handbook of clinical strategies.* Champaign, Ill.: Research.

Sidman, M., and Stoddard, L.T. (1967). The effectiveness of fading in programming a simultaneous form discrimination for retarded children. *Journal of the Experimental Analysis of Behavior* 10: 3–16.

Siegel, R.K. (1977). Stimulus selection and tracking during urination: auto-shaping directed behavior with toilet targets. *Journal of Applied Behavior Analysis* 11: 255–265.

Singh, N.N. (1987). Overcorrection of oral reading errors: a comparison of individualized group-training formats. *Behavior Modification* 11: 165–181.

Skinner, B.F. (1968). *Technology of teaching.* New York: Appleton-Century-Crofts.

_____ (1982). Contrived reinforcement. *The Behavior Analyst* 5: 3–8.

Smith, R.M., and Neisworth, J.T. (1975). *The exceptional child: a functional approach.* New York: McGraw-Hill.

Solnick, J.V.; Rincover, A.; and Peterson, C.R. (1977). Some determinants of the reinforcing and punishing effects of time-out. *Journal of Applied Behavior Analysis* 10: 415–424.

Stanford, G., and Perry, D. (1976). *Death out of the closet: a curriculum guide to living with dying.* New York: Bantam.

Stein, S.B. (1974). *About dying: An open family book for parents and children together.* New York: Walker.

_____ (1976). *About handicaps: An open family book for parents and children together.* New York: Walker.

Stevenson, D.W.; Kaiser, W.W.; and Ruben, D.H. (1984). Constructional approach to pre-vocational training in the reduction of stereotypic behavior. *Behavioral Engineering* 10: 25–30.

Stokes, T.F., and Baer, D.M. (1977). An implicit technology of generalization. *Journal of Applied Behavior Analysis* 10: 349–367.

Striefel, S., and Wetherby, B. (1983). Instruction-following behavior of a retarded child and its controlling stimuli. *Journal of Applied Behavior Analysis* 6: 663–670.

Suinn, R. (1977). *Manual: anxiety management training (AMT).* Colo.: Rocky Mountain Behavioral Sciences Institute.

Sultz, H.; Schlesinger, E.; Mosher, W.; and Feldman, J. (eds.) (1972). *Longterm childhood illness.* Pittsburgh: University of Pittsburgh Press.

Sulzer-Azaroff, B., and Mayer, R.G. (1972). *Behavior modification procedures for school personnel.* Hinsdale, Ill.: Dryden.

_____, and Mayer, R.G. (1977). *Applying behavior-analysis procedures with children and youth.* New York: Holt, Rinehart and Winston.

Sundel, M., and Sundel, S.S. (1975). *Behavior modification in the human services: a systematic introduction to concepts and application.* New York: Wiley.

Terrace, H.S. (1966). Stimulus control. In W.K. Honig (ed.), *Operant behavior: areas of research and application.* New York: Appleton-Century-Crofts.

Thompson, T., and Grabowski, J.G. (1969). *A primer of operant conditioning.* Glenview, Ill.: Scott, Foresman.

Thorpe, R.G., and Wetzel, R.J. (1969). *Behavior modification in the natural environment.* New York: Academic.

Timberlake, W., and Allison, J. (1974). Response deprivation: an empirical approach to instrumental performance. *Psychological Review* 81: 146–164.

Timm, M.A.; Strain, P.S.; and Eler, P.H. (1979). Effects of systematic, response-dependent fading and thinning procedures on the maintenance of child-child interaction. *Journal of Applied Behavior Analysis* **12**: 308.

Travis, G. (1976). *Chronic illness in children.* Stanford, Calif.: Stanford University Press.

Tweeney, J.W. (1972). Training letter discrimination in four-year-old children. *Journal of Applied Behavior Analysis* **5**: 455–465.

Vulelich, R., and Hake, D.G. (1971). Reduction of dangerously aggressive behavior in a severely retarded resident through a combination of positive reinforcement procedures. *Journal of Applied Behavior Analysis* **4**: 215–225.

Wahler, R.G.; Breland, R.M.; and Car, T.D. (1979). Generalization processes in child behavior change. In B. Lahey and A. Kazdin (eds.), *Advances in clinical child technology (vol. 2).* New York: Plenum.

Walen, S.R.; Digiuseppe, R.; and Wessler, R.L. (1980). *A practitioner's guide to rational-emotive therapy.* New York: Oxford University Press.

Walker, H.M., and Buckley, N.K. (1975). *Token reinforcement techniques: classroom applications for the hard to reach child.* Champaign, Ill.: Research.

Weihner, R.G., and Harmon, R.E. (1975). The use of omission training to reduce self-injurious behavior in a retarded child. *Behavior Therapy* **6**: 261–268.

Weiner, H. (1964a). Conditioning history and human fixed-interval performance. *Journal of the Experimental Analysis of Behavior* **7**: 383–385.

_____ (1964b). Response cost effects during extinction following fixed interval reinforcement with humans. *Journal of the Experimental Analysis of Behavior* **7**: 333–335.

_____ (1969). Controlling human fixed-interval performance. *Journal of the Experimental Analysis of Behavior* **12**: 349–373.

Weintrauh, A., and Ballard, L. (1977). *Public policy and the education of exceptional children.* Va.: Council for Exceptional Children.

Williams, G.E., and Cuvo, A.J. (1986). Training apartment upkeep skills to rehabilitation clients: a comparison of task analytical strategies. *Journal of Applied Behavior Analysis* **19**: 39–51.

Wilson, M.D., and McReynolds, L.V. (1973). A procedure for increasing oral reading rate in hard-of-hearing children. *Journal of Applied Behavior Analysis* **6**: 231–239.

Zimmerman, J., and Levitt, E. (1975). Why not give your client a counter: a survey of what happened when we did. *Behaviour Research and Therapy* **13**: 333–337.

Index